# LIBRARY PUBLIC RELATIONS, PROMOTIONS, AND COMMUNICATIONS

## A How-To-Do-It Manual

## Second Edition

## Lisa A. Wolfe

## *HOW-TO-DO-IT MANUALS FOR LIBRARIANS*

## *NUMBER 126*

NEAL-SCHUMAN PUBLISHERS, INC.
New York, London

Published by Neal-Schuman Publishers, Inc.
100 William Street, Suite 2004
New York, NY 10038

Printed and bound in the United States of America.

The paper used in this publication meets the minimum requirements of American National Standard for Information Sciences—Permanence of Paper for Printed Library Materials. ANSI Z39.48-1992. ∞

Library of Congress Cataloging-in-Publication Data

Wolfe, Lisa A.
  Library public relations, promotions, and communications : a how-to-do-it manual / Lisa A. Wolfe.— 2nd ed.
      p. cm. — (How-to-do-it manuals for librarians ; no. 126)
  Includes bibliographical references and index.
  ISBN 1-55570-471-9 (alk. paper)
  1. Libraries—Public relations—United States. I. Title. II. How-to-do-it manuals for libraries ; no. 126.

Z716.3.W58 2005
021.7—dc22                                    2004025944

# DEDICATION

To my colleagues and clients from whom I have learned much about public relations.

# CONTENTS

# LIST OF FIGURES

# LIST OF SUCCESSFUL PUBLIC RELATIONS SAMPLES

# PREFACE

Things change! And in the eight years since the first edition of *Library Public Relations, Promotions, and Communications: A How-To-Do-It Manual* was published, much has changed in the library community, in the public relations profession, and in our world as a whole.

Libraries face challenges never dreamed of in 1997. The advent and rapid adoption of the Internet has been both a boon to libraries' ability to provide information and a threat to their very existence. Public libraries must deal with funding cuts as a result of the current economy and with community leaders who assume that access to the Web's vast resources obviates the need for publicly funded library service. Access to the Internet in libraries brings about discussions of intellectual freedom that are polarizing communities and resulting in legal action, going as far as the U.S. Supreme Court in some cases. Electronic publishing causes similar changes in copyright legislation and, as with any information issue, libraries are often at the epicenter of these controversies.

From a public relations perspective, the technology revolution also provides a whole new set of communications tools. For example, in the first edition, I suggested that libraries might e-mail press releases to those editors who had e-mail access—and it sounded like an innovation. Today I seriously doubt that most reporters open their "snail mail," and I sincerely hope that libraries aren't paying postage to mail press releases. Technology has changed the entire public relations landscape—not only can you get your message out there more quickly, you can save the copying and postage costs that were incurred in the past.

I devoted one page to "Web site development" in this manual's earlier edition. At that time, few libraries had Web sites. Patrons weren't using the Internet, so why would a Web site be a communications tool? Rest assured much more ink is devoted to that and other technology communications strategies in *Library Public Relations, Promotions, and Communications: A How-To-Do-It Manual, Second Edition.*

Today we live in an era where many homes have more computers than televisions, and libraries boast unprecedented increases in use. Total nationwide circulation of public library materials tops out at nearly 2 billion annually or 7 items per capita and public library visits total 1.1 billion or 4.3 per capita. Oprah shook up the publishing industry with her book club—sending viewers running to their libraries for the most recent selection—and the Harry Potter phenomenon sparked kids' reading habits—children are demanding intriguing titles to tide them over till the next book in the series is published.

Despite the increase in usage, libraries still grapple with the age-old challenges:

- patrons who simply cannot understand why controversial material belongs in a public library collection
- city council members who think that professional librarians can be replaced with volunteers.
- principals who see the school library program as a way to provide classroom coverage for teacher prep periods

The list goes on and on.

And then, because of their integral role in society, libraries are also subject to the dramatic changes in our overall cultural landscape. On September 11, 2001, our country changed forever, and that tragic turn of events presented a whole new set of challenges for libraries. Our federal government now asks libraries to share confidential patron information to help protect national security. Librarians who refuse are called "unpatriotic" and even accused of aiding and abetting terrorists—a sad set of circumstances, but one that we see reported in the media on a weekly basis.

Various and sundry solutions exist to deal with these issues, but at the core of any successful strategy is a cohesive, well-planned communications effort. All of these old and new challenges faced by libraries are often overcome—or even better, avoided—by telling the library's story and communicating its role and importance on an ongoing basis. *Library Public Relations, Promotions, and Communications: A How-To-Do-It Manual, Second Edition* is a tool designed for developing the story and communicating it effectively.

The world of public relations has changed as well since 1997. When I first started in this business nearly 20 years ago, many still perceived PR as fluff and considered a communications strategy as something to be used only when traditional advertising wasn't affordable. It's true—it is easier to communicate your message when you simply buy the space and publish it, but with editorial coverage comes credibility. Paid advertising is, in some instances, an important part of the communications mix, but for all types of libraries, it is often prohibitively expensive and doesn't necessarily demonstrate the most prudent use of public or institutional funds.

The recent "dot-com" era helped to build the credibility of public relations. Leaders that emerged from the dot-era, such as Microsoft, saw the value of communicating their message editorially when building their brand; they made deep investments in public relations, rather than in advertising. And many of today's other major brands, including Starbucks and Wal-Mart, followed suit, investing heavily in building positive public perception rather than traditional advertising.

In many ways, libraries were innovators in using public relations as the core of their communications strategies. For some, PR was simply a matter of economics—advertising was not in the budget.  For others, it was a legal issue—as in my experience working in Washington, where we were not allowed to spend public dollars on paid advertising. And for many, it stemmed from an understanding that the best possible way to build community support is through clear, consistent communications, particularly media relations.

I, too, have changed since I wrote the first edition of this book; I had spent the majority of my career in the world of public and school libraries—always involved in public relations and communications—but focused entirely on the government and not-for-profit world. Shortly after the first edition was published, I moved from the public to the private sector, taking a position at a public relations agency in Chicago where I managed education market public relations for a major corporation. Today, I run my own small public relations company dedicated to working with the education and library markets.

Admittedly, when I first began to work on *Library Public Relations, Promotions, and Communications: A How-To-Do-It Manual, Second Edition*, I wondered if I still brought the right perspective to the library community. What I have found is that my recent experiences have broadened my perspective on public relations strategies and my overall view of communications. I see the communications challenges and opportunities that libraries deal with from both an internal and external perspective, and I bring those new experiences, fresh ideas, and approaches to this edition.

# USING *LIBRARY PUBLIC RELATIONS, PROMOTIONS, AND COMMUNICATIONS: A HOW-TO-DO-IT MANUAL, SECOND EDITION* TO GUIDE YOUR LIBRARY'S COMMUNICATIONS

While this new edition deals with emerging communications issues and strategies, it is still a "how-to-do-it" manual that offers librarians an introduction to basic communications concepts, presents a step-by-step process that develops and implements a library public relations/communications plan, and provides details on effective communications tools and strategies. It is intended to guide both the PR novice and the seasoned professional as they develop and implement communications efforts for any type of library—public, academic, school, or special.

Part I, "Planning and Evaluation," features six chapters, including "Thinking About Public Relations and Communications for Your Library," "Defining Your Library's Messages and Audiences," "Developing Your Library's Public Relations/Communications Plan," and "Evaluating Your PR Program." It also includes two special chapters, "Positioning Libraries in a Changing Environment" and "PR in Different Types of Libraries."

Part II, "Strategies and Methodologies," provides step-by-step details for 11 ways to get your message out, including improving media relations, developing press materials, utilizing volunteers, expanding outreach, building programming, and networking with professionals. This part includes whole new chapters addressing increasingly important communication strategies. Chapter 7, "Building Your Library's Brand," offers an overview of branding as a marketing/PR tool, discusses ways to assess your library's current brand, and presents strategies for building the brand that your library will need for its very survival in the new century. Chapter 10, "Using Technology as a PR Tool," offers in-depth tips for using technology to broaden your library's communications. In addition, a separate chapter on "Coping with Communications During a Crisis" is included as Chapter 16 in this new edition.

Throughout *Library Public Relations, Promotions, and Communiciations: A How-To-Do-It Manual, Second Edition,* you will find real-life examples of effective communications strategies at all types of libraries and several major case studies of libraries that I believe have strong, integrated communications programs.

If your library is one of the many that has told its story effectively while using PR and communications to build your brand, the information and success stories in this book will help you refresh your approach with new strategies and best practices from other successful libraries. If your library is just developing a cohesive, ongoing approach to communications and public relations, *Library Public Relations, Promotions, and Communications* will take you through that process step by step.

# PART I
# PLANNING AND EVALUATION

# 1 POSITIONING LIBRARIES IN A CHANGING ENVIRONMENT

When the first edition of this book was published, the year 2000 was close, but we still thought of the "21st century" as more of a concept than a reality. Now here we are, almost halfway through the new century's first decade and grappling as a society with all of the challenges and opportunities presented by the new decade.

Reflecting society, libraries face many of the same—often conflicting—challenges and opportunities that other institutions and organizations face:

- pervasive access to technology vs. the digital divide
- vast resources of the Internet vs. quality and accuracy of Internet resources
- new and innovative funding models vs. decreasing public funds
- legislative support for access to technology vs. caveats that come with that support

The list is endless! And the challenge for libraries is to determine their role in this new environment and to communicate that role to the public. However, that role cannot be defined in a vacuum. Libraries belong to their communities and determining the place that libraries hold in today's society must be a community process. When public institutions dictate their mission to the communities they serve, they are usually unsuccessful in fulfilling that mission.

## EVALUATING AND MEETING COMMUNITY NEEDS

The first step in any successful public relations program is working with the community to determine its needs and how the library can meet those needs. Several years ago, a library in a poor, rural community in West Virginia had a collection of formal gowns that girls in the community could borrow to wear to school dances and formals. When this story was picked up by the national media, some library leaders criticized the program as being outside the mission of a public library. No matter what your opinion is, however, there is no denying that this library looked at its community, assessed its needs, and then went about meeting them. Perhaps those girls who visited the library to check out a prom gown had never been there before, and perhaps they also went home with a book or two or did some research on careers or colleges. Sometimes innovative community outreach strategies get library patrons in the door.

Assessing a community's information needs and determining what your school, public, or academic library can do to best meet those needs does not require hiring outside consultants or conducting expensive or time-consuming surveys. Assessment methods may be as simple as hosting a few small focus groups at your library and asking community members what they need or expect from the library, conducting a few informal surveys of both library users and nonusers, or closely monitoring the local media to see what kinds of information needs are surfacing. For example, when a community is dealing with the closing of a manufacturing plant, the library may reallocate its collection resources to purchase additional materials that will help workers find new jobs or explore new careers. And, of course, the library must then publicize those new materials so that the workers know they are now available.

On an ongoing basis, leaders at any school, public, or academic library should answer the following questions:

- What is the most important issue in our community at the moment?
- What is our library doing to help community members address this issue?
- What services and programs are our patrons making the most use of?
- What services and programs are our patrons not really using?
- What patron request are we most frequently not able to fulfill?

The answers to these questions will guide you as you determine your positioning in the community on an ongoing basis. You will find the answers to these questions from your frontline library staff—the people working the circulation and reference desks. You'll get the answers from your Friends of the Library, the teachers in your school, and the faculty members at your college or university. You'll read them in the local newspaper and hear about them when you attend the local Rotary Club meeting. For libraries to be successful—for them to survive—library leaders must keep their ears to the ground in their communities and be aware of both what the information needs are and how the library is perceived in terms of meeting those needs.

Public relations will also help your library stay on top of community needs and perceptions. Communication is always a two-way process and once you reach out to tell the community your library's story, the community will talk back. The key is to listen to what they are telling you. For example, say you launch a major campaign to publicize the library's genealogy collection and that campaign is successful in terms of garnering major media coverage and presentations at community groups. But if the use of the collection doesn't increase as a result of the campaign, it may be time to reevaluate the resources that you devote to that collection. Perhaps a career center is more appropriate for your community, or perhaps your users are more interested in leisure reading materials than in research materials.

# COMMUNICATING CORE LIBRARY VALUES

While successful libraries reflect community values and community needs, there are also some "bottom lines" for libraries that present additional challenges. At the core of these library values is intellectual freedom. The diversity of a library's collections and the audiences that it reaches are at the very foundation of libraries in this country. The challenge is explaining intellectual freedom to community members who, in some instances, have the best of intentions but not always the best information.

Ongoing public relations is the best tool for explaining to the public the values that all libraries uphold. A current challenge for many public libraries has been the USA Patriot Act which says that the federal government can request patron records when investigating terrorism. Some libraries have publicly announced that they would not comply with the act; others have remained quiet on the subject. This is obviously a touchy topic in a country where we are rightly concerned about national security. Many members of the public simply do not understand why libraries would deny government access to these records, and many librarians have eloquently explained the issues associated with patron confidentiality in the national and local media. However, in communities where patron confidentiality was discussed before the crisis of the USA Patriot Act presented a possible challenge, it is likely that the community has a better understanding of the issues and the library's stance.

# THE FUNDING DILEMMA

As hard as it may be to believe, the competition for public funding is even more competitive today than it was five years ago. The interim period was a time of a prosperity economy, but we are now once again in tight times. In 2003 nearly 30 states reported that they would have a tax deficit and needed to make significant cuts in public services and programs.

A new wrinkle, however, in public funding for libraries has been brought on by the development of the Internet. Ill-informed public officials are now questioning the necessity of public and school libraries; they assume that the information and resources that peoplew need are available online. Even more sadly, they assume that students and community members can simply evaluate those resources independently—that the librarian played no role in helping library users decide which materials best met their needs. Governors in at least five states have either eliminated or greatly cut back the funding for state library services.

The bottom line is that competition for tax dollars now presents an even greater struggle for libraries, and telling the story of the importance of libraries and librarians in schools, communities, colleges, and universities plays an even more critical role in garnering the funding needed to provide high-quality library services.

## THE UP AND DOWN SIDES OF THE INTERNET

Through deep state and community investments, and through such federal funding programs as the E-Rate, most school and public libraries are now wired and offer access to the Internet. "The National Council on Educational Statistics Quarterly, Spring 2002: Public Libraries in the United States: Fiscal Year 1999" report states that 92 percent of public libraries nationwide had access to the Internet. As many as 83 percent made the Internet available to patrons directly or through staff, 5 percent made the Internet available through staff only, and a mere 4 percent made the Internet available only to staff. [1]

Connectivity is just as pervasive in schools. Since 1990 U.S. school districts and states have invested more than $40 billion in computers, software, and connectivity. According to a report by Quality Education Data, Internet access has become the rule in K–12 schools, with 96 percent of K–12 teachers in public schools stating that they used the Internet as a teaching resource, up from 90 percent in 2001 and 86 percent in 2000. The same report reveals that 99 percent of America's public schools and 91 percent of public school classrooms are connected to the Internet.[2]

The Web plays a huge role in the educational environment at today's colleges and universities. Entire courses are taught online, professors post their syllabi and other course resource materials on secure Web sites, and many schools provide campuswide wireless connectivity. Yet, campuses still have brick-and-mortar library buildings and, in some instances, librarians play a role in planning for connectivity and the provision and acquisition of online resources. While students may access the resources from their dorm rooms or on the lawn in the quad, academic librarians need to play an ongoing role in the selection decisions and in helping students evaluate those resources that best meet their needs.

Finally, home Internet access in the United States is increasing daily. According to the Benton Foundation's Digital Divide Network, 41 percent of U.S. homes are connected to the Internet. Nearly 65 percent of college graduates have home Internet access. Interestingly, 33 percent of those people not connected have chosen not to go online with the biggest reason cited as "lack of need."[3] For those who have made the choice to "get connected," many libraries offer remote home access to online databases or the ability to put a "hold" on a book that they want to check out. Today's patrons can make use of a variety of library services without ever leaving their homes.

The bottom line is that the playing field for libraries has changed! Yet, even with ubiquitous access to the Internet, users need assistance evaluating the resources available on the more than three billion Web pages published on the Internet. Who better to provide that assistance than librarians? Unfortunately, however, much of the public and many legislators think that filters offer a better solution. As a result, federal and local funding for libraries is now often tied to the deployment of Internet filters. Librarians, however, know that just isn't true. Librarians and library staff are uniquely qualified to help patrons locate and evaluate all types of information—both in print and online.

So how do we get that message out? By investing in public relations and educating communities about the role of libraries and librarians in our society. The fact is that with the proliferation of free and original sources available online, it is even more important than before to fund training for professionals to help community members make the most of that information.

The following example is from ten years ago—before we even dreamed about the Internet in libraries. However, it still demonstrates the education process that is necessary and the role that public relations can play in that process.

A public library system was considering whether it could afford to continue providing outreach services to inmates at the county jail. The library system approached the county commissioners to ask for county funding to continue the service. One of the commissioners, who also happened to be a surgical nurse, suggested that perhaps the service could be continued using volunteers instead of library staff. A community member testifying at the hearing remarked, "Perhaps when the hospital budget gets into trouble, it could just use volunteers for some surgical services." Obviously, that person understood the value of professional librarians and trained, experienced paraprofessionals, and knew that library service is more than just checking out books. The citizen's analogy convinced the commissioner to vote to authorize funding for the service. Such a crucial understanding doesn't just happen; support like that comes from a well-planned and well-executed public relations program.

# CONCLUSION

At first, you might think that it will be difficult to make a case for implementing a public relations program for your school, public, or academic library. But when you consider the issues that you are faced with in today's changing environment, you will quickly realize that you can't afford not to move in that direction. As you will see in future chapters, you can start small or you can go gangbusters with a big, glitzy program. However, communicating with the public about your library's programs, services, values, and plans is critical to your ongoing success and, perhaps, to your very survival. So turn the page and learn more about planning and implementing a public relations program that will meet the needs of your library and, most important, your community.

# NOTES

1. National Council on Educational Statistics, "NCES Quarterly, Spring 2002: Public Libraries in the United States: Fiscal Year 1999." Available *http:// nces.ed.gov/pubs2002/quarterly/spring/q5-1.asp*.
2. Quality Education Data, "Internet Usage in Teaching for the 2002 School Year" (September 2002).
3. Benton Foundation, "Digital Divide Basics Fact Sheet" (2004). Available *www.digitaldividenetwork.org/content/stories/index.cfm?key=168*.

# 2 THINKING ABOUT PUBLIC RELATIONS AND COMMUNICATIONS FOR YOUR LIBRARY

The first step in implementing a public relations program for any library is to develop a plan that maps to your communications needs and resources. It is important to look at all of your programs and services and evaluate the communications needs associated with them. Some may need to be promoted, others must be explained to the community, and others might require a crisis communications plan. All programs and services must support your overall system messaging and communications strategy.

For example, summer reading happens every year at Anytown Public Library and every year the staff does the same things to promote it—news releases, flyers, children's librarians visiting school classrooms. Every year, the program is implemented, attendance is high, circulation increases slightly, and by the end of August the children's librarians are exhausted. Through outreach in the schools and flyers at the library, children throughout the city are reached and on an annual basis about 50 percent of the community's children participate in the program in some way. Not a bad result, right?

The library never had a written public relations plan for summer reading and the efforts were never evaluated. No one ever sat down and thought about how the promotion of summer reading fits into the rest of the library's public relations efforts. While they may be doing exactly what works, they might not be getting the most effectiveness from their efforts or the most bang for their buck. Attendance levels might be as high as they can reasonably get or as the tired children's librarians can handle. Getting coverage for the summer programs and events in the local newspaper and on television might not increase the already high participation levels, but it would demonstrate to community members— particularly those without children—the important services that the library is providing.

By carefully planning the summer reading promotion and considering where it fits in the library's overall public relations efforts, Anytown Public Library will be able to achieve better results and make its limited dollars go further. Evaluating efforts based on the plan will help improve strategies for next year. For example, perhaps by looking at all the other public relations activities in the library, staff may discover that three other activities are being heavily promoted with the local media during the same time period as summer reading. That discovery may provide an answer to the children's librarian's constant query, "We are doing really creative programs. Why don't we ever get any news coverage?" Library-wide planning will help Anytown Public Library avoid competing with itself for news coverage or other types of public attention.

In your library, a public relations/communications plan will also be a guide as you get involved in the hectic pace of working on your project. By referring to the plan, you can see what you have done, what you need to do, and (based on the experiences you have had thus far, and your timing or budget constraints) what elements of your plan might need to be changed. You have a record of where your time and energy have gone and you can evaluate your efforts and decide where they might be best directed in the future.

Above all, developing your library's public relations/communications plan forces you to sit down and think about where you have been, where you are going, and what you want to do. It gives you a reason to consider thoughtfully the communications tools available to you and how to use them.

You will have to decide whether to do a comprehensive or a project-based public relations plan. Several factors should influence your decision. If this is your first public relations effort, a project plan may be the best place to start. You can build on that with future efforts. If you are in a library where lots of project-based public relations efforts—planned or not—are already occurring, a comprehensive plan is probably what you want to develop. It will provide an opportunity to bring the various activities into one cohesive and complementary effort. Be careful when deciding what kind of plan to develop not to take on more than you can handle. Set yourself up for success by developing a goal and a plan that are manageable based on your experience and fiscal and human resources.

Planning will put your public relations efforts into a context where they will support your overall program rather than derail it or contradict it. Planning will make the process of telling your story and garnering public understanding more efficient, more effective, and more fun!

## STAFFING FOR PUBLIC RELATIONS

Once you have decided that planned public relations/communications is a priority for your library, it is critical that one person be designated to coordinate implementation of your plan. This doesn't mean that one person has to do everything, but it is necessary to have a lead person who oversees the plan's implementation and follows up on the completion of scheduled activities.

A public relations staff, or at least one full-time person devoted to managing your public relations, is the ideal. There are two schools of thought about what a public relations manager's training or background should be. Some maintain that only a professional librarian can accurately represent the library's philosophy, programs, and services. Others hold that it is most important for a library public relations manager to have a background in public relations, communications, or journalism. Whoever you hire should be an effective communicator, one who is well organized with creative ideas and lots of energy, and one who understands and believes in the value of library service.

A full-time public relations staff may be ideal for many libraries, particularly larger public libraries and academic libraries. However, the ideal may not always be practical when other budget and staffing needs are taken into consideration. You may have to reassign the duties of a current staff person so that person can spend a portion of his or her time working on your library's public relations program. If you have decided that public relations is a priority for your library, it is critical that the person appointed receive release time from regular duties in order to handle public relations activities. Your public relations efforts will not be effective if they are merely added to a staff member's already massive workload. By freeing up staff time for work on public relations and by devoting human resources to your efforts, you are making a statement about your library's commitment to telling its story.

For school library media specialists, public relations may indeed be another job responsibility in an already unmanageable workload. You can, however, think about what tasks, including some of the public relations activities, can be delegated to volunteers. With the current strong emphasis on parental involvement in schools, you may find public relations professionals available to help with your efforts. Check with the PTA/PTO or volunteer office for your school or district.

Creating a relationship with public relations/communications staff at the school district level is another way to lighten your load. Such a relationship also provides you with an opportunity to see where your building or departmental plans fit within the school district's overall public relations plan.

Academic librarians may have some of the same opportunities for shifting workloads that public librarians have. And like school librarians they have the opportunity to work closely with the college or university's public relations office to coordinate efforts. Again, however you staff your public relations activities, one key person should coordinate and oversee all efforts so that your library takes a big-picture approach.

Another staffing-related issue to consider is who will supervise the public relations person. Whether you have a full-time public relations person or a staff member who is coordinating your efforts on a part-time basis, the chain of command for this person could have a significant impact on the success of your plan. In the corporate world, public relations directors often report directly to the chief executive officer. If they aren't direct reports, they typically have direct access to that person. The reason for this relationship is obvious: it is always important that the person telling the organization's story receive a clear message from the top about what that story is. A library's public relations efforts and the goals of its administration must be tightly interwoven and not working at cross-purposes. A public relations person who reports to the library director knows the organizational priorities and can follow them. When competing priorities are presented, the public relations person has the ability to say, "The library director said we are going to do it this way." That kind of clout can be very important to effective public relations.

In a school environment, the principal should have a clear understanding of the school library media specialist's public relations efforts. The principal might even participate in the implementation of public relations activities. Such support speaks loudly to the rest of the faculty, to parents, and to school board members about the importance of the school library media program. It also provides the school librarian with help in reshaping job duties so that he or she can devote some time to public relations activities. A school librarian with a strong interest in public relations should garner the support of the district public relations person—and perhaps even volunteer to serve on a districtwide public relations advisory committee or to work on districtwide public relations activities. Such activities provide more chances to tell the library's story from a districtwide public relations perspective.

Again, the academic librarian's situation is a combination of that of public and school librarians. The person responsible for public relations in a college or university library should report to the library director for that part of his or her duties, but a strong relationship with the college or university's public relations staff is also necessary. Volunteering to be involved with institution-wide public relations efforts is a good strategy for an academic librarian; such involvement provides a broader perspective and offers opportunities for integrating the library into the institution's overall public relations efforts.

The most important thing about choosing staff for your library's public relations efforts is to look for someone who is passionate about your library's services, programs, and role in the community, and who has the ability to communicate that passion. A person with these qualities will be able to recruit volunteers for your efforts, garner staff support for the importance of public relations, and, ultimately, achieve your public relations goals.

## BUILDING INTERNAL SUPPORT FOR PR

While it is important to have a person who takes lead responsibility for your library's public relations activities, planning and implementation of public relations and communications should be a collaborative effort among the library staff and volunteers—even if they only serve in an advisory capacity. You may want to form a library-wide task force or committee to plan your public relations efforts, and then involve the same group or a new one in implementing and evaluating the plan.

Other library staff will bring significant concerns and information to your communications activities, but involvement of a wide variety of staff will also encourage all of the staff to take ownership in your efforts. Public relations activities may be something that your principal or library board has asked you to become involved with, possibly causing difficulties for staff in general—more work, additional confusion in the middle of a busy work-day, and the need to drop everything to help you deal with reporters. It is important that all staff understand the value of what you are doing *before* public relations activities interrupt their work schedules. For example, if your communications planning committee members agree that unless you get the word out and increase your library's circulation statistics and gate count, the city council is going to cut your budget in the next fiscal year, library staff members who serve on the committee will understand that dropping everything to help you deal with a reporter isn't an interruption of their work, but rather a key to their survival. Staff who serve on the planning committee for communications activities will develop such an understanding and be committed to your efforts. In addition, they can share that commitment with their coworkers.

Serving on a planning or advisory committee can be an excellent educational opportunity for library staff. Frontline staff will learn more about the challenges of getting the word out, while you learn more about what really happens at a public service desk. One example of a communications activity that could have proved problematic if not for the "buy-in" of frontline staff involved a public library that was asked by a radio station to help in a promotion. The radio station was giving away free tickets to a Rolling Stones concert by hiding them in various places around the city and then giving its listeners clues to finding them. The station's promotions manager approached the library's communications director and asked to hide tickets in a book at the library. This was an excellent opportunity to promote the library—particularly to the radio station's listeners, ages 20 to 40—and it created an image of the library as a fun, hip place. The communications director agreed, but there was a catch—she wasn't allowed to tell anyone because the hiding place was a secret. On the morning that the clue was announced on the air, over 100 people were waiting for the library to open. They ran into the building and began looking for the book where the tickets were hidden. The staff stood helplessly by and looked befuddled. The tickets were found and the chaos ended.

The library staff could have been upset about not being forewarned. But, after years of successful communications activities and many library staff serving on various communications planning and advisory committees, the majority of the staff recognized the opportunity and understood why the communications director had taken advantage of it. They were quick to squelch the complaints of the "naysayers." The process of education and buy-in that had taken place over nearly a ten-year period had paid off—and both the staff and the radio station's listeners had a little bit of fun while spreading the word about the public library.

Another reason to involve other library staff in your efforts is that in most cases you alone cannot implement your plans. For example, if you are trying to increase use of your academic library's Internet services by community members, you can develop and promote training events, but you will need to work with a variety of people—the library's technology coordinator to plan and implement the training, the custodian to set up the room for the training sessions, and perhaps the circulation manager if you are going to offer community members free library cards when they come for the training. While the goal of this project might be to change community members' perception about the university and the role that it can play in their neighborhood, it will take a collaborative effort to plan, promote, and implement this activity that was developed in support of your goal.

## FUNDING YOUR EFFORTS

True commitment to library public relations will mean choosing to spend money on public relations. Once your plan is developed, you will need a budget to support it. If you can't afford what you planned, then hard decisions must be made and your plan will need to be pared back or alternative funding sources, such as grants, will have to be investigated. The problem with grants, or "soft" money, is that they go away; if your public relations efforts are funded entirely by grant funds, when the grant is over, so are your public relations activities. When you make public relations a priority, a separate budget for those efforts is important to your success. It doesn't have to be a huge amount of money, but it must be realistic in terms of what you are planning to do. About two to five percent of your overall library budget is often a good target.

When you are convincing your library board, school-based management team, or university library director that this is an important expenditure, think about trying to place a value on the results of the public relations efforts. Of a $2 million budget, $100,000 will seem like a drop in the bucket if it has the potential to increase public support and pass an upcoming bond issue of $40 million, or if it might increase your circulation to such an extent that the city council will appropriate an extra $1 million for your library budget next year. On a different level, $250 out of a school library media center's $5,000 budget might not seem like much to spend on public relations efforts, but, school and academic libraries may also have the opportunity to build on the overall public relations efforts of their school districts or universities. The important thing is to make a commitment to a level of spending for public relations that is commensurate with your overall library budget, and to consider that commitment as important as any other line item in your budget. Some day your public relations/communications efforts may be critical to your library's very survival.

A word of warning is in order, however. Your public relations plan has the potential to achieve great things for your library, but there are no guarantees. It is an obvious gamble for those making the funding decisions. Nevertheless, if you have a detailed public relations plan and ask for a reasonable amount of money based on that plan you have a better chance of having your budget request granted and of achieving your public relations goals—so that you can return the next year with bigger goals, a bigger plan, and possibly a request for more funding.

## DEFINITION OF TERMS

The terms *public relations, marketing, promotion,* and *advertising* are used frequently and often interchangeably in the profit and nonprofit worlds, including the library community. While these terms are all communications strategies, they are not interchangeable. Before you can develop a successful public relations/ communications plan, clear definitions of these terms are needed. Not only will these definitions help you design a plan that is most appropriate for your library's needs, they will help you when you sell the plan to other staff, and to board and community members.

The following definitions will give you a place to begin thinking about public relations, marketing, promotion, and advertising as distinct but overlapping concepts.

**Public relations:** The business of trying to convince the public to have understanding for and goodwill toward a person, firm, or institution. Also, the degree of understanding and goodwill achieved.

**Marketing:** Actually selling or purchasing in a market. Also, a combination of functions involved in moving goods from producer to consumer.

**Promotion:** Trying to further the growth or development of something. Especially, trying to sell merchandise through advertising, publicity, or discounting.

**Advertising:** Calling something to the attention of the public, especially by paid announcements.

None of these terms is a new concept; the etymologies date the origin of the term *advertising* to 1762 and *marketing* to 1561. *Public relations* is the newest—having been coined in 1807. Yet, as a result of our increasingly competitive marketplace, particularly in the area of information services, they should be and are becoming more and more a part of our society's common vocabulary. And, during the current information explosion, under-

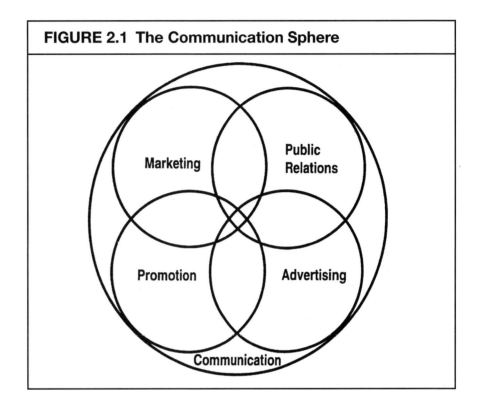

**FIGURE 2.1 The Communication Sphere**

Marketing

Public Relations

Promotion

Advertising

Communication

standing and application of these concepts is key to the future of library services in this country, particularly for school and public libraries.

Figure 2.1 illustrates the relationships among these complex concepts. As you can tell, none of them can really exist without at least one of the others and they are all required for effective marketing. The diagram demonstrates the idea that public relations, marketing, promotion, and advertising used in any combination are all interrelated *communication* activities.

## PUBLIC RELATIONS

In 1975 the Foundation for Public Relations Research had 65 leaders in the profession write their own definition for public relations:

> Public relations is a distinctive management function which helps establish and maintain mutual lines of communication, understanding, acceptance and cooperation between an organization and its publics; involves the management of problems or issues; helps management keep informed on and responsive to public opinion; defines and emphasizes the responsibility of management

to serve the public interest; helps management keep abreast of and effectively utilize change, serving as an early warning system to help anticipate trends; and uses research and sound and ethical communications techniques as its principal tools.[1]

This comprehensive definition may sound complicated, but basically public relations works to create positive perceptions of your library. It is related to marketing when it is used as part of a marketing plan, but it also exists in its own right as a critical tool for creating goodwill toward your library and its services. At times, public relations is reactive. For example, if the local newspaper is writing a story on the new circulating DVD collection at your library, it is your job to make sure that the reporter puts a positive spin on this new service. The reporter may want to talk about how the library is now competing with private enterprise—the Blockbuster on the corner. In order to have a story that creates a positive perception of your library and its programs, you need to work with the reporter to ensure that he or she accurately reflects the purpose of the DVD collection, understands the importance of providing information in a variety of formats, and still gets a story that will be interesting to readers. This is not a simple challenge. Chapter 8 deals with learning how to work effectively with the media. Effective media relations are an important part of positive public relations.

At other times, public relations is proactive. For example, if your university library will now be open 24 hours, you may want the campus newspaper to do a positive article that stresses the security measures that will be part of your late-night open hours. By encouraging news coverage of your new open hours, you also risk criticism. Perhaps the reporter will interview students who will say that they feel the library is not safe and secure during your daytime open hours and that they would never feel safe there at night. The students may or may not be telling the truth—perhaps they are just anxious to be quoted in the campus newspaper. Nevertheless, you have a media opportunity that could become a negative one if you don't handle it correctly. Again, working effectively with the reporter to tell your story is important for successful proactive public relations.

Good public relations plans include multiple approaches to achieving their goals. They acknowledge the different ways of reaching an audience and the diversity within even a clearly delineated audience. For example, if you want community members of ages 30 to 45 to learn about and understand the importance of continuing to fund library service to the elderly in nursing homes, and if you know that your target demographic group reads the local newspaper, you might try to have the paper run a human interest story about this service. That is one approach to achieving your goal, but it should be only one component of your overall plan for communicating the message. Other components might include working with a local talk radio station with the appropriate demographics to do a story that includes interviews of elderly people who value your service, launching a television public service announcement campaign of spots with nursing home patrons talking about what library services mean to them, or even developing a volunteer program so that community members can join your staff on their monthly visits to the nursing homes. In concert, these components could create a multidimensional public relations plan for reaching your goal.

To be most effective, public relations efforts should be time intensive—they should happen in a concentrated period of time. For example, in the approach described above, the efforts will have the greatest impact if they occur within two to three months rather than two to three years. The messages we remember most are the ones we hear at least three times within a limited time frame. If the length of time you plan to reach your goal is too long, your message will be obscured by other messages.

Careful planning is extremely important for successful public relations. Planning doesn't preclude taking advantage of serendipitous opportunities, like an offer from a television station to produce free public service announcements that further your efforts. In fact, such opportunities will be even more meaningful if your library has a clear overall plan for public relations. Careful planning means that you and the other staff will all have a clear road map toward your public relations goal and will be able to concentrate efforts on reaching that goal rather than taking a scattershot approach. It will help you develop clear, consistent messages to deliver over and over again to your constituency. A plan also provides you with a mechanism for evaluating your efforts.

In the past, public relations had a somewhat negative reputation. P. T. Barnum is sometimes referred to as "the father of public relations," and his trademark, "There's a sucker born every minute," has dogged the practice of public relations and public relations practitioners for years. Public relations practitioners were referred to as "spin doctors" and "flacks." Our increasingly sophisticated society has had a tendency to be suspicious of public relations.

In addition, libraries are viewed by many as institutions that should be above the kind of practices that the negative connotations surrounding public relations imply. Yet, thoughtful taxpayers can be convinced that their tax dollars for library programs and services will be ill-spent if the community doesn't know about and understand those services. Unfortunately, though, the first step in your library's public relations plan might need to be creating a positive public perception of the importance of public relations for libraries, especially if you are planning to devote significant human or fiscal resources to your effort.

The good news, however, is that over the past 20 years, public relations has gained greater acceptance. In their 2002 book *The Fall of Advertising and the Rise of PR*, Al Ries and Laura Ries write, "Wherever we look, we see a dramatic shift from advertising-oriented marketing to public relations-oriented marketing."[2]

John Cotton Dana is considered the father of library public relations. Dana, a librarian who pioneered using public relations to promote library use, was the first director of the Newark museum, the first president of the Special Libraries Association, and the 11th president of the American Library Association. He established the first children's room and the first U.S. branch library for the business community. The sidebar outlines ten ways that John Cotton Dana improved his library—they all hold true today. Since 1946 the American Library Association has annually presented the John Cotton Dana Library Public Relations Award for outstanding library public relations.[3] Figure 2.2 provides examples of today's libraries putting John Cotton Dana's time-tested principles into action.

Positive public perception of the library is more important than high gate counts or circulation when you need the community's help in funding a new service or the school board's support for an increased materials budget for the school library media program. A good example of this is a public library board member who served for more than eight years. He readily admitted that he didn't use the library's services—he bought his own books. But he dedicated countless volunteer hours to his work on the board and to the library's capital campaign. Why? He said he recognized the importance of high-quality library service in a community—even if he didn't use it himself. He never added to the gate count or the circulation statistics, but he made a significant contribution to that library's success.

Developing positive perceptions of a school, public, or academic library does not happen overnight. And while public relations involves working to create that perception, it is critical that the reality the public faces when they come to use your services matches the positive perception you've instilled in your community.

---

### Ten Ways John Cotton Dana Promoted His Libraries: Tips from the Past

*This article was originally excerpted on the University of Illinois Graduate School of Library and Information Science Web site, "UI Current LIS Clips," at www.lis.uiuc.edu/clips. This Web site is a great resource for annotations of and links to articles on a variety of topics of interest to libraries and libraries.*

John Cotton Dana was one of the most innovative and influential librarians of the twentieth century. From his first library job in Denver where he opened the first public library, until his death in Newark in 1929, Dana successfully used public relations and marketing strategies to promote his libraries. He believed the library was there to be used and the more people who used it the better. In 1946, the library profession honored him with a library public relations award in his name. The John Cotton Dana contest is the oldest annual competition in the United States recognizing excellence in library public relations. To promote his library in Denver, John Cotton Dana:

1. sent circulars advertising the services of the first Denver public library to editors of a variety of local and national journals and newspapers;
2. made personal visits to every editor and every leading clergyman in Denver;
3. reached out to the business community by developing a business library in the Chamber of Commerce building;
4. established the first children's room in a public library in the U.S.;
5. granted teachers the opportunity to check out up to 50 books for use in the classroom;
6. developed a picture collection of art works and illustrations and let these to schools for classes;
7. collected foreign language materials that reflected the ethnic groups in the community;
8. provided meeting room space to local clubs;
9. published a monthly newsletter about the library;
10. developed an apprenticeship program to train inexperienced library staff.

*Excerpted from Deborah Fink and Bonnie McCune, "Marketing Libraries," Colorado Libraries 27 (Winter 2000): 5–40. Reprinted from "UI LIS Clips" September 2003. © Board of Trustees of the University of Illinios.*

**FIGURE 2.2 Simply the Best . . .**

**Two Years of John Cotton Dana Winners**

There is no better way to develop a strong public relations and communications program for your library than to study the work of the masters. The libraries below received John Cotton Dana Awards in 2003 and 2004 for the programs described. The program descriptions include links to the libraries' Web sites. As you can see, libraries of all types and sizes develop and implement successful, creative public relations programs.

The John Cotton Dana Library Public Relations Award recognizes and honors outstanding achievement in library public relations. This annual award jointly sponsored by the H. W. Wilson Company, Bronx, N.Y., and the Library Administration and Management Association (LAMA), a division of the American Library Association (ALA)—has been awarded annually since 1946.

Check out these libraries and their PR programs—in the library PR world, they are "simply the best!"

2004 John Cotton Dana Award Winners

- Halifax Public Libraries (Dartmouth, N.S., Canada) for its complex and layered "Summer Reading Quest," featuring seven fantasy characters in an original, interactive adventure and a dynamic Web site designed to attract the reluctant reader.

- Orange County Public Library (Santa Ma, Calif.) for the imaginative Egyptology Lecture Series, a program of scholars and other luminaries that was developed from a unique partnership with the American Research Center in Egypt

- Edmon Low Library, Oklahoma State University (Stillwater, Okla.) for a stellar commemorative celebration, "That was Then... This is Now," focusing on the successes and challenges marking 50 years of building pride.

- Dr. Martin Luther King, Jr. Library (San Jose, Calif.) for a building dedication campaign, highlighting a groundbreaking partnership between the San Jose State University and the city's public library.

- Pioneer Library System (Norman, Okla.) for an intriguing and visually appealing campaign that promoted libraries as prominent cultural agents. The Red Dirt Book Festival celebrated the Oklahoma literary experience.

- Las Vegas—Clark County Library District (Las Vegas, Nev.) for Reading Las Vegas, Books: A Sure Bet!—a catchy public relations and branding campaign using casino imagery to promote the library's second annual adult reading program.

- Barrington Area Library (Barrington, Ill.) for "Simple Living," a series of lifestyle programs featuring the concept of paring down, making choices, and staying focused, designed in response to the changing economic climate.

**FIGURE 2.2** *continued*

2003 John Cotton Dana Award Winners

- Genesee District Library (Flint, Mich.) for opening a 3,800-square-foot demonstration location inside a busy shopping center to take their services to the people. Since their initial opening, this new location has averaged over 7,000 visitors per month and registered over 2,000 new cardholders.

- Guernsey Memorial Library (Norwich, N.Y.), for a delightful celebration of the library's centennial anniversary. The celebration focused on genealogy, local architecture, and history, successfully creating a positive image for the community.

- Halifax Regional Library (Dartmouth, N.S., Canada), for its redesigned Summer Reading Program. With a skateboarding dog, Booker T. Beagle, and animal "Book Buddies" for younger children, the program creatively used a consistent graphic identity, a dynamic Web site, and targeted marketing to reach the intended audience.

- Julia Rogers Library, Goucher College (Baltimore, Md.), for the public relations program "25 Years of Jane Austen," designed to bring increased attention to this unique collection. The identification of strategies for the campaign, along with target audiences, was precise and comprehensive, ranging from a resident scholarship to digitizing the collection for access by a worldwide audience.

- Library System of Lancaster County (Pa.) for its stimulating public awareness campaign promoting the Pennsylvania online world of electronic resources (POWER), which successfully enhanced local resources.

- Las Vegas-Clark County Library District (Las Vegas, Nev.) for its outstanding public relations campaign celebrating Asian Pacific American Heritage Month. Part of the library district's "Celebrate Cultural Diversity" initiative, the event attracted more than 6,000 people and generated positive media coverage.

- Saint Paul (Minn.) Public Library and the Friends of the Saint Paul Public Library (Saint Paul, Minn.) for a multifaceted public awareness campaign to celebrate the reopening of their newly renovated historic Central Library.

- Sarasota County Library System (Sarasota, Fla.) for its successful program "Celebrate Freedom @ your library" which refocused public attention on how libraries contribute to a free society. This program, developed in answer to the challenges posed by 9/11, helped to erase the doubts raised by that tragic event by reinforcing the knowledge that libraries stand for freedom of information and access for all.

- Toronto Public Library (Toronto, Ont., Canada) for an innovative performing arts lecture series and public relations program that contributed to the city's literary and cultural life while also enhancing the library's community profile.

Program descriptions from American Library Association John Cotton Dana press releases.

## MARKETING

Marketing seems to be today's buzzword in terms of library promotion. Many library directors talk about developing marketing plans, when what they really need to develop is a public relations or communications plan. Public relations and promotion are both components of a comprehensive marketing plan, but they don't necessarily involve the intensive market research and study that marketing requires. In libraries, marketing might be used to influence a citizen's behavior, rather than just change his or her perception of the library. For example, a marketing campaign might be used to get citizens to check more videos out of the library. You would do research to discover what kind of videos the public wants, you would purchase them, and then promote them. The goal of a public relations campaign, on the other hand, can be simply to create a positive public perception of your library.

In fact, the corporate world acknowledges the value of including public relations as part of corporate communications. In *The Marketer's Guide to Public Relations*, Thomas Harris coins the term "marketing public relations." He cites a number of corporate successes (such as the Cabbage Patch Kids phenomenon, the sale of Reese's Pieces candy following the release of the film *E.T.*, and Pillsbury's increased sales after its annual Bake-Off) as examples of corporate marketing goals that were met by public relations efforts. He defines marketing public relations as "the process of planning, executing and evaluating programs that encourage purchase and consumer satisfaction through credible communication of information and impressions that identify companies and their products with the needs, wants, concerns and interests of consumers."[4] Based on that definition, the public relations efforts of your library will often be marketing public relations. By creating the positive public perception of your library, you will encourage your public to use your services.

Comprehensive marketing begins before the service is developed or at a time when changing the service can be considered. Marketing begins with the identification of customer needs. If people don't need what you are planning to provide, there is no market. Through careful analysis of the results of market research, library services or collections are designed and promoted to the customer. The goal of marketing in the for-profit world is increased profits. In the library world, the goal might be increased circulation, gate count, or program attendance.

This is a rather simplistic description of a complex concept. For a more in-depth description of how to develop and implement a marketing plan, *Library Marketing That Works!* (Neal-Schuman, 2004), by Suzanne Walters, provides a step-by-step guide for using marketing to develop library services uniquely suited to your customers.

## PROMOTION AND ADVERTISING

The terms promotion and advertising are also used interchangeably. Advertising, however, is a component of promotion, marketing, and public relations. For the purpose of this discussion, advertising will be limited to something you must purchase, such as television advertising spots that you purchase time for, ads that you place in the local newspaper, and billboards that you rent. If you have the budget to purchase advertising, it may be an effective public relations/communications strategy for your library. In addition, most outlets that sell advertising (such as newspapers, television and radio stations, transit advertising, and billboard rental companies) offer nonprofit rates that your library might be eligible for. Unreserved space is sometimes available gratis if you produce the artwork for the advertisement.

Interestingly, though, the public has become increasingly skeptical of advertising over the past 20 years or more. Ries and Ries state, "PR has credibility. Advertising does not. PR provides the positive perception that an advertising campaign, if properly directed, can exploit."[5]

So, while there may be instances when advertising—or paid placements—are the appropriate communications strategy for your library, they must always be linked to your greater public relations/communications plan and overall institutional message. Advertising just for the sake of getting your library's name in print is not an effective strategy and, in some circumstances, may even backfire. Community members may ask, "Why does that library think they need more funding when they can buy advertisements in the local newspaper?" This negative outcome can even occur when you secure a discounted or gratis ad—the public sees advertising as an expense, no matter how it is funded.

Promotional efforts can be part of your public relations/communications plan. When you promote a service or program, you are usually trying to cause people to act. For example, you promote preschool storytime so that people will bring their children. It isn't enough for them simply to know about storytime and think it is a good thing; you are trying to get them to participate. As another example, you might have a regular plan for promoting new titles in your collection—so that people visit the library, check out materials, and increase your circulation count.

You may decide that promotion and/or advertising play a role in your library's overall public relations efforts. No matter what strategies you include, it is critical that you think carefully about your goals and develop an overall plan that will help you meet those goals. In Chapter 4, you will learn how to assess what you want to achieve and how to develop a plan for getting there.

## CONCLUSION

By picking up this book, you have indicated that you are thinking about library public relations. At this point, you may even think that your library needs a public relations plan. As a 20-year public relations professional, I believe that all organizations—big or small, and particularly those that serve the public and are publicly funded—need to have a public relations/communications plan. This plan is the only way that you can explain to the public the ways that you serve the community and the value that libraries have in society. In today's competitive environment, it isn't enough just to work hard and do great work—you have to tell the public about it so that they continue to use, recognize, and, ultimately, fund your library.

Deciding to commit the resources necessary to make communications a priority for your library will be the next step. Then, you will need to develop a detailed plan for your efforts. This plan will help you to identify your message and your communications goal, and to think carefully about the activities that will help you to achieve your goal.

As you explore developing effective public relations, promotions, and communications for libraries, you will learn that the definitions for public relations, marketing, promotion, and advertising are not clear-cut and that there is a lot of overlap and ambiguity. The following example from *Promoting Issues and Ideas: A Guide to Public Relations for Nonprofit Organizations* sums up the vagueness of the distinctions:

> If the circus is coming to town and you paint a sign saying "Circus Coming to the Fairground Saturday," that's advertising. If you put the sign on the back of an elephant and walk him into town, that's promotion. If the elephant walks through the mayor's flower bed, that's publicity. And if you can get the mayor to laugh about it, that's public relations.[6]

# NOTES

1. Scott M. Cutlip, Allen H. Center, and Glen M. Broom, *Effective Public Relations*, 6th ed. (Englewood Cliffs, N.J.: Prentice Hall, 1985), 4.
2. Al Ries and Laura Ries, *The Fall of Advertising and the Rise of PR.* (New York: Harper Collins, 2002), xi.
3. Connie Vinta Dowell, "A Revamped John Cotton Dana PR Award Turns 50," *American Libraries* 26 (October 1995): 908–911.
4. Thomas L. Harris, *The Marketer's Guide to Public Relations* (New York: John Wiley & Sons, 1991), 12.
5. Ries and Ries, xi.
6. Public Interest Public Relations, *Promoting Issues and Ideas: A Guide to Public Relations for Nonprofit Organizations* (New York: The Foundation Center, 1987), 1.

# 3 DEFINING YOUR LIBRARY'S MESSAGES AND AUDIENCES

The two important building blocks for your public relations/communications plan are message and audience. Effective public relations activities communicate a clear, consistent message to a carefully selected target audience. The message is reflected in the services and programs your library provides, and the methods used to communicate it are appropriate for the audience you want to reach. Your public relations/communications efforts will be more successful if you spend extra time in your planning process thinking about the specific messages you want to communicate and the audiences you want to reach. In addition, once you determine your key messages and your audience, the strategies and tools for your communications plan will become apparent.

Wanting to tell everyone in your community that your library is good and that they should use it is an admirable goal. But how do you go about achieving it? Would time and resources allow you to reach everybody? What outcome do you want? Narrow that goal to increasing library use by parents of students enrolled in the local public schools. Focus your message on telling them about the high-quality resources and activities that you offer for families.

## DEVELOPING YOUR MESSAGE

Clear, consistent messages are key to the success of your communications efforts. After you answer the question "What do you want to tell people?" and even after you develop your public relations/communications plan, you will want to spend time developing and refining your message. It cannot be ambiguous and you must work to ensure that all of your materials carry the same messages, if not the same words. Ambiguity is created and mixed messages are communicated when your message is not consistent with reality.

Your messages should also be focused. Don't try to tell people everything at once or in one communications effort. If you are simply trying to change perceptions, then your messages should communicate whatever perception you are trying to create. But, if the aim of your message is to get people to act, then make sure your message tells them what you want them to do. If you want them to check out more books, communicate that action: "Anytown Public Library—Check Us Out!" If you want people to think your library is a safe place, develop a message that says "Anytown Public Library—A Safe Place." Don't let clever words and slogans get in the way of your message. It is better to be clear and get the word out than to be clever and confuse a lot of people.

A communications plan should have no more than three key messages. Your messages should be concise, bulleted statements. To develop your key messages, answer these questions:

- What do I want my audience to remember from this PR campaign?
- What action do I want them to take?
- How will taking this action require them to change their thinking and behavior?

Continuing with the example of a campaign to increase public library use by families with school-age children, let's answer the questions.

- What do I want my audience to remember?
  Answer: The library offers programs and resources targeted specifically to families with school-age children.
- What action do I want them to take?
  Answer: To attend our programs for families and children and take advantage of our collections and resources for families and children.
- How will taking this action require them to change their thinking and behavior?
  Answer: If the library isn't already on their busy list of activities, they will need to find room for it.

Based on those answers, the three key messages for the campaign might be:

- Anytown Public Library focuses on the family with special programs and collections targeted specifically at parents and their school-age children.
- Anytown Public Library is the best bargain in town for families. Library cards, programs, and services are all always free. Check us out!

- Anytown Public Library's convenient hours, including on Sundays and in the evenings, allow parents and families to fit library visits into their busy schedules.

Once you have developed manageable messages, specific communications activities, such as having your branch libraries set up information booths at school parent nights, will begin to emerge as possible ways of communicating your message and accomplishing the goal.

Messages and audience are the two components of your public relations/communications plan that should be set in stone before your plan is developed. You may want to change your strategies or approach or make your goal more manageable, but once you determine what you want to say and who you want to say it to, staying the course is the best bet for achieving your goal. (The only exception would be if you discover that you have not chosen the right audience or that your message doesn't reflect the reality of your situation.) By reading the rest of this chapter and thoughtfully answering the questions about your message and your audience, you should be able to develop a message and target audience early in your planning process and then work toward strategies for getting the word out.

## LIBRARY POLICIES, PROCEDURES, AND ENVIRONMENT AND YOUR MESSAGES

Not only do your messages need to be clear and consistent; they also need to reflect the reality of your library's policies, procedures, and environment. Don't try to tell the public one thing about your library when your practice tells them something completely different.

For example, if you want people to think of your public library as a community center, you need to look at all of your library's public relations materials and make sure that they convey that message. In addition, you may need to examine library policies and procedures to be sure that they reflect that message. Library policies and practices cannot contradict your message. If they do, you need either to change the policies or change the message. For instance, you can't try to convince the public that your library is a center for the community if your meeting rooms are locked at 6 p.m. every day and unavailable for community group meetings. A policy change will be necessary before you can effectively communicate the message that the library is a community center.

Your messages must also be reflected in the staff's attitude and behavior. For example, if you are trying to encourage neighbors from the area surrounding your university library to use your services and resources, but staff give a look that says "Who are you and what are you doing here?" to everyone who doesn't appear to be a student or a faculty member, your message is contradicted by staff behavior. Part of your communications plan must include working with the library staff to convince them of the importance of a good relationship with university neighbors. In addition, a new library policy about providing service to nonuniversity patrons might need to be established and implemented. Communicating a message that isn't reflected in policy and practice is misleading, damaging to your credibility, and ultimately a waste of time and money.

The perception you are trying to create and the messages you are trying to communicate must also be reflected in the library's environment. For example, an elementary school library media specialist who has just purchased a collection of parenting materials and is trying to encourage adults from the neighborhood to visit the library and use the collection should provide chairs that are comfortable for adults in addition to the little chairs designed for the regular patrons. Perhaps the parenting collection should be set to one side in the library so that parents can come in unobtrusively and use the materials out of the student traffic and commotion. The collection needs to be on a shelf that is a good height for adults and labeled clearly. Parents, who come in response to the flyer inviting them to visit the school library to use the collection, will see an environment that reflects the message presented in words on the flyer.

Another example is a public library that wants to encourage teenagers to use its services. Lots of wonderful, teen-appropriate promotional materials are designed and distributed through the schools and other youth organizations. Yet, when the teens arrive at the library, they find their area is a corner of the children's room and the furniture is about the right size for fifth graders. In addition, the materials in the young adult collection aren't age appropriate and they are battered and worn. The promotional materials communicate one message and the environment—the reality—reflects another.

Another public library received a grant to have its cardholder information translated into Asian languages, such as Vietnamese and Laotian. Translation was costly, but it was done and the materials were made available in the different languages. News releases were sent out announcing that cardholder materials were now available in languages for new immigrants. When a reporter arrived to do a story, however, the real story was that, while the library had registration materials in Vietnamese and Laotian, there were no materials in the library's collection in those languages. Registration materials were geared to welcome new users, but the collection did not provide them with any resources.

The bottom line is this: If you don't have it, don't try to sell it! Communicating messages that are inconsistent with your library's policy or environment sends your audience mixed messages and leaves them confused and doubtful about your library and its credibility.

## VISUALS AND YOUR MESSAGES

You will probably use some type of artwork—perhaps photographs, drawings, or graphic designs—to tell your story. Again, your visuals must reflect your messages. If you want teens to think the library is a place where they should hang out, don't develop a Web site featuring only pictures of preschoolers or senior citizens. Develop a Web site with pictures of teenagers in the library.

In the example of the parent collection in the school library media center, the flyer sent to parents needs to be designed for parents, not children. Cute teddy bears might not be the best artwork to promote a serious collection of materials that will help your students' parents develop their parenting skills.

Remember that if you want your library to be perceived as a friendly place, the people featured in any drawings or photographs you use should be smiling and look friendly. Be sure that drawings and photographs reflect cultural diversity and include both genders. It is important for people to be able to identify with the people they see in your artwork. For example, if the words on your brochure say "Anytown Public Library Is a Great Place for Senior Citizens," a photograph of an older African American female patron smiling and working with a library staff person will reinforce your message. On the other hand, a 45–year-old frowning woman sitting alone at a reading table doesn't do much to tell your story. Visuals should complement and enhance your messages, not detract from or contradict them.

## BUDGET AND YOUR MESSAGES

Quality communications materials are important to the success of your efforts. "Quality," however, does not necessarily mean "expensive." Pay close attention to what you are spending on communications materials, particularly if your message has any budget connotations.

For example, if you are launching a campaign to encourage the community to pass an operating levy for your library and your message is "Anytown Public Library: The Best Bargain in

Town," developing and distributing four-color brochures might not be the best way to spread the word. A simple, one-color piece is effective and speaks loudly. It says, "Anytown Public Library Does Quality, Cost-Effective Work."

A public library once published a "wish catalog" of items for which it wanted people to consider donating money. This catalog was elegant, with photographs, expensive paper, and three colors of ink. Library patrons complained that the money spent printing the catalog could have been used to purchase several of the items the library was "wishing" for. While the catalog was a beautiful printed piece and even won national awards, its extravagance was inconsistent with the library's message—"We Need Donations."

## CREDIBILITY AND YOUR MESSAGES

If you promise people something, be sure you do it! It may be a great idea to ask people to donate money to your library's "Buy a Book" program and promise that their name will appear on a bookplate in your collection in exchange for a $25 donation. But, be sure that you follow through—so that when Mr. Jones shows up to see the three books that his $75 bought, you can show them to him. If you don't follow through you destroy your credibility—the next time you try to communicate with Mr. Jones he will be skeptical. It is better not to promise an outcome than to promise one and not follow through on it.

An example of damaged credibility is a public library that conducted a bond issue campaign for new buildings. A charming photograph of two library patrons using bookmobile services was included in the informational materials. The words in the materials did not state that bookmobile services would be continued after the bond issue passed, but the photograph's inclusion in the bond issue informational materials implied that to many community members. The library's credibility suffered significant damage when, three months after the bond issue passed, bookmobile services were discontinued. There may or may not have been a plan to stop running the bookmobile at the time that the bond issue materials were developed. But, some community members viewed using the photograph in the materials as a blatant way of manipulating bookmobile patrons into voting for the bond issue.

Library suggestion boxes are an excellent example of an area where your message must be consistent with your actions. For example, a library has a suggestion box for patrons with a sign that says, "When you talk, we listen." Patrons who complete the suggestion form, put it in the box, but never see any responses posted or mailed to them are shown that "When you talk, we don't care." Rather than send that message, the library would be better off without a mechanism for patron suggestions.

## THE MEDIA AND YOUR MESSAGES

Always make sure reality is consistent with your message when dealing with the media. Don't make an exception to a policy for a reporter or change practice to provide him with assistance unless you want to see it on the six o'clock news. If a reporter asks for access to your patron database, don't provide it and tell him it will be your "little secret." The same policies apply to the press as apply to the general public.

You can, however, work to ensure that when a reporter comes to cover a story, you present the story in the best possible light. An example of this would be writing and sending out a news release that talks about your successful summer reading program and how your libraries are constantly full of children. You get a call from a television reporter who wants to come that afternoon and do a story based on this release. This is a great opportunity. Obviously, choose a time when you are certain that children will be in the library. You may want to announce during story hour that a television reporter will be doing a story on your summer reading program on Wednesday at 3 p.m. Watch how many kids show up! Don't risk telling a different story by having the reporter show up at the Main Library only to find an empty children's room.

## CONSISTENT, NOT COMPLICATED

All of these warnings—about making sure that your messages reflect reality and aren't contradicted by your library's practice—may imply that telling your library's story is terribly complicated. It really isn't. You can develop clear and simple messages, ensure that they aren't contradicted by reality, communicate them clearly and consistently, and implement an extremely successful public relations/communications plan. Common sense and good judgment are the only skills that you need to develop a message that will tell the community what your library is really all about.

Once you decide what your messages are going to be—what you want to tell people and possibly ask them to do—then ask the following questions:

1. Are we currently doing everything we are talking about?
2. Are we telling the complete truth?
3. Do any of our policies, procedures, or practices contradict this message?
4. If we are promising something, can we follow through?

5. Does our environment reflect what our message is saying?
6. Would I believe this message if I heard it? Would I act in the way that I am being asked to act? Why or why not?

Your answers to these questions will help you to more clearly define your messages. If there are conflicts, you can decide either to change your messages to reflect reality or change reality to reflect your messages. It is a good idea to convene a mini–focus group of library employees to evaluate your messages based on these questions. You will find the different perspectives, particularly from those who weren't involved in the message development process, very helpful as you determine whether you need to make changes. Plus, this is another opportunity to build staff support for your PR activities.

The most important question to consider is the final one: Would I believe this message if I heard it? Would I act in the way that I am being asked to act? Why or why not? If your message doesn't seem consistent with reality to you or to other library staff, then you cannot expect to convince an external audience that it is true or to act on it. The responses to these questions may tell you to start over completely in terms of developing messages, or they may tell you that you are on the right track and provide you with information that will be helpful as you develop strategies for communicating your messages.

# TARGETING YOUR AUDIENCE

Deciding "who" you want to communicate with is equally important as deciding "what" you want to say. Answering the question "Who do we want to tell?" may seem simple. However, choosing your target audience(s) is essential to the success of your public relations/communications efforts and must be given thoughtful consideration. You can develop a clear, consistent message that reflects reality, and a wonderful public relations/communications plan with great strategies, and implement that plan without a hitch. But if you aren't communicating to the right audience(s), it will all be for naught. If you want to pass a bond issue, you can't waste time and energy telling your story to teenagers who can't vote or to citizens from another county. When time and resources are limited, it is important to carefully target your audience(s) and then work hard to get your message out to that audience(s).

Choosing an audience(s) is much easier when you have project-based messages. If you are working on promoting preschool storytime, then parents of preschoolers are your target audience. As a university library trying to increase gate count, your obvious audience is students and faculty members. However, you might want to consider focusing on community members instead, depending on your overall communications goals.

Even when you have a message that needs to be communicated to a wide audience(s), it might be better to focus on one segment of that audience(s) at a time. A school library media specialist's overall communications goal might be to convince the faculty in her school that Internet resources can contribute to the curriculum. However, she might decide that, for the first three months, the target audience will be third-grade science teachers. She will focus more energy on that audience for a short period of time.

The bottom line is that the "scattershot" approach to communications does not work. You can't just develop your message, send it out there, and hope someone receives it. The whole purpose of developing a public relations/communications plan is to ensure that you make careful decisions about what your messages are, how you communicate them, and to whom you communicate them. Any marksman knows you don't accomplish anything if you just close your eyes, fire your gun, and hope for the best. You need to aim it at a target. The same goes for your library's communications efforts: if you aim, you have a better chance of hitting the target.

Carefully selecting target audiences for your message will help you to choose strategies and tools for communicating it. If your target audience is senior citizens, the local rock radio station is probably not the best media outlet for you to work with on communicating this message. And if you choose to get your message across via a newsletter, you might want to consider using large print.

Targeting an audience or audiences will help you to spend your limited human and fiscal resources in the most effective way. It gives you a focus for your efforts.

## HOW TO CHOOSE YOUR AUDIENCE

Libraries and librarians have a tendency to want to be all things to all people. So, choosing target audiences may not come naturally to most librarians. While it would be nice to be able to tell everything to everybody, time and resource constraints don't make that practical.

Before selecting the target audience for a particular PR program, however, it is a good exercise to brainstorm a list of your library's possible audiences. List them under two headings—internal and external. An internal audience is an audience within your organization. Further, it is an audience that you will need to help you to communicate your message. An external audience is an audience outside your organization that you want to reach with your message. For a public library, internal audiences might include staff, library board members, Friends of the Library, and volunteers. A school library might include teachers, the principal, other school staff, and volunteers as its internal audiences. External audiences for a public library would be community members, city council members, state and federal legislators, the national library community, and more. Friends of the Library and volunteers could also be on a public library's list of external audiences. A school library's external audiences might be the community, the school board, parents, and students.

Confusing? Definitely. Unfortunately, defining your audience is not a cut-and-dried activity. Like developing your message, determining your target audience(s) is a judgment call. Once you brainstorm the list of possible audiences, think about them in terms of the message and answer the following questions:

1. Who is the message geared toward? Is it geared toward them as an internal or an external audience?
2. How much time do you have to communicate this message?
3. Do you need action on this? If so, who is capable of acting?

First, think carefully about who your message is targeted at. Are you talking to adults or children? Are you working to convince policy makers or the general public? You can't afford to spend time telling the story to people you don't necessarily need to reach.

Second, the amount of time that you have to communicate your message will also help you to select your target audience(s). For example, if you have years and a very broad message, you might want a very broad target audience—perhaps community members, from infants to age 90. You can then develop a plan with objectives that target the different age groups.

The third question should really help you to narrow your focus. Is this a message that requires action? If so, who can act? Promoting preschool storytime to increase attendance by sending flyers to senior citizens in nursing homes doesn't make much sense. However, sending flyers to parents through local preschools does make sense. Answering this question honestly will help you focus your efforts on the audience who can most help you achieve your goal.

After answering these questions, you should have a narrower list of audiences for this particular message. Consider audiences carefully. Is it realistic to target all of them, considering the time and resources available? If the answer is yes, move onward. If it is no, would it be better to do a more comprehensive job of telling your story with a smaller target audience? Or perhaps some audiences should be "major" targets for your plan while others should be "minor." (Major targets would be the focus of most of your efforts; some activities would address the minor target audience, but they wouldn't be the focus of your plan.)

## THE IMPORTANCE OF INTERNAL AUDIENCES

When you are developing your plan and considering your target audience(s), give serious thought to your internal audiences. The library staff is the best communications tool available to you. What a circulation clerk says over his back fence about your library will have much greater impact than any flyer or slick brochure that you produce. Convening a staff advisory committee for your communications efforts and including staff at all levels in the decision-making process is a great way to ensure buy-in for your efforts. At times, however, such a committee isn't advisable or practical. In those cases, at the very least, make sure that staff receives information before it is distributed to the public. In addition, give staff the same time and consideration for questions about an issue that you would give to a reporter from the local television station. Your efforts are guaranteed to pay off and be reflected in staff attitudes toward you and your efforts.

Above all, never, ever, overlook your internal audience. It is critical to the success of your external communications. Before you launch any type of campaign or public relations effort, be sure that your internal audience is working for you. Provide them with clear, consistent information and take their ideas and suggestions under careful consideration. Remember that they are on the front lines dealing with the public. They hear the concerns, comments, and perceptions of the public on a daily basis. The information and insight that they have will be invaluable to you as you develop and implement your public relations/communications plan.

## "WHO" DETERMINES HOW

Once you have identified your target audience(s), you will be ready to think about how you want to communicate with them. If you are looking at using print or broadcast media, the demographics of the various media outlets will help you decide which ones to target. The age and ability levels of your audiences will help you decide what type of approach to take to communicate your message, what your print and graphic design should look like, and what types of special activities might help to tell your story.

For example, if a primary target audience is the new readers involved in your library's literacy program, you will want to ensure that materials are written on a level they can understand. If you want to reach senior citizens you will need to pay special attention to typeface size. If your target is school-age children, it is easy to reach them through school. The list of possible communications tools and strategies begins to develop once you have defined your target audiences.

# CONCLUSION

Determining the messages for your PR program and selecting target audiences for the program are hard work, but it is the first important step toward meeting your communications goals. Once you have established "what" you want to say and "who" you want to say it to, you will be able to determine "what" are the best tools for reaching your audience. This is the part of public relations work that is really fun. Selecting and developing your communications tools are opportunities to use your creativity and to work directly with a wide variety of people in your community.

In the chapters that follow, various communications tools and strategies will be described and approaches for using them will be discussed. As you consider how you will communicate your message, always remember to consider your audience(s) carefully. Think about each tool or strategy in terms of "Will this work with teenagers? senior citizens? parents of preschoolers? teachers? students? faculty members?" By building on each component in your public relations/communications plan, you will develop an approach that is geared to your audience(s) and that aims your message directly at your target audience(s).

But the next step is to develop your public relations/communications plan. Turn the page to Chapter 4 and get started.

# 4 DEVELOPING YOUR LIBRARY'S PUBLIC RELATIONS/ COMMUNICATIONS PLAN

Many organizations take the same approach to their communications efforts that Mickey Rooney and Judy Garland brought to planning theatrical productions in their 1940s movies. They say, "Let's do a newsletter, let's do flyers, let's do a news release"—just as Mickey and Judy used to say, "Let's do a show!" And, just as in those old movies, they may have the resources to produce those materials, but those communications tools may not be the best use of those resources in light of the communications goal. Without a careful plan that includes a clear goal, consistent messages, and targeted audiences, producing a newsletter, developing a brochure, or creating a Web page, are not public relations. And without coordinating these types of communications efforts, you can, at times, do more harm than good.

At this point, you have read Chapter 3 and have begun to think about your messages and target audiences. Obviously you have some idea of what your PR goal is, but it likely needs refining and clarification. You are ready to move on to that next step in PR planning.

## CLARIFYING YOUR LIBRARY'S PUBLIC RELATIONS GOAL

You probably have some idea—no matter how vague—of what you want to achieve with your public relations efforts. Answering the following questions in the next section will help you to clarify your public relations goal.

## WHAT DO YOU WANT TO TELL PEOPLE?

This is your message. You need to determine what you want people to know or understand. Often your message will have a quality that is more subjective than just conveying information. For instance, you won't just want people to know about your books-by-mail service—you'll also want them to believe that it is a valuable community service. At other times, you will just want to convey information, such as how the library's new overdue policy works. It is important to try to keep your message as simple and focused as possible. As discussed in Chapter 3, you may have more than one message to communicate, but try to keep it to no more than three.

## WHO DO YOU WANT TO TELL?

Determining the audiences for your message is critical to your success. Think about who needs to know what you are communicating. If your message is preschool storytime hours, then your primary audience is parents of preschoolers and your secondary audience may be day-care providers. Deciding who needs to receive your message will help you determine how to communicate it. Remember to consider your internal audiences. Chapter 3 provided more information on thinking about who your communications audiences are for your PR campaign.

## WHEN DO YOU WANT TO COMMUNICATE YOUR MESSAGE?

Timing is everything. Trying to spread the word about school library services is probably more appropriate during the school year than during the summer when families, teachers, and students aren't focused on school. If you are promoting an event, it is important to communicate your message intensively in a concentrated time period before the event. Sometimes it may take you longer to plan your public relations/communications efforts than to implement them.

## WHY DO YOU WANT TO TELL PEOPLE ABOUT THIS? DO YOU WANT THEM TO DO ANYTHING?

These questions go back to the subjective nature of your message. Once people learn what you are trying to communicate, do you need them to act? Is this a proactive message? Do you want them to attend an event? Actively support the retention of a library service? Vote for supplemental funding?

Look carefully at your answers to these questions. They should form the foundation for a public relations goal. Remember that a goal should include a statement of what you want to achieve, delineate a time frame for achieving it, and indicate how you will measure your success.

Figures 4.1–4.3 provide examples of using the above questions to formulate a public relations/communications goal. Look carefully at each example and you will see how easy it is to formulate a public relations/communications goal. The answers to the questions can be turned into a measurable and focused goal statement. Spend thoughtful time answering the questions and formulating your goal. It will be the foundation on which you build your plan, and it is important to your success that you clearly articulate what you want to achieve.

# REVIEW YOUR CURRENT COMMUNICATIONS

Now that you know what you want to achieve, you can begin to think about how you are going to achieve it. Your goal looms

---

**Figure 4.1 Formulating a Public Relations/Communications Goal: School Library**

1. *What do you want to tell people?*
   We want to tell parents and the school board that our current, limited, online resources are enhancing learning for our students and that an additional investment would have an even greater benefit..

2. *Who do you want to tell?*
   Parents, teachers, and school board members

3. *When do you want to communicate your message?*
   Spring 2005

4. *Why do you want to tell people about this? Do you want them to do anything?*
   We wat to do this so that the school board will increase our budget for online resources by 20 percent for the 2004–2005 school year.

**Goal:** Communicate to parents, teachers, and school board members the important role that online resources play in education for children. Increase the funding for online resources by 20 percent for the 2004–2005 school year.

---

**FIGURE 4.2 Formulating a Public Relations/Communications Goal: University Library**

1. *What is it that you want to tell people?*
   We want to tell students and faculty members that even with wireless access to our online resource they can—and should—visit our library that is now open 24 hours.

2. *Who do you want to tell?*
   Students and faculty members

3. *When do you want to communicate your message?*
   September 2004—the beginning of the academic year and the kick-off of the new hours

4. *Why do you want to tell people about this? Do you want them to do anything?*
   We want to tell students and faculty members so they will understand the value of having access to professional librarians and a quiet study place 24/7 even with campuswide access to our online resources. We want to increase our gate count by 15 percent.

**Goal:** Create faculty and student awareness of the continued value of in-library services. Achieve a 15 percent increase in the library's overall gate count by the end of academic year 2005.

---

**FIGURE 4.3 Formulating a Public Relations/Communications Goal: Public Library**

1. *What do you want to tell people?*
   We want to make people aware of the public library's programs and services.

2. *Who do you want to tell?*
   Community members

3. *When do you want to communicate your message?*
   2005

4. *Why do you want to tell people about this? Do you want them to do anything?*
   Circulation and gate counts are down. We think people are using our services online from home, but the city council wants us to justify our open hours. We need to increase both circulaton and gate counts and promote the value of in-library services or our funding will be cut.

**Goal:** Increase public awareness of all library services and programs—not just online resources—by developing and implementing a year-long comprehensive public relations plan. Achieve a 15 percent increase in circulation and a 20 percent increase in gate count.

large before you and you are ready to begin developing a plan to reach it. Your next step is to think about your goal and other public relations efforts that you have conducted. What worked? What didn't work? An audit can help take the guesswork out of your public relations/communications planning. The financial records kept by your library's accounting department are audited on a regular basis. It is also important that you audit your communications efforts and carefully evaluate your past efforts before investing time, energy, and money in another public relations campaign. An audit will help you determine what you are doing well and what you need to improve. It will also help you decide what communications tools have worked best in the past and what might be effective in the future. An audit will also provide a benchmark against which you can measure future communications efforts. You will know where you started when you developed your plan.

Communications audits measure perceptions of your organization by your key audiences. Ideally, a communications audit is performed by an outside PR firm or consultant. In the sidebar, library communications consultants Peggy Barber and Linda Wallace recommend that approach. If your budget allows, it is the best route. Only an outside individual can objectively assess your current efforts and make recommendations for the future. If funds are tight, perhaps this is something that your Friends of the Library organization would be interested in funding. Your local chapter of the Public Relations Society of American or a local PR firm might be willing to provide someone to conduct the audit pro bono. A local college or university might have an upper-level student studying PR who could conduct your audit as a senior project. While I don't recommend funding your ongoing PR activities in this way, a communications audit is an isolated activity and so you don't need to build ongoing capacity to support it.

Another possibility is to turn to another city department or to the university communications office for support. While this individual may not be part of the library staff, he or she is a member of your larger organization and therefore may not bring the same level of objectivity to your audit as someone from the outside.

In fact, as Barber and Wallace state, even if your library already has a PR agency, you should hire a different agency or consultant to conduct the audit. That is how you will get the most value for your investment. Typically, I believe that libraries and other locally funded organizations should hire local consultants if available; in the case of a communications audit, however, I

## What's the Message? Is Anyone Listening? A Communications Audit Can Help You Find Out

### By Peggy Barber and Linda Wallace

Remember the line . . .

"I know you think you understood what I said, but what you don't understand is that what I said is not what I meant."

Most of us can relate. When it comes to library communications, we are often unaware of how the messages we send are received by others. We may not even be aware of all the messages we're sending—or whether they are reaching their intended audience.

Many libraries have adopted the regular use of customer service surveys to ask "How are we doing?" Focus groups have also come into more widespread use. But regular review of our communications and their impact on key audiences is still rarely done.

One of the most valuable tools for evaluating the effectiveness of our communications is the communications audit. Performed by an outside PR/communications professional, the audit is an objective assessment of both what and how a library communicates. In the broadest sense, the audit includes an analysis of everything from the facilities (e.g. signage, displays, lighting) to publications, media relations, telephone voice message, electronic communications (Web site, email lists), customer service and community outreach.

Among the most interesting and telling parts of the audit process are interviews with library board members, staff, representatives of business, government, the media, educators, users, nonusers and other groups the library wishes to learn more about. What many won't tell you to your face, they will share anonymously to a third person.

You may feel you already get lots of input from board members and others. And that is not to be taken lightly. But people who love libraries tend to have strong opinions about them. So do people who don't. Too often we base our messages/actions on our own assumptions rather than taking time to learn what others are actually thinking or feeling.

An audit is a chance to find out, and it's not just about what's wrong. It is about what works. It can confirm which strategies have been most effective and suggest corrections or possible new courses. An audit is not a do it yourself job. Nor is it one for the PR agency/consultant already employed by the library. The value of the audit lies in its objectivity.

Similar to a feasibility study conducted for fundraising or election campaigns, an audit can be as broad or as narrow as you wish. It can focus on internal audiences—staff, board and/or Friends. Depending on the focus of the project and existing data, the audit may or may not include focus groups, direct mail or telephone surveys and other research.

The end product is a detailed report of research findings along with strategies and recommendations for improving communication. The final audit report provides a foundation for the library's marketing and communication planning, one that rests on factual, authoritative information—not personal opinion, assumption or speculation.

Most PR agencies or consultants are familiar with the audit process. Seeking out an audit means you are open to doing it better.

Where do you start? If you're interested in hiring public relations/marketing professionals to conduct a communications audit for your library, you will want to seek recommendations for those who have this capability. You will also want to prepare a Request for a Proposal (RFP) that clearly describes the library's goal and objectives, areas of particular concern, and the assignment. For example:

The XYZ Library seeks proposals to evaluate and improve the effectiveness of our communication. Our goal is to increase overall awareness of the library and its role in our community. We are also concerned about identifying and reaching out to those who may not know or understand how they might benefit from library services. Groups of particular concern are the business community, young people between the ages of 10 and 18 and the small but growing number of Hispanic residents in our community.

Proposals should outline steps toward the following objectives:

- A thorough analysis of how the library communicates both internally and externally.
- Research to determine how the library is currently perceived in the community and key audiences for its services.
- Suggested messages and strategies for reaching key audiences.
- Recommendations regarding staffing and budget.

The request should also include brief, basic data about your library and the community, as well as any pertinent background information, e.g. you have a bond issue pending, you're planning a fundraising campaign or budgets have been cut. You may also want to specify the amount budgeted for the project, a timeframe, number of meetings with board/staff, and criteria for selection, e.g. experience with libraries and/or non-profit organizations, reference checks, interview with administrative staff or library board.

It's important to meet with the firms you are considering, even before requesting a proposal and budget. Discuss your short list of objectives. Get their input. Make sure you find out which staff will be working on your project. Look at their portfolio. Ask if they have had experience with libraries or other education or not-for-profit clients. Much depends on "chemistry" and you need to feel comfortable and confident about the people you hire.

The good news. This needn't be a wildly expensive or time consuming activity. We recommend appointing a staff team to work with the PR specialists. The director must take a lead role in communicating this activity to board, staff and others if it's to work. You should also check in with the city's public information staff (if you work with such). Seek their advice. Involve them in the project.

More good news. Your communications project will, in itself, raise public awareness of the library. When you ask people what they think, you create an opportunity to educate them and increase their sense of ownership.

Building library use and support depends upon good two-way communication. As more libraries adopt a marketing approach to promoting their services, it is critical that we take time to listen—to our customers, potential customers, funders, trustees and other key groups. In other words, it's not about us, it's about *them*.

We recommend the communications audit because we hired them for the American Library Association—more than once. We've also conducted audits for libraries and library organizations. We know they work. But only if you are committed to listening and translating what you learn into action. For those who are, the communications audit can be a powerful tool.

*Peggy Barber and Linda Wallace are founders and principals of Library Communications Strategies (LCS), a consulting practice dedicated to providing creative, practical, and effective communication services to libraries and library organizations. Barber was formerly Associate Executive Director for Communications for the American Library Association (ALA) and Wallace was director of the ALA Public Information Office. The LCS Web site is* www.librarycomm.comn.

also recommend that the consultants come from outside your community. Again, this brings you objectivity—and no hidden agendas or preconceived notions about what your community needs. Barber and Wallace are highly regarded, experienced consultants in this field, and there are other firms out there as well.

# CONDUCTING YOUR OWN COMMUNICATIONS AUDIT

If you are in a small library or a school library with limited resources, some activities, such as focus groups and surveys, can help you to evaluate your current efforts without hiring an outside firm. Begin by determining what audience you want to assess. For example, a university library conducting a communications audit might want to measure the perceptions of university faculty, staff, and students. Or, if one of the library's communications goals is to reach an audience beyond the university campus, it might be important to measure the perceptions of a particular group of community members, such as parents of school-age children, or a cross section of the entire community.

The next step is to determine how you currently communicate with this audience. Make a comprehensive list of all communications tools. This list might include newsletters, brochures, flyers, mailings, news releases, electronic communication, signage, cable television programming, community presentations, and programming.

Based on your defined audience, the perception that you want to measure, and the communications tools that you have employed in the past, you can develop a research instrument for your audit. On a college campus, you might have faculty members or graduate students who can assist with this phase of your audit. In fact, you might have a communications graduate student who is willing to take on the entire audit as a project. Public or school libraries might also have access to these types of resources at a local college or university,

Then you are ready to assess the effectiveness of these efforts with your defined audience, and to find out how the audience perceives your organization and where that perception comes from.

A little bit of research into the current perceptions of your services and resources can provide you with a lot of information to use in your communications planning. By gathering information from users and nonusers, you can conduct a simple audit of your communications efforts and learn what information you are communicating effectively, what you need to communicate, and what misperceptions you might want to work to change.

## FOCUS GROUPS

One way to gather information is to hold several small focus groups. A focus group is basically a guided group discussion. You gather a group of people who are willing to discuss the topic (such as library services in your community) and a facilitator leads them through a discussion of that topic. In the for-profit sector, focus group participants are usually paid a small fee for participating. It may not be possible or necessary for your library to pay individuals to spend one or two hours discussing your services. But perhaps you can come up with a special perk for attendees, like a voucher that waives a certain amount of overdue fees or free admission to the next Friends' book sale. You should always provide refreshments and be sure to follow up by sending a thank-you note to each participant.

Host both user and nonuser groups. The success of a focus group is dependent on the careful selection of the participants and the skills of the facilitator. Focus groups should never exceed about ten participants and it is often helpful to have a neutral party—not a library employee—facilitate the session. Again, graduate students might be willing to donate their time to have the experience of leading the groups, or your city or school district might already employ skilled facilitators. Work with the facilitator to develop several leading questions for the participants and then let participants discuss their perceptions. The same questions should be asked at each focus group meeting so that results are comparable. You might begin a public library focus group with a question such as "What is the most valuable service this library provides and why?" Or you might start a focus group of students who are nonusers of a college library by asking them to "Name one reason that you don't use the library and tell us what we could do to change it."

You will want a record of the discussion at your focus group meetings. You might have a staff person attend and summarize the high points of the discussion (using PowerPoint or a flip chart), or you might make an audio recording of the meeting.

The results of the focus groups will tell you where your strengths are, what needs to be changed, and, most important for your communications efforts, what areas of service and resources are not valued or viewed in the proper way by your constituents. By carefully examining those services, you may discover that nothing is wrong with the services—you just need to communicate the value of the services more clearly and positively.

## SURVEYS

Another way to gather information is by survey. A short questionnaire, asking participants to describe their perceptions of current services and materials or what services and materials they would like to see in the future, can provide you with the background to plan your upcoming communications efforts. If you have the time and resources to conduct both focus groups and a survey, you can use the findings from your focus groups to develop questions for your survey.

The key to surveying is to keep it short and simple. But, always be sure to gather demographic information so you have a sense of who you have surveyed. Depending on the focus of your survey, demographic questions may determine who should complete the entire survey. For example, if you are trying to increase library use by single people under 40, ask for age and marital status early in the survey so you don't waste their time and yours.

Personal interviews are an excellent way to get information. You can stop library users when they come into the library and ask them if they have a minute to answer a few questions. Just remember that if you conduct the survey in the library, you are only talking to library users. You may want to get permission from a local shopping mall to survey customers so that you talk to a broader segment of the population.

People like to share their opinions and are typically pleased when someone asks them thoughtful questions and listens to them. If you are trying to survey a limited number of people in a small environment, such as a school, you might simply want to distribute a questionnaire and ask participants to complete and return it. Under these circumstances the questionnaire must be easy to complete and easy to return, and it should ask about something that the audience cares about (for example, teachers would probably respond readily to a questionnaire asking about curriculum resources in the library).

Another cost-effective option is a Web survey. With a Web survey, you eliminate the time needed to interview people personally. A survey can be designed and set up on your Web site so that each visitor is asked to complete the survey. Again, put the demographic information up front so you can weed out the people who don't fit your target group. However, remember—like surveying people in the library—you are likely to reach only library users with a Web survey on your site. One way to broaden your reach is to ask the city or school district if you could place the survey on its site. Then you would reach all visitors to their sites as potential survey respondents.

Once you have done your simple research, examine the results thoughtfully. Determine the most important message to be communicated by the library and the most effective way to communicate it. Decide if you are going to develop an overall public relations/communications plan for the library or one focused only on a specific area or service.

# DEVELOPING A PUBLIC RELATIONS/ COMMUNICATIONS PLAN

When you begin to develop a public relations/communications plan, it is best to start from scratch using the results of your research. If you have been producing a newsletter for years and the results of your audit showed that it is an effective communications tool, keep it. Perhaps your research provided some suggestions for improving the newsletter. If so, apply them and you may end up with an even more effective communications tool.

A public relations/communications plan can have a narrow goal (such as to promote use of the library's video collection to children at East Township Branch), or a broad goal (such as to communicate effectively to the community the services and programs of East Township City Libraries). You may determine this goal as a result of something you learned from your research. For example, perhaps you discovered that the children you interviewed don't even know you have a DVD and video collection and think you should add one—you may want to inform children about your collection. Or your communications goal may be determined by other factors. For instance, your library board may want to increase circulation or program attendance statistics, or your building principal may think that parents need to know more about the important role that school libraries play in education.

A thoughtfully developed public relations/communications plan will be a road map for your efforts over the time period it addresses, and it will provide you with a way to measure the success of your work. If you use the information obtained in your research as you develop each objective and activity, your public relations/communications plan will likely lead you to your goal.

The major components of a public relations/communications

plan are goals, objectives, and activities. You have already worked to define your goal earlier in this chapter. That goal should be the guiding force behind the development of all your objectives and activities. As you determine objectives for the plan, you need to ask, "What relationship does this objective have to our goal? Will it help us to achieve that goal?" Every objective should be clearly stated and measurable, with a clear time frame. If your objective is "to promote circulation," you would have no way of knowing if you were successful or not. On the other hand, if your objective is to increase circulation at your branch library by 5 percent in the next 12 months, that is measurable and you can develop communications activities to support that objective.

When writing objectives, it helps to state them as a verb in the infinitive form. For example, "To place three stories about the library's online resources in the local media during March, April, and May 2006" is an objective. Activities are the steps that you will take to achieve each objective. "Develop press kits describing the library's online resources and distribute them to all local media outlets" might be an activity to support the above objective. Identifying the primary person responsible for completing each activity will be critical to the success of your plan. The tasks outlined will then be clearly delegated and people will be more likely to complete the necessary tasks when they understand the expectations and can see them in relationship to the overall goal.

An outline for a public relations/communications plan and two sample plans based on the goals determined earlier in this chapter appear in the Appendix. In the outline, each component is briefly described. The sample plans provide an idea of what a public relations/communications plan for your library might look like. Other activities could be substituted for those presented or other supporting activities could be added. Both sample plans are project-based rather than comprehensive.

Remember that your public relations/communications plan is always a work in progress. Revisit it on a regular basis and assess where you are going. You may want to change directions, or you may decide that you were too ambitious and want to pare it back a bit. Use it as a road map and refer to it often, but remember that if an unexpected opportunity or new challenge arises you can always take a different route to achieve your goal.

# 5 EXPLORING PR IN DIFFERENT TYPES OF LIBRARIES

Effective PR campaigns can be developed and implemented in any size organization. You don't need big budgets or flashy four-color materials. The same goes for libraries of all types and sizes.

Different types of libraries—public, school, and academic—all have a lot in common. They follow the same philosophies of service and adhere to guiding principles such as the Library Bill of Rights. The public relations/communications planning process described in Chapter 4 is applicable to any type of library, and the communications tools and strategies described later in this book are available and appropriate in varying degrees for public, school, academic, and special libraries. However, each type of library serves a different audience and a unique purpose; as a result, each faces some different communications challenges and opportunities. In this chapter, public relations/communications activities at public, school, academic, and special libraries are explored through hypothetical "success stories." These stories may not all have fairy-tale endings, but all of the efforts result in some degree of success. They offer realistic insights into the challenges of public relations in each type of library and the fact that, at times, success can be dangerous.

## PUBLIC LIBRARIES

### SUCCESS STORY

Middlefield Public Library serves a city of 45,000 citizens from two branches and one kiosk in a shopping mall. Susan Miller is the reference librarian responsible for public relations at Middlefield Public Library. She has 14 hours per week to devote to her public relations activities. Susan carefully and thoughtfully assembled a public relations advisory committee for her library, and they are in the midst of implementing a recently developed public relations/communications plan.

Susan finds it hard, however, to find the time to deal with the communications activities detailed in the plan. A city funding crunch, a flood at one of the system's branch libraries, and a censorship challenge have put the library in the media spotlight and have taken up the small portion of time that Susan has to devote to public relations. In addition, just as she was about to launch a major promotion of the library's summer reading program, a community group launched a campaign against allowing children to use the Internet at the library. Instead of headlines touting the exciting new summer reading program, the paper carried stories proclaiming that the public library was a "dangerous place for children." In fact, two of the corporate sponsors for summer reading reneged on their agreements in light of the Internet controversy.

Susan has seen some success from her planned public relations efforts. A promotional effort to increase homebound service has increased that program's circulation by 15 percent and a special mailing to parents of preschoolers has increased storytime attendance by twice the goal of 20 percent. Also, the library's overall circulation has increased by more than 25 percent, which, ironically, the staff attributes to renewed interest as a result of the news coverage provoked by the Internet and budget controversies.

## PUBLIC LIBRARY PR CHALLENGES

This story might seem a bit extreme, but it is indicative of the kind of communications challenges that public librarians, particularly those who are only part-time public relations people, face. Issues arise that weren't planned and it seems there aren't enough hours in the day to deal with all of them. Creative public relations librarians, like Susan, do learn to capitalize on such issues and still achieve their goals, even if the approach is a little different from what they had planned.

In addition, public libraries face different public relations challenges according to their size. Small libraries usually have very small staffs and have the most difficult time finding time to engage in public relations activities. But they are also usually in small enough communities that obtaining coverage in the local media is easier and promotion of library programs and other events can occur by word of mouth as well as through planned public relations activities.

The bureaucratic structures that are usually a part of a large public library system can often get in the way of effective public relations. By the time a staff person receives clearance to give an interview or participate in an event, the moment of opportunity may be gone. The best and most effective public relations often happens in medium-size libraries. They are big enough to have the staff to manage the activities and yet they are small enough that they aren't restricted by a large bureaucracy and lots of red tape.

Another major challenge for public libraries is focusing their message. Public libraries have traditionally wanted to be all things to all people. Often, when developing a public relations/communications plan, public library staff want to promote all of the library's programs and services. It is important to think carefully about what your library's PR priorities are throughout the year. Also, be sure that if you successfully promote a program or service, it can tolerate increased attendance or use. For example, if you launch a huge promotion of your books-by-mail service, you first need to be sure that you have the budget available to cover the costs of increased use. Or if the space you have for preschool storytime is already filled each week with three-year-olds, you should note that your public relations efforts would probably be better focused on a different program or service. (It is not that preschool storytime isn't a valuable program that deserves promotion, but at the moment you don't have a lot of room for growth.)

Targeting a specific audience is another challenge for public libraries since they serve all members of a community. Again, careful thought is necessary to determine what group the library really wants to reach. Public libraries not only serve all members of the community, but they can, at times, become a target for various community groups. Censors attack the library's collection, the genealogy club thinks that its collection should take over the entire first floor, a group of concerned citizens is upset that the library is throwing away withdrawn items. Because it is the "public" library, the public feels it has the right to voice its concerns over every practice in the library—and they do! The positive aspect is that members of the community who are aware of what is happening at their library and expressing their concerns are taking a great deal of ownership in this community-based institution. Creative public relations can take advantage of this ownership, particularly in times of crisis.

Securing the resources for public relations activities is always a challenge for public libraries. Community members, library board members, and others often have a difficult time understanding why a library needs a public relations program; they are hesitant to fund such a program when, as they see it, the money could be used in another area, such as the materials budget. The best strategy for changing mindsets regarding public relations is to develop a targeted, relatively inexpensive public relations/communications plan, to implement it, and to demonstrate your success to the library director, library board, city council, and other decision makers. Develop a goal for this plan that achieves the type of things that decision makers tend to like, such as increases in circulation, gate count, or attendance. Then, next time, develop a slightly more expensive plan and increase your funding incrementally, each time sharing your successes. Over time, chances are that the decision makers will see that the small investment in public relations activities is worth the increased use of the library, the changed public perception of the library's value, and the positive impact that it has in times of crisis.

Finally, public libraries sometimes practice "stealth PR." They think it is important to promote their programs and services, but are loathe to admit that they actually have a PR plan—let alone a PR person. In a recent discussion on an ALA PR listserv, people serving the "PR function" in their libraries engaged in a lively debate about what their titles should be. The suggestions ranged from Public Information Officer to Community Services Manager and Community Relations Director. No one, however, suggested PR Manager. The fear was, of course, that members of the community would be upset if they thought their tax dollars were being spent to support PR. There may be some foundation for these concerns, but do remember that PR has a great deal more credibility in today's world. And, in my opinion, if you believe it is important and are devoting resources to PR, you should be upfront about it and ready to defend your position. Your community can spend millions of dollars on library services and materials, but if the public doesn't know about them or use them, that isn't a very good investment, is it?

## SCHOOL LIBRARIES

### SUCCESS STORY

Bob Hadley is the school library media specialist at Kennedy Middle School. Kennedy serves 800 students, grades 6–8, in an economically disadvantaged neighborhood. This past school year, his public relations/communications goal was to encourage families to visit the school library with their children in the afternoons and evenings, so that children could get help with their homework and research and adults could take advantage of the parent collection. It is the end of the school year and Bob has seen a lot of success.

In September, when he first started keeping the library open two evenings per week, eight parents visited each evening. As the school year progressed and Bob implemented his plan, attendance increased to 50 parents per open evening—and one night a record 102 parents visited the library with their children.

Bob is also exhausted. In January he lost the funding for the library assistant who helped him during the evening hours. He had to recruit and train two volunteers to help. Throughout the school year, he continued to serve on the school-based management team and to meet with the teaching teams from each grade level on a regular basis. He also coached the school's basketball team.

In April Bob's principal decided that there aren't sufficient funds to keep the library open in the evenings next school year. The parents who had taken advantage of the library's services spoke up and the teachers that Bob worked with went to the school-based management team and suggested other areas in the school's budget that could be cut. The result was that the principal made some budget adjustments and the Kennedy Middle School library will be open three nights per week next year and Bob will have a library assistant—in addition to his two volunteers—to help out on all of those evenings.

## SCHOOL LIBRARY PR CHALLENGES

The school library media specialist faces the same challenge of finding time for public relations activities as public librarian, Susan Miller, in her success story. However, Susan is given some release time for her work and Bob Hadley has to take on whatever public relations work he wants to get done in addition to his duties as a member of the school's instructional team. Yet, similar to the public library's circumstances, ongoing public relations for a school library may be the key to its survival in times of budget cuts.

Library media specialists face the challenge of promoting the value of their programs in the community and also in their building and school districts. As the success story demonstrates, it is important to do such promotion on a consistent basis and not just when there are questions about whether to fund the school library media program.

As in all types of libraries, some people think that the resources and role of the school library media program can be replaced by computers, Internet access, and a technology coordinator. Or the district administration may view the role of the school librarian as one of checking out and shelving books and may decide that volunteers or clerical staff can take care of those tasks, thus eliminating the need for the more expensive school library media specialist position. As a result, school library media specialists are often in the position of having to do "personal public relations." They must be vigilant about promoting the value of their role in the instructional program. They need to continue to learn about new technology and to become resources for both teachers and students in those areas.

The challenge is that school library media specialists often become so busy doing the work that they forget to spread the word. In addition to being contributing members of the school's instructional team, school library media specialists must be self-promoters. They need to volunteer for school committees and to speak up when they have something to offer. They continually need to offer the library as a meeting place for the PTA, the school-based management team, or visitors from out of town. The energy of the school library media specialist must be focused on his or her work as an instructional leader in the school and not on checking out books and keeping them neatly shelved.

# ACADEMIC LIBRARIES

## SUCCESS STORY

When the Clarence University Library increased its open hours to 24 hours per day throughout the academic year, circulation librarian Kara Richardson was disappointed in the student response. The skeleton staff scheduled to work the 11 p.m.–7 a.m. shift was lucky if they saw five students during the evening, and the staff spent most of their time chatting and drinking coffee. Kara decided that the answer was to get the word out, and she asked the library director if she could take on the responsibility of promoting the nighttime hours in addition to her other duties. He readily agreed and Kara set about forming a public relations task force and developing and implementing a plan.

Only six weeks after the beginning of Kara's public relations activities, there were so many students in the library at 2 o'clock on a Wednesday morning that there weren't any seats left in the study rooms. Soon, the library director had to add staff to the night shift. By the next academic year, there were questions about whether the library could afford to continue its 24-hour schedule.

## ACADEMIC LIBRARY PR CHALLENGES

Kara's public relations efforts were successful beyond what the fiscal resources of the university could support. Overwhelming success can also happen in other types of libraries. A service or program is promoted beyond what anyone can afford to provide. However, in this instance, when Kara began promoting the 24-hour schedule, the university's resources were being wasted as staff whiled away the time. Chances are that if the night hours aren't available next academic year, the university will hear about it from its paying customers—the students. And the university understands that time and resources for studying are critical to the students' academic achievement, which plays a role in the university's overall public relations efforts.

In some ways, academic libraries have more of a guaranteed place in their setting than school libraries do. In addition to providing resources for students, academic libraries often provide resources for faculty members engaged in "publish-or-perish" research projects. The struggle for the academic library is to maintain a balance between its role as a research center for students and faculty and a warm, welcoming place where students can do research and study.

Like the other librarians described above, Kara added public relations activities to her other duties. The increases in circulation that may have occurred from the increased use at night, however, may have helped her to lobby for more circulation staff.

Like school libraries, academic libraries face the challenge of positioning themselves positively in their community as well as selling themselves to the students. Hosting special events, ensuring that there is a library presence at campuswide events (such as the homecoming parade), and attracting alumni donors are all activities that are time-consuming but important to a positive position. Academic libraries need to position themselves to prospective students as an institutional drawing card; they should be a part of the admissions tour for prospective students and should be included in the university's recruitment material.

In addition, universities often offer their library as an enticing benefit in their "town and gown" relations programs, for example allowing members of the local community to use the library for no fee or for an extremely low fee. If this happens, the academic library immediately gains another audience, and it will need to design public relations activities to address that audience. Not only will the library face the challenge of promoting its services to this new target audience, but it will have to deal with integrating this new group with the audience it currently serves. Faculty members and students who are in the library studying and conducting research may not be too enthusiastic when people from the neighborhood visit just to look around. A public relations/ communications program that includes tours, orientation sessions, and other activities for this new audience will help the library meet this challenge.

# SPECIAL LIBRARIES

## SUCCESS STORY

Tom Patrick is the head librarian at the corporate library of the Princefield Environmental Engineering group. He leads a staff of two librarians and four clerical staff members who provide library service and research assistance for the group's 200 engineers. Tom's recent internal public relations challenge was to communicate to engineers that they could request that specific materials be purchased for the library. (His predecessor considered himself an expert on environmental engineering and he made all of the collection development decisions.)

Six months ago, Tom approached his staff and suggested that they develop a public relations/communications plan to communicate their willingness to work with the firm's engineers to develop a print and online collection to meet their needs. At first, the staff thought Tom was crazy. They told him that Princefield was a small firm and all he needed to do was send out a memo. But Tom asked them to give his idea a chance and to work with him on the plan's development. The group skeptically worked with Tom on the plan's development and initial implementation. After the first few weeks of enthusiastic response, they began to think about ideas for future internal public relations activities. Not only did the engineers begin to bring their purchase requests to Tom, but he eventually formed a selection committee of engineers from different areas of expertise in the firm.

Use of the Princefield Corporate Library and its resources has increased by 25 percent because now the materials more closely meet the engineers' needs. And the president of Princefield has increased the library's collection development budget by $150,000 because the heads of the firm's departments recommended that their small departmental reference materials budgets be pooled for the library to purchase materials for everyone's use.

## SPECIAL LIBRARY PR CHALLENGES

Special libraries can disappear from the corporate landscape if they don't make themselves an integral part of the organization's operations. Like Tom's library, they can increase their funding and services if they prove that the service they provide is critical to the work of others in the organization. In some ways, they are in a position that public, school, and academic libraries might envy. Their budgets can be increased as the organization's revenues and their perceived value increases. On the other hand, they can also be cut or eliminated, and there isn't a large community to rally to their aid. If the special library hasn't proven its value in the past, a quick public relations campaign probably isn't going to help. Therefore, ongoing, consistent public relations activities are critical to the survival of special libraries, just as they are to public, school, and academic libraries.

# SHARED PUBLIC RELATIONS CHALLENGES

Different types of libraries do indeed face some different challenges to their public relations/communications activities. But they face many of the same obstacles. School, public, academic, and special libraries all strive to provide the highest quality of service to their users. All four face the hard choices of which services to promote and to whom, which programs to fund and why; and they must all find that delicate balance between promoting and over-promising. In addition, all four types of libraries often exist within the context of a larger organization. School libraries are in schools in school districts; public libraries are often a department of a city or county government; academic libraries are part of a college or university; and special libraries are part of the organization that they serve. As a result, their public relations/communications activities often come under the auspices of these larger organizations. The freedom to develop and implement their own plans may not exist under these circumstances. In fact, a library's public relations activities might be stymied by the larger organization so that its other public relations goals can be met. This is a difficult challenge to face. The only answer is to begin with a strong internal public relations program designed to demonstrate to the larger organization the positive perception that the library can help create for everyone, and then to build incrementally.

Developing and disseminating a clear, consistent message is another challenge for all types of libraries. No matter how hard the people developing and implementing the public relations plan might try, there are many obstacles along the way to disseminating the message to the target audience. A library board member might go to the press and tell a story that is the exact opposite of the one you are trying to spread. A parent challenging a book in the school library might put an entirely different spin on the community outreach program that the school library media specialist is trying to implement. The key here is patience and education. Bringing as many people as possible on board in the development and implementation of your public relations plan will help you to avoid such obstacles. Obstacles will still happen, but the people who understand and support your message will help you stay on course.

Another challenge for all public relations professionals, especially those in libraries and nonprofit organizations, is time. As demonstrated in the success stories above, librarians are often asked to develop and implement public relations activities in addition to their other duties, with little or no release time. They get stressed out and begin to realize that, as public awareness and library use increases, all that their success brings is more work. This is a critical issue, it can only be resolved when library directors and other decision makers are persuaded to make public relations a priority by devoting staff time to it. School library media specialists must establish priorities for their workloads and put public relations at a higher level.

Finally, funding for public relations activities is a challenge faced in all types of libraries. Any library has limited funds, and when the pot is divided public relations often gets short shrift. It is a difficult decision. If you don't fund collections and programs sufficiently, you won't have anything to promote. Yet, if the library's programs and collections aren't used by the community and viewed as important and valuable, the library's overall funding may be cut. Librarians must work hard to convince those who make the budget decisions that funding for public relations is essential to the organization's survival.

# CONCLUSION

Libraries developing and implementing effective public relations plans face a lot of challenges and obstacles. Yet, the rewards make the effort worth the battle. The goal of any library is to serve its community, and public relations activities are the key to creating public awareness of the availability and value of that service.

Effective public relations and communications take time and patience. There will be great leaps forward and small steps backward, and there will be times when you will be ready to give up. But, no matter what type of library you are in, the investment of carefully developed, ongoing, and consistent public relations for your library will eventually pay off. Your constituency will increase its use of your library's programs and resources. Users will come to your defense during funding crises and intellectual freedom challenges. They will view your library as a "community value."

# 6  EVALUATING YOUR PR PROGRAM

You are finished! You have developed and implemented your communications plan within the time frame that you originally developed. You completed all of the activities to meet your objectives and you made the midcourse corrections that you deemed necessary. There is nothing left to do, right? Wrong! The next step is critical for planning future communications efforts. You need to look with a critical eye at what you accomplished and evaluate your efforts.

Your public relations/communications plan is the key to your evaluation. While it provided the road map for your efforts during implementation, it will also provide you with a mechanism for looking at what you did and determining what worked and what should be improved or changed in the future. Remember, however, that public relations is not an exact science. It is subjective, and your evaluation of your efforts will also be somewhat subjective.

Without investing large amounts of money in survey research, it will be hard to determine whether you have actually changed public perception of your library and its services. Determining this will be easier in a more isolated environment, such as a school or university library, as opposed to a public library system that serves a large community. Careful study of your success in meeting your public relations/communications goals and objectives will provide you with useful information for future planning, no matter how large your target audience might be.

When evaluating your program, it is important to remember that the number of newsletters or flyers produced and the numbers of news releases mailed are not effective measures of success. You want to think of evaluating your efforts in terms of perceptions and behavior, not things. The guiding question for your entire evaluation should be "How have people behaved differently as a result of our efforts?"

You will also want to evaluate your efforts in terms of adherence to your plan. That doesn't mean that taking advantage of public relations opportunities (such as the passage of a library bond issue in a nearby community) aren't valid efforts, but you must consider how much such opportunities interrupted or furthered progress toward your public relations goal.

# EVALUATION ANXIETY

It probably goes back to our first report cards in grade school, but many of us suffer from evaluation anxiety. We view any kind of evaluation as a judgment that says "You succeeded" or "You failed." When evaluating your PR efforts, you must think about evaluation as just another PR tool. Every time you complete a campaign or program and evaluate your efforts, you will come up with strategies that will improve your next effort. That is the true purpose of evaluation.

Also remember that the success of any library's public relations efforts never rests on the shoulders of one individual or group; it is a team effort that involves all of the players who are part of the library's community. In a public library, the work toward the goal is accomplished by all of the staff, the director, the library board, volunteers, the city or county administration, and the community at large. In a school, it is the entire faculty, the principal, the PTA, the students, parents, volunteers, and others who contribute to the success of the public relations program—not just the school library media specialist working in isolation. Similarly in an academic library, PR success is obtained through the efforts of library staff, faculty, and the support of administration.

So don't think about evaluating your PR program like you might a performance review. Evaluation is an opportunity to look critically at what we accomplished so that we can accomplish even greater things the next time around.

# TIMING YOUR EVALUATION

Evaluating your communications efforts after you have completed them seems logical. However, depending on your goal and the time frame for achieving it, you may wish to conduct some formative evaluation efforts during implementation of your plan. For example, if your efforts are directed at obtaining additional funding for your library and the decision will be made on a specific date by a designated group of people (for example, a bond issue election or school board budget meeting), timely assessment at milestones will help you make midcourse corrections, before it's too late. If the current path doesn't seem to work, you can evaluate your plan and make revisions based on your experience thus far.

In other situations, your goal may be broader and more intangible, such as "Build awareness of the Middletown Public Library as a community center." You know that the time frame for achieving this goal is relatively long and that there isn't a specific end date. Evaluating this public relations program at the end of a designated time frame or on an annual basis is more practical.

Even if you are going to evaluate your efforts at the completion of your campaign, you will want to start planning and conducting your evaluation early on—definitely before the completion of an annual plan. You don't want your communications activities to stop just because the time frame for your plan ended. Implementing two successive plans would help avoid this situation, but you want to be sure that the plans overlap so that the community and press continue to hear from you while you are evaluating your efforts. You may have implemented a tremendously successful PR campaign, but if it just stops dead with no further efforts, you may be doing more damage than if you had never done any PR at all. Your audiences will be confused and wonder what happened. They will think, "Hmmm . . . is that library not that great any more?" Or, "Whatever happened to Middletown Public Library? Maybe they ran out of money?" Okay, so those are pretty preposterous leaps for them to make, but stopping communications completely after a PR campaign creates confusion and sends out mixed messages.

# REVISITING YOUR PUBLIC RELATIONS/ COMMUNICATIONS PLAN

Pull out that public relations/communications plan. It should look pretty well used, like any road map after a long journey. Tattered a bit, torn and covered with your notes and marks, it will guide you through the evaluation process just as it guided you through your communications activities.

The final element in your plan should describe a process for evaluating your efforts. Look carefully at that item. Now after implementing your efforts, is that still the most effective way to assess your accomplishments? Will it really tell you what happened, or do you need to think about other factors? Chances are that the technique you described will play a major role in the overall evaluation, but you may also decide to gather other information to help shape your future efforts.

If you worked with a library-wide task force or committee to plan and implement your public relations/communications plan, you should involve that group in the evaluation process. The discussion in this group about what you achieved and what still needs work will be useful. Bring them together and talk about plans for evaluation. Ask them what they would suggest. Should this group lead the evaluation, or do they recommend that you form a different committee—perhaps of staff, board members, and community members?

## CELEBRATE FIRST!

Remember, however, that even before you evaluate, your planning committee needs to celebrate! You worked hard implementing your public relations plan and you should celebrate your accomplishments. Make a list of what you achieved during the implementation of your plan. Include everything from the tangible accomplishments, like "issuing 15 press releases" to such things as "surviving more than 2,000 kids in summer reading." Host a party or other celebration and display the media coverage you garnered, materials you developed, and other noteworthy items. We are often too quick to criticize our efforts without taking a moment to pat ourselves on the back and say "Look what we did!"

## KEY EVALUATION QUESTIONS

- *What did you set out to accomplish?*
  The answer to this question is simple. It is your public relations goal, your message, and your target audience. Reaching a specific audience with a particular message to achieve your goal is what you set out to accomplish.
- *What did you do to accomplish it?*
  To answer this question, carefully review your public relations plan. Look at each activity and each objective. Did you complete each activity? Why or why not? Do you have examples of your work (such as newsletters, photos from a special event, newspaper clippings)? Whether or not you completed all of the activities under an objective, did you achieve the objective? In your opinion, why or why not? Think about whether you were too ambitious when planning your activities.
- *Did you choose the right message(s)? Did you communicate the message(s) you chose?*
  Look carefully at the messages(s) that you wanted to communicate. Did they say what you wanted? Did you com-

municate them through your public relations activities? Should these messages still be part of your future public relations efforts?

- *Was your target audience appropriate for your message(s) and activities?*
  The target audience might have been the right one for the message(s) you wanted to communicate, but your activities might not have matched your audience. For example, if your target audience was senior citizens and you wanted them to know that they can use the library's services without leaving their homes, it might seem logical that electronic communications would be a good tool for reaching them. But maybe you didn't reach your goal because you quickly discovered that only 5 percent of the senior citizens in your community have a computer or access to the Internet. Think carefully about whether your audience, your message(s), and your activities were in sync.

- *Did you accomplish your goal? Or how much progress did you make toward achieving that goal?*
  This question will either be easy or extremely difficult to answer. For a finite goal, such as "Increase library circulation by 10 percent from January to December 2004," you will have a "yes" or "no" answer to whether your PR efforts were successful. However, if you have a broader, less tangible PR goal, you will likely have a more subjective answer. Research, such as you may have conducted during your planning process, may be necessary to answer the question in this case.

- *What happened during the implementation of your plan that you didn't anticipate?*
  This question is a particularly good one for your planning committee to consider. The group should think about "What unanticipated events contributed to the achievement of our PR goal?" and "What unanticipated events took us off the course of achieving our PR goal?" For example, a snowy winter might have derailed efforts to increase attendance at adult programs. Or maybe a local television station hired a new station manager who loves libraries and he asked that his 6 p.m. newscast carry at least one library story per week. Both of these events are out of the library's control, but they may have had an impact on progress toward your goals.

- *How are things different now compared to before you implemented your PR plan?*
  The answer to this question may or may not have a rela-

tionship to your efforts. If your school has a new principal or your city has a new mayor, that environmental change may have had an impact on your efforts. If your main library's gate count has increased by 125 percent, some of that increase may be attributed to your work; but some increase may also be because two of your branch libraries were closed for renovations for six months during the project period. Displaced patrons simply used the main library and then returned to the branches when they reopened. Think about changes in personnel, changes in environment, changes in behavior, and changes in perceptions that have occurred during the implementation of your plan.

- *Were budget and resources sufficient for the implementation of your plan?*

  If you spent the project period working 90 hours per week and haven't seen your family in two months, then perhaps your plan was too ambitious for your resources. If this was a targeted effort, such as a bond issue or other funding campaign, it may have made sense to exploit your resources to reach your goal. But if this was an ongoing PR/communications program that you intend to implement on an annual basis, you need either to rethink your goals, objectives, and strategies or to dedicate more resources to PR. The same thing applies, of course, to fiscal resources. If your spending exceeded your budget allocation by 50 percent, you may need to scale back next time. If you underspent, then you have to wonder if you really executed all of the planned activities.

- *What will you do differently in the future? What will you do the same way?*

  Think carefully about what worked and what didn't. Maybe you developed a wonderful PR Web site, but it is hidden deep on the library's site and you didn't do anything to promote the unique URL. Or maybe you sent out so many news releases that the press felt inundated and didn't cover your library at all. Think about what you did right and what you would change. The answers to this question will provide important information for planning your future efforts.

Prepare a document based on the group's discussion or your consideration of these questions. This document is a qualitative evaluation of your public relations/communications efforts. You may also wish to ask three or four other library staff members or members of your Friends of the Library group to answer the same questions. While the answers may seem highly subjective to you, they will provide valuable information for planning your future public relations/communications efforts—and they may serve as ammunition when you go to the board or other administrative body for library PR funding.

Remember when answering the questions and compiling your written evaluation—don't beat yourself up! Just embarking on a PR campaign of any kind is a big undertaking and you deserve congratulations for that. To become a polished PR pro requires time and experience. And, like so many other things in life, in PR, we often learn more from our failures than from our successes.

## EVALUATION RESEARCH

If you used research during your PR planning process, you may wish to replicate that research while evaluating your work. This research will provide useful quantitative information as you assess your efforts and plan for the future.

Holding focus groups comparable to those used during your planning process will provide you with insight into whether public perception of your library has changed. Conducting the same survey—in the same location—that you used to assess perceptions during the planning process will also provide perspective on changed perceptions.

If you conducted a communications audit during your planning process, revisit that process as well. You will likely see how far you have come in just a short time.

## WHAT'S NEXT?

So it's over! You developed, implemented, and evaluated a successful library PR program. Are you tired? Let's hope not, because the next step is to go back to the beginning and start again. Your next plan may simply be an extension of the plan that you just completed, with an extended time frame and some changes in the activities based on your experiences. Or, if you had a finite goal and achieved it, you may develop a plan with an entirely different focus.

The important thing to remember is that no matter how close or far you were from achieving your goal, your experiences during the development and implementation of your previous plan should inform your future efforts. Changing public perceptions and communication your library's message to your targeted audiences is a building process. It is not a one-shot deal. You can't say "Been there, done that, got the t-shirt." It is a cyclical process of assessment, planning, implementation, and evaluation. Each time you go through the process, you will learn a little more, understand your audience a little better, and improve on your efforts, so that, we hope, one day no one will ever have the experience of this character in the comic strip, "FRAZZ."

**FIGURE 6.1   FRAZZ Comic Strip©**

FRAZZ reprinted by permission of United Feature Syndicate, Inc.

# PART II
# STRATEGIES AND
# METHODOLOGIES

# 7 BUILDING YOUR LIBRARY'S BRAND

In the first edition of this book, this chapter was called "Developing a Corporate Identity for Your Library." But today "branding" is all the rage and while building a brand means something bigger and broader than just building a consistent visual image, that visual identity still plays a key role in "branding." In *The Fall of Advertising and the Rise* of PR, Al and Laura Ries say it simply, "Everything is a brand. Coca-Cola is a brand. The United States of America is a brand. Public relations is a brand."[1]

Today certain celebrities, such as Tom Hanks, Oprah Winfrey, and (perhaps dubiously at the moment) Martha Stewart, have become "brands." In fact, Tom Hanks talks openly about the importance of protecting the Tom Hanks brand. The state of Vermont thinks it's a brand too and is developing regulations to stop out-of-state companies from falsely appropriating the "Vermont" cache.[2]

So how do you go about building your library's brand? Remember that a brand is not a logo. Simply put, a brand is the value behind that logo—what you provide to your customers. For example, your library may have a deep, well-rounded collection and state-of-the-art technology, but the most important thing that you have to offer your community is high-quality customer service—and your brand must communicate your service values. What do your customers think of when they hear the name of your library? What do they think of when they see that eye-catching logo that you invested time and resources to develop? "Branding your library" doesn't just mean developing a logo and plastering it all over your facilities, print materials, and Web site. It means thinking carefully about what you do, who you do it for, and why you do it.

## THE LIBRARY MISSION STATEMENT

The first step in developing a brand for your library is developing a clear, focused mission statement. This is important whether your library is a large university library, a school library serving 1,500 high school students, or a small, rural, public library. You must know why you are there—what your mission is. In *Market-*

*ing Concepts for Libraries and Information Services*, Eileen Elliott de Saez provides an in-depth discussion of mission statements for various types of libraries and processes for developing mission statements.[3]

A wide number of other resources, including books, Web sites, and consultants, can help your library define its mission. However, essential to developing a mission statement for any organization is a process of inclusion. For there to be organizational buy-in, key individuals at all levels must be involved in the process. Library board members, Friends of the Library, and all levels of staff should have some voice in the process. And once the mission statement is developed, it must be clearly communicated and explained to all library stakeholders. Every library staff member is a "brand manager" who plays an important role in communicating your brand through his or her daily actions.

One note of caution. Your library's mission statement should communicate who you are, what you do, and how you do it with commitment and passion, but it doesn't need to be lofty or unrealistic to provide the foundation for your brand. A mission that is attainable and understandable to the customers you serve is much more important than one that is unrealistic or so steeped in library buzzwords that it doesn't mean anything to the audience you are trying to reach. And remember that you are a library—not all things to all people—and so your mission should be defined within the scope of what your customers need and what you are capable of providing. While the credo of the Hard Rock Café, "Love All, Serve All," may be an attractive idea at first blush, few libraries—if any—have the resources available to meet this lofty goal. In fact, if you aim in that direction, it is most likely that your brand image will be one of an organization that does lots of things and none of them well.

Say it simply—three sentences should do it. If you follow those simple guidelines, you will have a mission statement that provides a firm foundation for your library's overall brand, corporate identity, and messaging. It is obvious that the library and community leaders who developed the sample mission statements in Figures 7.1–7.4 did. While they may vary in voice and tone, note that each statement defines the unique way—the individual brand—that the library serves its community.

Once you have finalized your mission statement, share it. Post it on your Web site, and include it in your newsletter, annual report, and other publications. Print copies for display at service desks and at the desks of library staff members. You might even ask all staff members to include the mission as a tagline below their e-mail signature.

---

**FIGURE 7.1 Sample School Library Mission Statements**

**Forest Oak Middle School, Gaithersburg, Md.**
The Forest Oak Middle School Library Media Center's mission is to support curricular instruction by providing staff and student access to a collection of print, nonprint and electronic media, along with training and support that will promote efficient and responsible use of all available resources. Reprinted with permission of Forest Oak Middle School, Michael Warner, Library Media Specialist.

**Highland High School Media Center, Anderson, Ind.**
The mission of the Highland High School Media Center program is to continually encourage academic excellence by providing service and instruction to students and staff members, to collaborate with staff in designing learning opportunities with resources, information, and technology which enhance learning and teaching, and to promote life-long reading. Reprinted with permission. Toni Overman, Media Specialist.

**North High School Library, Downers Grove, Ill.**
Our mission is to develop students who are independent and effective users of information. These information management skills are integral to academic achievement, to responsible participation in a democratic society and to lifelong learning. The library will supply access to materials in a variety of formats, provide instruction in use, and promote appreciation of reading with the collaboration of other educators. Reprinted with permission. Community High School District 99—North High School.

---

**Figure 7.2 Sample Academic Library Mission Statement**

**Peabody Library, Peabody College of Vanderbilt University, Nashville, Tenn.**
The mission of the Library is to provide an inviting environment for scholarly inquiry and for social and cultural activities. The Library draws upon the knowledge and energy of its staff and the Peabody faculty to prepare students as informed citizens of the world. As a divisional library within the Heard Library system, the Peabody Library functions as a resource for the greater Vanderbilt community. Reprinted with permission.

If you are going to develop a mission statement and say, "Great, that is done," without communicating it far and wide, don't bother. If you are truly committed to building a brand for your library, you will define your mission and then it will drive every decision, every policy, and every customer interaction in your library.

---

**Figure 7.3 Sample Public Library Mission Statements**

---

**Evanston Public Library, Evanston, Ill.**
The mission of the Evanston Public Library is to promote the development of independent, self-confident, and literate citizens through the provision of open access to cultural, intellectual and informational resources. Reprinted with permission.

**Saskatoon Public Library, Saskatoon, Sask., Canada.**
Saskatoon Public Library is an autonomous community-oriented institution ensuring quality cost-effective services to its public. The system provides educational, informational, recreational and cultural opportunities delivered by qualified and committed staff, as directed by Board Policy. Reprinted with permission of Saskatoon Public Library.

**Las Vegas–Clark County Library District, Las Vegas, Nev.**
We enable the people of our community to pursue lifelong learning through our responsive collections, electronic resources and innovative services. Our inviting public libraries are the cornerstones of our diverse communities where children and adults can experience personal enrichment and connect with one another. Used with permission of the Las Vegas-Clark County Library District.

**Redwood City Public Library, Redwood City, Calif.**
The Redwood City Public Library is the learning center of our community and the place people turn to for the discovery of ideas, the joy of reading and the power of information. Community needs drive our services and we take a personal interest in ensuring that they are delivered in a welcoming, convenient, and responsive manner. Reprinted with permission.

---

**Figure 7.4 Sample Mission Statements from Other Library Organizations**

---

**Friends of the Virginia Beach Public Library, Virginia Beach, Va.**
The mission of the Friends of the Library is to promote the mission and services of the Virginia Beach Public Library through advocacy and financial and programming support. Reprinted with permission. Friends of the Virginia Beach Public Library.

**South Carolina State Library, Columbia, S.C.**
The South Carolina State Library's mission is to improve library services throughout the state and to ensure all citizens access to libraries and information resources adequate to meet their needs. The State Library supports libraries in meeting the informational, educational, cultural, and recreational needs of the people of South Carolina. Reprinted with permission.

# DEVELOPING YOUR CORPORATE IDENTITY

You do, of course, need a visual corporate identity to support your brand. The biggest brands today have strong visual identities or logos. Nike has its trademark "swish." McDonald's has the Golden Arches. Others, like Microsoft and Apple, have type-driven logos that we recognize without actually reading the words.

In *The Pursuit of Wow!* Tom Peters details a variety of reasons for considering the design or the "look" of your communications materials. While Peters is addressing primarily a corporate audience, all of his 142 definitions of design can be applied to libraries; these definitions should be thought-provoking as you consider developing a graphic corporate image for your library.[4]

Whether you are managing communications efforts for a large public library system or a library media center in a small elementary school, you will want to develop a graphic corporate identity for your library. That identity and the style elements that accompany it will serve as a guide as you develop all of your communications materials, including print and electronic materials, bookplates, signage, and identification stickers on your library van.

By developing a graphic identity or look for your library, you will be working to create a particular public perception of your library, driven, of course, by your mission statement. For example, if your primary mission is to serve the local business community, you will want the colors and design of your corporate identity to be conservative. You might use white paper and have your corporate colors be blue and gray. If you are creating an identity for your academic library, but your service mission includes making the library a fun and interesting environment, you might choose brighter colors and a more casual style for your materials.

# THE IMPORTANCE OF DESIGN

Even before you decide that you want to develop printed communications materials for your library, you will want to begin thinking about design. The corporate graphic image that you develop will guide you in designing communications materials to meet your public relations goal. Someone who looks at a brochure produced by your library should immediately recognize that it is yours before reading any of the information. Occasionally, you will want to create unique materials that stray from the dictates of your library's corporate style in order to attract special attention. For example, if you are trying to attract teenagers to your public library, you may want to use a flyer that doesn't look like it came from a library. But, in general, you will want to establish a look for your library and stick with that look for all of your printed materials, your Web page, and your library's stationery.

Think about the corporate identities of companies such as Apple, Microsoft, Nike, McDonald's, or Coke. They may have different advertising campaigns and their materials may have slightly different looks, but you always know immediately who the ad comes from. A mixture of looks, colors, and paper types for your library's printed materials not only makes your literature racks unattractive, it also projects an image of a cluttered organization that doesn't know where it is going.

When you design your print materials or any item for your library, think about different types of design. Peters lists examples of the simplicity of design, the eclectic nature of design, and the importance of design. His diverse list (which even includes bad examples of design) emphasizes the importance of developing a look—a design—that belongs exclusively to your organization.

Your library's corporate identity is the foundation on which much of your communications efforts will be built. Since it will be featured in most of your communications materials, you might want to hire an outside graphic design or public relations firm to assist you. Design firms charge anywhere from $500 to $5,000 to develop the type of corporate identity package that a public library might want. Academic and school libraries may want to work with their parent institutions' communications offices as they do with other parts of their communications efforts, to develop an identity that complements the organization's overall identity. A simple addition to the parent institution's materials, such as an icon attached to the logo or an additional color, would create an identity for a school or academic library that is distinctive but also consistent with the overall image of the organization. If you can't afford an outside design firm, perhaps a local design firm will be willing to do pro bono or reduced-fee work for your library. Just ask! Lots of people have warm feelings about what libraries have done for them and would welcome the opportunity to repay the library. A student at a local art or design school might be willing to develop your library's corporate identity as a class project, or perhaps a talented Friend or a staff member would be willing to volunteer.

Bear in mind that, however, you often get what you pay for, so carefully review the work of a designer who offers to work pro bono. Your corporate identity is an important part of building your library's brand and you will likely have to live with the results—particularly if they are donated. Tread lightly and be sure that the generous designer's work reflects the experience and style that you need for your materials.

Whether you are working with a volunteer or a paid design firm, it is important to start your process with a written agreement about what will be developed and on what timeline, how many times the artwork will be reviewed and by whom, and how many times alterations will be made. This agreement will guide your progress and will prevent any misunderstandings.

An overall corporate identity package includes:

- logo
- corporate colors
- style sheet for different uses of the logo and colors
- corporate typestyle
- stationery
- Web page template/design
- newsletter template (optional)
- brochure template (optional)
- program flyer template (optional)
- signage template (optional)

Be very specific with the designer about what you are trying to achieve and what you can afford to spend on your communications materials both now and in the future. You may have $5,000 to invest in the development of the corporate identity package, but if you can't afford to print stationery in the new design, then it's not the right design for your library.

From the beginning of the process, be sure that the designer meets with the key decision makers for your library. If your library director will have the final approval on the design, then the designer must meet with the director early in the process. While the designer should have your mission statement as a guide, he or she may also want to question the director about the desired projected image and may review some other corporate identity packages to get a sense of the director's taste. When you meet with the designer on your own, you may want to share other pertinent information, such as "Our library director hates pink." This may sound silly, but why go through an entire design process and end up with an element (such as a color) that simply won't be approved by the top decision makers? Make the best use of your resources and do your research first. The major question to answer throughout this process is "What image does this library want to project and will these materials help us to do that?"

During the design process, show the logo designs and colors to a variety of people for their reactions. This is a good way to find out how the public will react. It is best, however, that the final approval decision not be made by a committee or the library board. Design is a very personal matter, and it is hard for a group to agree on a design because individuals tend to respond in terms of their personal likes rather than what will get the job done. Some designers may even charge more if they know that the decision will be made by a committee or board, rather than one or two individuals, because they believe the work process will be more cumbersome.

## CHOOSING A DESIGNER

If you decide to work with a design firm to develop your library's corporate identity, be sure to select someone who will work well with you and your library. Do a Google search for graphic designers/advertising firms in your community. Their Web sites will tell you a great deal about their design style and may provide links to the sites of their clients. If a designer doesn't have a Web site, don't consider that firm. Online images are too critical to libraries today to consider working with a Luddite graphic designer. Look carefully at client lists to determine the kinds of organizations the firm has worked with. You may want to consider firms with nonprofit or government organization experience over those that worked only have with the corporate world. They will likely have a greater understanding of the resource constraints and similar limitations that institutions like libraries face.

Larger communities may have special directories of designers, including more information about each firm and samples of their work. Word of mouth may be the best way to find a good designer, however. Look at the communications materials of other organizations in your community. When you find something you like, call the organization's communications director and ask who did the design. People are usually pleased to make referrals to firms especially when they are happy with the work. Another great source for referrals to designers is the people who sell printing or paper to your library. They often work directly with designers and know a lot about firms in your community.

Once you get some referrals, call the designers and tell them about your project. If the firm is interested, ask them to send you a few samples of their work or to direct you to examples on the Internet. If you like what you see, call them back and schedule a meeting to discuss your project. Ask each designer to bring a portfolio to your meeting so that you can see a variety of work. You may also want to visit the designer's studios to get a sense of the atmosphere and work environment. After you find two or three firms that might be appropriate to design your library's corporate identity, ask each to provide a proposal and quote based on the job that you describe. If you have a set budget or budget range, share it with the design firms upfront. Some of them may be out of your budget league from the start, and it doesn't make sense to waste anyone's time. Others will develop a proposal that fits within your available budget. Compare the quotes and make your decision. If your policy doesn't dictate that you go with the lowest bidder, be sure to consider how you feel about the designers. If all three designers quote the same fee, but you seem to "click" with one of them, hire that one! Design is largely an intuitive process and it is important to trust your intuition when hiring a designer.

# BUILDING THE PACKAGE

Once you have selected the designer for your library's corporate identity, it is time to begin building the package. The designer will want to work closely with you on each stage of development so that the materials meet your library's communications needs. Each element in the package builds on the next. The first decisions you make will be about a logo, colors, and stationery.

## WORKING WITH A DESIGNER

Don't worry if you have never worked with a designer before and know nothing about graphic design. Operate under the maxim "I don't know much about art, but I know what I like." Show the proposed designs to others, and remember to voice your opinion when you don't like something even if you aren't sure why. On the other hand, trust the designer you hire as the expert. If you don't like something, express your opinion, but rely on the designer to correct the problem. Don't spend your time trying to change or redesign the logo yourself. If it becomes apparent that this designer really isn't producing ideas that will work for your library, talk to the designer. There might be someone else in the firm who can take over your account or the designer might recommend that you find another firm that can better meet your library's needs.

## LOGOS

Working with a designer to develop a logo for your library is a chance to design a graphic image that supports your brand. Like your mission statement, a good logo is simple. It is eye-catching, and reproduces as well in black and white as it does in color. The complete name of the library must be integrated into the artwork.

You may want your library's logo to include something representative of your community. If you hope to reach people outside your community, be sure that they recognize and respond favorably to any local image that is part of your logo. The public library system that I used to work with had a logo that was a local tent-like landmark on top of a book. Locals knew what it represented. Individuals from out of town, however, thought it looked like a spider doing push-ups on a book. Needless to say, we developed a new logo that resonated both locally and nationally. *Print* magazine publishes an annual issue of logos from around the world, including library logos. In addition, *101+ Great Ideas for Libraries and Friends* (Neal-Schuman, 2004) includes sample logos, particularly for Friends groups. You may want to look at these resources before you begin your logo design process.

If your library already has a logo but it is dated, you may wish to have the designer update it rather than start from scratch. This is an especially good strategy if the current logo is well known and your library has a good reputation. By simply updating your current logo, you are using it to communicate the message "Our library isn't changing, it is simply updating its brand."

### Style Sheet for Logo Use

Developing a style sheet for the use of your library's logo is important to maintaining the integrity of your corporate identity. This style sheet will provide you and other library staff with guidelines for how and when to use the logo. If it is a three-color logo, the style sheet can specify how the logo should be used in a two-color application, a one-color application, or black ink only. It will describe how the logo should be reduced and enlarged, where it should be placed on materials, and how it can or cannot be altered. The guidelines provided by the style sheet will help to ensure the consistency of your library's graphic images. Copies of the style sheet should be distributed to anyone who might use the logo on any materials.

## CORPORATE TYPESTYLE

A specific type font will be used for the copy included in your logo. It may be a standard font or a font that is specially altered for your use. In addition, your designer will want to determine one or two fonts for use in all of your communications materials. The designer will determine what sizes and styles of font (bold, italics, reverse) you should use and when. This information will be included on your style sheet. By following these guidelines, you will produce materials that have a "family" look instead of looking cluttered or messy.

This typestyle should also be used on your Web site and other online communications to maintain a consistent look and feel. In fact, you may even want to ask library staff to use this typestyle in their e-mail communications.

## Stationery

When people receive a letter from your library, the first impression that they get will be from your letterhead. You will want it to have a design that communicates your brand. If you want people to perceive your library as a dignified research institution, your letterhead should have a very corporate look. If your message is that the library is a fun and exciting place, your letterhead should reflect that image. The point is be sure that your colors and paper type reflect, and don't detract from, your brand. The list of colors in Figure 7.5 and what they mean to most people will help you work with your designers to select proper colors for your library. Once you select those colors, they will be the corporate colors for your organization and should be used on many of your materials, including business cards, brochures, newsletters, and signage.

There are many wonderful kinds of paper to choose from for your letterhead. Be sure that you can afford the one you select. In addition, make sure that the paper will really meet your needs. Will it photocopy well? Will it work in the paper tray of your photocopier and go through your laser printer? It may be beautiful speckled paper, but do the speckles make the text printed on the paper hard to read? Remember that the look of your stationery is important, but it is a communications tool and the look shouldn't hinder communicating.

The design of your letterhead shouldn't get in the way of your message either. Some letterhead designs are graphically interesting but not very practical. If the designer presents you with letterhead that has printed information at both the top and the bottom of the page or in both the right and left margins, there may not be much space left for the letter itself. Think carefully about how restrictive this type of design will be before choosing it.

---

**FIGURE 7.5  Color as a Symbol**

Color can create a mood, symbolize ideas, and provoke emotions. Your library's colors should be carefully selected based on the image you want to project. Consider the following impacts of colors when making your selection:

| Color | Idea/Emotion |
|-------|--------------|
| Red | Happiness, excitement, bravery, danger |
| Blue | Dignity, serenity, loyalty, honesty |
| Black | Death |
| Yellow | Cowardice |
| White | Purity or innocence |
| Purple | Royalty or wealth |
| Green | Life or hope |

Source: Robert O. Bone, Robert E. Sintons, and Philip R. Wigg, *Art Fundamentals: Theory and Practice* (Dubuque. Iowa: William C. Brown Co. Publishers. 1968), 95.

---

Another consideration is the information that you want to include on your letterhead. Traditionally, you would include your library's name, address, phone and fax numbers, and Web site URL. Some libraries also print the name of the library director and/or library board members on their letterhead. This is a nice touch, but can get expensive since your letterhead becomes obsolete with every name change. If you put all of this information on your letterhead, it will be informative, but making it not look cluttered may be a challenge to the designer. Consider carefully what is the most important information to include.

**Templates**

Particularly if you or other staff members are skilled at desktop publishing, you may want to have the designer develop a variety of templates for print materials using your library's corporate identity. Possibilities include templates for a newsletter, brochures, program flyers, signage, and, of course, Web pages. The designer will provide a look for these items and you can "fill in the blanks" when the need for a brochure or flyer arises. The designer should develop a style sheet for each template, telling you what typestyle and sizes to use and detailing other design considerations. Using the template and the style sheet, you will be able to create materials that support your library's public relations activities and reflect the organization's overall corporate identity.

**INTRODUCING NEW MATERIALS**

If your library already has a logo and supporting corporate identity materials, and you are now updating or totally redoing your image, you will want to consider how to introduce your new materials. The best way to start using your new materials is to discard all the old items. (First be sure that you can afford to do that and that your timeline is long enough to meet your deadline.) You might have a special event to "unveil" your new logo and colors. You could hold a press conference or do this at an already scheduled event, such as a board meeting or parent's night at your school. Such an event is an opportunity for your library director or board president to talk about why these materials were developed, what image your library is trying to project, and why.

Developing a corporate identity is a first step in building your brand. You will be able to design materials that communicate the library's mission—and that design can pervade all of your communications materials. As Tom Peters says, "Design is at least as important for corporations grossing $250,000 a year as for those grossing $25 billion per year."[5] Indeed, design is as important for libraries with a $50,000 budget as for those with a $50 million budget.

# CONCLUSION

Once you have developed your library's brand, including its mission statement and visual identity, you are done, right? Cross that off the list! Hardly! Like all communications, your mission statement and other tools that support your brand must be revisited on an ongoing basis to ensure that they are still relevant. However, that doesn't mean completely changing your focus and your values. It means updating them, tweaking them to reflect the current cultural environment. If you are constantly changing directions, your audience will quickly become confused and your brand will communicate that confusion.

In *Brand Warfare: 10 Rules for Building the Killer Brand*, David F. D'Allessandro's third rule is "A great brand is like a bucking bronco—once you're on, don't let go."[6] Remember that. The bottom line is that once you have established who your library is, what you do, and how you do it and once you have developed the tools to communicate that, stick with it. Get out there, achieve your mission, and spread the word about your library.

# NOTES

1. Al Ries and Laura Ries, *The Fall of Advertising and The Rise of PR* (New York: Harper Collins, 2002), 280.
2. David F. D'Alessandro, *Brand Warfare: 10 Rules for Building the Killer Brand* (New York: McGraw Hill, 2001), xiii.
3. Eileen Elliot de Saez, *Marketing Concepts for Libraries and Information Services* (London: Facet Publishing, 2002), 15-27.
4. Tom Peters, *The Pursuit of WOW! Every Person's Guide to Topsy-Turvy Times* (New York: Random House, 1994), 120–127.
5. Peters, 122
6. D'Alessandro, *Brand Warfare*, 26.

# 8 PREPARING FOR SUCCESSFUL MEDIA RELATIONS

Media coverage—an article in your local newspaper, a story on the six o'clock news—is often the most inexpensive and effective (and, at times, destructive) communications tool available. The only expense is the time that you spend preparing the press materials, pitching the story to reporters, managing the interviews, following up, and monitoring for coverage. Inexpensive, right? Not always!

While media coverage is many times the ultimate goal of a public relations campaign, it is important to weigh the time invested against the story you are pitching. For example, you might send your quarterly press release announcing the preschool storytime schedule to all of the local media, but only pitch the editors who handle calendar listings. Then once the storytimes start, it might also be worth calling the photo editors who might be looking for feature photo opportunities. But if you are opening a new branch library or cutting the ribbon on your new school library, you will want to do call-downs to all of the local reporters and keep trying until you reach them.

Ultimately measuring the value of media coverage is an art—not a science. Some PR agencies place the value of advertising space on media coverage when reporting back to their clients. For example, if you secure a 15-column-inch story in your local newspaper, then the value of the article would be the same as a paid advertisement of the same size. This technique of measuring your efforts might be valuable when dealing with a board or other staff members who are skeptical about your library's investment in public relations. However, while news coverage is, in many instances, more credible with the public, you don't have control over the content as you do with paid advertising. So, in the end, measuring the value of coverage in this way is comparing apples and oranges and not recommended as an ongoing strategy. Instead, you might prepare a short written report describing each local newspaper story in terms of the article's tone, what it covered, and who the potential audience was. This approach provides a more honest assessment of the success of your efforts—even if it isn't as scientific.

Positive coverage from the media can help you achieve your

public relations goal. If your story isn't presented in a positive light, it can set back both your public relations efforts and progress toward your library's goals. It is just as important to plan in advance how to handle unanticipated media coverage as it is to seek media coverage. Building effective relationships with reporters, editors, and photographers allows you to help each other achieve your goals—they get their stories and you get to tell your story!

## WHO TALKS TO THE MEDIA?

It is important to have an overall philosophy and a policy about how you will handle inquiries from reporters. If you are in a school library, a university library, or a public library that is governed by a city or county policy, your challenge may not be to develop a philosophy and policy, but to determine how to interpret the parent or governing body's policy. Many large organizations insist that all inquiries be directed to an office of communications or public relations before they are referred to the appropriate individual. If that is the case in your organization, do not view that as a detriment to coverage. The referral process can buy you much-needed time to gather information, and can protect you when you don't want to comment on a negative story. On the other hand, you hope that your communications office will refer the reporter appropriately to talk to an expert on, for example, the role of school library media programs in education. You may wish to spend some time educating your school district's or university's communications director so that he or she understands the library issues and knows where to make referrals.

If you are in a smaller organization that doesn't have an overall media relations policy, develop one. Often the library director or assistant director is the first contact. Once the interview is cleared with the appropriate spokesperson, the reporter might be referred to someone who knows more about the topic. For example, if it is a story about summer reading, it is most appropriate for the reporter to talk with the children's librarian. But, if the reporter is calling with specific questions about the library budget, it is important that the interview be cleared and possibly held with, the library director or public relations person. A media relations policy prevents a reporter from putting your circulation clerk on the spot with a question about a recently challenged book—the staff person can simply tell the reporter that the interview must be cleared by the library director. Such a policy protects the staff and helps ensure that the message you are communicating is clear, consistent, and, above all, accurate.

## CHOOSING A LIBRARY SPOKESPERSON

Obviously you will need to work within your organization's policy on media spokespeople, but following those guidelines you will want to identify overall spokespeople and then spokespeople for each major story/issue. Depending on the size of your library, it may make more sense for the children's services coordinator to be the spokesperson for summer reading than the library director. However, if the library director is new in town and you are trying to build the director's profile, you may want to use him or her. If your school library is cutting the ribbon on its new space, the principal or superintendent is likely the best spokesperson.

Sometimes—particularly with controversial issues—a tiered approach to spokespeople works best. If your library is making the decision about whether to install Internet filters, the library director might be the most appropriate spokesperson to explain the issues and the decision-making process to the public. However, when the decision is made, a representative of the board—the group that holds the ultimate authority and made the decision—should announce the decision and field questions.

## PICK THE BEST SPOKESPERSON FOR THE STORY

Chances are that for most stories you have a variety of spokespeople to choose from. For summer reading, you have your system's entire children's team—not just the director of children's services. When you are launching a new circulation system, you might use the director of the technical services, collection development, technology, or circulation as the spokesperson. You might read this and gasp and say, "But won't the children's services director be offended if I use another children's librarian as the spokesperson? Won't the circulation services director's feelings be hurt?" Obviously it is a slippery slope, but if you work with them to identify the best possible spokesperson and garner successful coverage, it is a win for everyone. And, often, the people who aren't particularly good public spokespeople know it and are relieved when they discover they don't have to take on that responsibility.

When selecting a spokesperson, look for people who are:

- confident
- enthusiastic
- articulate

- professional
- calm
- well-groomed
- dynamic
- flexible
- warm
- fast-thinkers

## MEDIA TRAINING

Before you send out that first press release, call the first reporter, or set up that first interview, you must be sure that your key spokespeople are trained to work with the media. If you move forward with a media relations program without training spokespeople, skip the rest of this chapter and go to the chapter on crisis communications (Chapter 16).

Once you identify the spokesperson/people—whether it is you, your library director, your principal, or your board members—evaluate their experience talking with the media. Most people are willing to admit that they are interested in learning strategies for a successful interview—particularly those who have had a negative experience in the past. In fact, veteran spokespeople are often the most willing to participate in training, even if it is refresher. Use them to help convince your less-experienced spokespeople that training is critical.

If your budget allows and if you are new to public relations/media relations, it is well worth it in the long run to invest in a professional media trainer. Most communities have professionals in this field—sometimes they are former reporters. Some newspapers and radio and television stations are willing to send their reporters to media training sessions to talk about how best to work with them. Having these individuals talk to your spokespeople—particularly the skeptics—is a great strategy because they often have great horror stories to tell about ineffective media relations.

You might also contact your local chapter of the Public Relations Society of America to see if they have a resource for media training. They often have libraries of books and videotapes that can help you plan your training, and they might even have a member who would be willing to provide some gratis training for the local library.

# SUCCESSFUL MEDIA RELATIONS

There are two types of media relations—proactive and reactive. When you are involved in proactive media relations, you are encouraging coverage of stories. Reactive media relations is when a reporter calls and wants to do a story on a topic that you didn't necessarily want covered or you simply weren't focused on at the moment. A reporter might call wanting to do a piece on Black History Month resources at your library. It is a great story, but not necessarily one that you were pitching. Or a reporter might call and want to know your library's reaction to the USA Patriot Act. Again, you might not have been seeking this coverage, but you can manage the inquiry to work to your library's advantage.

## BUILDING A TARGETED MEDIA LIST

You are ready to start talking with the media—now what? Pick up the phone and start calling? No! You need to research the media in your community and develop a list of reporters who are appropriate for covering your library.

The Web provides a lot of information for building this media list. You likely already know what the major print and broadcast media are in your community, and their Web sites may contain the information that you need for your database. Using the forms in Figures 8.1–8.3, start pulling together your media list and compiling the background information that will help you target the right reporters. By gathering this information right up front, you will have the background you need for building media lists for each story that you want to pitch. When the information on a media outlet's Web site doesn't give you what you need, pick up the phone and call! Just don't do it on deadline! Also many communities have groups that publish guides to the local media as a fundraising project and these guides are usually available for a nominal fee. Check with your own reference librarian—your library may already own a copy.

A variety of commercially produced software programs, such as MediaMap, are available for managing media lists. But they come with a high price tag and are likely more than what your library or library system needs. Microsoft Outlook has a "Contacts" feature that you use to manage your media contacts, depending on the size of your media list. Another option is to develop an Excel document that contains all of the pertinent information. Or you might want to invest in an inexpensive "contacts" program to manage your media contacts; such databases usually provides space for personal information, the best time to call, and a

---

**FIGURE 8.1 Sample Media Fact Sheet: Newspaper or Magazine (Print or Online)**

**Name of Publication**

| | |
|---|---|
| Focus | What is the primary focus of the publication's content? Local news? National news? Community events? |
| Publication Schedule | Daily, weekly, monthly? If daily, what time of day? |
| Circulation | How many people does this publication reach? |
| Staff/Work Hours/Topics Covered/ Best Time to Contact | Your contacts and their individual phone and e-mail addresses. Find out the best time to call them and what "beats" they each cover. |
| Street Address | |
| Location | Directions for getting there! |
| Phone/Fax | General phone and fax |
| Web site | |
| Coverage | Include at least a bulleted list of past coverage (maybe the past year or so) of your library, with your assessment of the tone (e.g., positive, negative, neutral) |

---

record of previous contacts. Finally, if you are still a "paper person," a filing system or a notebook with listings in alphabetical order works as well. No matter what tool you select for managing your media information, it is important to have it all in one easy-to-use, accessible location.

**FIGURE 8.2 Sample Media Fact Sheet: Television Station**

**Name of Station**

| | |
|---|---|
| Affiliation | For example, ABC, NBC, FOX, CBS, PBS, or local independent |
| News Broadcast Schedule | What time(s) of the day does the station air its news? |
| Reach | How far does this station's signal reach? |
| Public Affairs or Interview Programs | List any programs that might be places for library staff or other supporters to appear. Be sure to include the contact person for each program. |
| PSA Submission Lead Times/Requirements | Does the station accept PSAs? If yes, how far in advance does it need to receive them? Are there specific PSA requirements? |
| Staff/Work Hours/Topics Covered/ Best Time to Contact | Your contacts and their individual phone and e-mail addresses. Find out the best time to call them and what "beats" they each cover. |
| Street Address | |
| Location | Directions for getting there! |
| Phone/Fax | General phone and fax |
| Web site | |
| Coverage | Include at least a bulleted list of past coverage (maybe the past year or so) of your library, with your assessment of the tone (e.g., positive, negative, neutral) |

**FIGURE 8.3 Sample Media Fact Sheet: Radio Station**

**Name of Station**

| | |
|---|---|
| Format | For example, Talk, Country, Rock, Classical, Christian, News? |
| Target Audience | What age range does this radio station try to attract? |
| News Broadcast Schedule | What time(s) of the day does the station air its news? |
| Reach | How far does this station's signal reach? |
| Public Affairs or Interview Programs | List any programs that might be places for library staff or other supporters to appear. Be sure to include the contact person for each program. |
| PSA Submission Lead Times/Requirements | Does the station accept PSAs? If yes, how far in advance does it need to receive them? Are there specific PSA requirements? |
| Staff/Work Hours/Topics Covered/Best Time to Contact | Your contacts and their individual phone and e-mail addresses. Find out the best time to call them and what "beats" they each cover. |
| Street Address | |
| Location | Directions for getting there! |
| Phone/Fax | General phone and fax |
| Web site | |
| Coverage | Include at least a bulleted list of past coverage (maybe the past year or so) of your library, with your assessment of the tone (e.g., positive, negative, neutral) |

### A Note About The Library Press

By all means, send the occasional release about a successful program or service to the national library press. In fact, include a color or black-and-white photo if you have a particularly good one from your National Library Week celebration or new building opening. As you know from browsing these publications, they do run these items and it helps create a national profile for your library. In addition, you will be able to show your library board, school board, and city council that your efforts merit national recognition. Do not, however, put the national library press on your mailing list for every single news release that you send out; it is a waste of time and money for you, and after a while they will dismiss an e-mail from your library as just another holiday closing—even though it might be an exciting story about a unique program at your library. Be selective in the releases and photos that you send to the library press just as you are for your local press.

### PROACTIVE "PITCHING"

PR professionals call contacting the media to garner coverage for a story "pitching." Typically you "pitch" a reporter after you have e-mailed him or her print materials on the story. If you have a press release announcing a special event, you have probably sent it to a list of local reporters. Then you call each of them to see if they received it and "pitch" the story. Or you might have a story that you think a particular reporter would be interested in and you have sent him a brief e-mail describing the story. A follow-up call is needed. However, before you pick up the telephone, you need to have some tools ready so that you are successful.

Review your media list. Be sure that the reporters on your list are appropriate for the story you are pitching. If you want something included in the community calendar, don't call the business editor. If you are pitching a board meeting, don't call the community calendar editor. Customize the media list for each story that you pitch. This strategy ensures the best use of your media relations time and lets the reporters know that you know what you are doing.

Then prepare your "pitch." Review the press release or your e-mail pitch and make a bulleted list of the top three things that you want to tell the reporter. Then identify the outcome that you want. Do you want the reporter to attend and cover an event? Do you want the preschool storytime schedule published in the calendar? Are you just letting him know that there is a board meeting next week? When you call the reporter, talk fast. Tell him the three things on your list and *request* your desired outcome. The reporter won't know what you want if you don't ask!

Give your spiel even if you get voice mail. Some reporters don't answer their phones unless they are expecting a call, so voice mail may be your only choice. Be brief, be articulate, and be enthusiastic—and always leave a call-back number. Until you become a real pro at media pitching, you may want to write all of this information down—like a script—and keep it in front of you when you are making calls.

If you are trying to schedule interviews with a spokesperson, have that person's schedule in front of you when you make your calls. That way if a reporter says, "Yeah, I can do that tomorrow afternoon," you can book the interview immediately and not risk losing the opportunity.

Make your calls at a time of day when you have the best chance of the reporter answering the phone. Finally, know when each reporter is on deadline. One way to ensure that your story won't get covered is to call when the reporter is on deadline—in fact, it is a good way to ensure that the phone won't get answered and you won't get a call back from the reporter.

## REACTIVE MEDIA RELATIONS

Any inquiry from the media should be viewed as an opportunity for your library. Whether the reporter is calling because of an interesting news release that you sent him or because a patron complained about a book in the collection, any inquiry is an opportunity to share your library's story and to continue to educate the community about the library's services, resources, and philosophy. It used to be that celebrities who received coverage in the tabloids sold in grocery stores took the attitude that "any press is good press." Today with the ubiquity of the media, particularly online media outlets that can publish a story in seconds, this old adage doesn't necessarily hold true. In today's media environment, it is more important than ever to manage the coverage that your library receives so that any media inquiry is an opportunity for positive news coverage.

It is always best to respond to a reporter's inquiry—even if you have to tell the reporter that the needed information isn't currently available. You are beginning to build a relationship that will benefit you down the road when you want coverage. Remember also that libraries have a variety of resources that can help people in the news business. For example, when a reporter calls looking for a local high school's 1966 yearbook photograph of a news figure, your prompt response may begin to build an impression in the reporter's mind that the library has many use-

## Top 10 (Okay, 11) Tips for Successful Media Pitching

Wendy Lienhart, a media relations pro with more than 20 years of experience pitching trade, local, and national media, wrote these tips for successful media. She currently manages media relations for L. Wolfe Communications and also has her own independent media relations consulting practice.

A former broadcaster, Lienhart has had pitching success with media outlets ranging from "The Today Show" and *Wall Street Journal* to weekly newspapers in small communities. I asked her to write 10 tips for successful media pitching, but she insisted that there were 11! So here are an experienced pro's keys to success:

1. Get to know who you are pitching. Most reporters have specific beats, or specialties, so make sure you are pitching the appropriate person. When in doubt, call the television assignment desk or a newspaper's city desk to find out who covers what.

2. Understand the hierarchy of a newsroom. For example, a news director of a television station is considered management and is probably not handling the day-to-day story assignments. The assignment desk, newscast producer, or beat reporters are the go-to people for this. At a newspaper, the editor-in-chief is the overall person in charge. Below the editor is the managing editor or editors of specific sections, such as education, features, and business. These folks assign stories to their staff of reporters.

3. You will have more success if you hone in on the story you are pitching. Don't give a reporter too much to consider, or the option to choose between story angle A, B, or C. A general or evergreen story idea does not have a sense of urgency. If you are very specific with the news angle, the reporter is more apt to do the story now than put your pitch on the back burner.

4. Reporters appreciate the personal touch, but what they need first are the facts—the who, what, when, where, and why. Skip the cold call and instead first e-mail, fax, or mail pitch materials. Keep a pitch letter short and sweet and to the point, and media alerts should be just that—the facts alerting them to a particular event or coverage opportunity. Then give the reporter a day to receive and read your pitch before making the call.

5. Emphasize a local angle in your pitch materials and phone follow-up. Include hometown facts or statistics as they relate to the broader topic, if at all possible.

6. It takes time, but work on establishing rapport with reporters. Read their stories or watch their reports on the news, so that next time you speak, if it's appropriate, you can refer to a recent story or special report.

7. Practice your phone pitch by calling a friend or family member first. If you're still nervous, save the biggies for last; start with a weekly newspaper first and work your way up to the dailies and television news desks.

8. Timing is everything! Know when to make, or perhaps more important when *not* to make your follow-up calls. Reporters generally have deadlines late in the afternoon, so it's best to call late morning to mid-afternoon. It's also not a good idea to call bright and early. Reporters often work late and use the morning to catch up on overnight news and enjoy their coffee. If you catch a reporter on deadline, apologize for the bad timing and ask when would be a good time to call.

9. Reporters and editors often play hard to get. But, an effective PR person knows when enough is enough. A good rule of thumb on follow-up calls is the three-voice-mails rule. If you've left three voices mails without any response, you are better off assuming the reporter isn't interested.

10. If a reporter sounds even remotely interested in your pitch and is involved in another story, or needs time to think about it or talk to an editor, never assume he will call you back. Make a note to check back in a week, or even two weeks. Persistence often pays off!

11. Don't get discouraged! Reporters can be abrupt and sound disinterested, but as much as they hate admitting it, they need us for story tips and to keep current on what's going on.

ful resources—you may have made a friend for the future when you want a story covered.

Sometimes you can turn a potential negative media opportunity into an opportunity to educate the reporter and the public. For example, a reporter calls your public library and asks for information about a patron in your database. You know that the library's policy on confidentiality of patron records prohibits you from sharing that information without a court order. Rather than simply telling the reporter, "No," and acting irritated, you can use this as a chance to explain the policy and the philosophy behind it, and maybe even fax the reporter a copy. The reporter may not use the information in this story, but you will have educated the reporter about how your library operates and why. This example appeared in the first edition of this book; as discussed in Chapter 1, in today's environment, the scenario is even more relevant today.

Be careful to share all information with reporters that the public has a right to know. For example, the budget for a public, school, or publicly funded college or university is typically public information. If you get a request from a reporter for a document and you are unsure about whether it should be shared, check with legal counsel for your library, school district, or college or university before sending the reporter away empty-handed. If you can't get an answer right away, tell the reporter you will get back to him or her. The last thing a library wants is to be accused by the media of withholding public information. Such an accusation will come back to haunt you when you deal with an intellectual freedom issue in the future.

Freely sharing public information does not mean that you should not present it in a context that tells the whole story. Be ready with a narrative document that supports your budget or new Internet use policy to provide background on the decision-making process and how it supports the community's needs. When you think an issue has the potential to be controversial or stimulate media interest, prepare these materials in advance and be sure that your key spokesperson is briefed on the messaging and potential questions.

At library board meetings, always be sure that there are extra copies of board materials for the media. Preparing several board packets and having them available on a table in the back of the room is a good idea. Handing them out as an opportunity to greet each reporter and offer your help in answering any questions that they may have is an even better idea. This personal touch helps you to build a relationship with these reporters and also lets them know that you are aware they are covering the meeting. Once you have an idea of the reporters that are in the room, you might want to give your board members a "heads-up" so that they are aware. Obviously, the board should always act is if there are reporters in the room, but a reminder never hurts.

Be sure that reporters get complete board packets—it is confusing if board members refer to materials that the media people don't have, and it may appear that you are trying to hide something.

## MANAGING MEDIA INTERVIEWS

Success! You have scheduled your first interview with a reporter from the local newspaper. Now what?

First, don't be afraid to ask the reporter what he or she wants to talk about in the interview. Drill down a bit and get a sense of the types of questions that might be asked, information or data the reporter might be looking for, and an estimate of about how long the interview will take. This information will help you brief the spokesperson prior to the interview. Figure 8.4 is an interview briefing form that you can modify to work for your needs and use as a guide when you are talking with the reporter and then briefing your spokesperson. Include in this document the questions that the reporter said he or she might ask in the interview, but also think carefully about other questions that might arise. In fact, it is important to think about the worst possible question that might come up and include that. If your spokesperson is prepared to answer that question, he can likely answer anything.

If at all possible, you should always verbally brief a spokesperson in case that person has any questions, but the interview briefing form also gives the spokesperson a resource to refer to while preparing for the interview. Of course, sometimes the interview will be in the next hour and you won't have time to write up a formal briefing document. But you can still use the form and its questions as a guide for your discussion with the reporter and for verbally briefing the spokesperson. One note: remember that this is a confidential document. Be sure that the reporter doesn't see it, or (gasp!) that it doesn't get mixed in with the press materials that you provide.

**FIGURE 8.4 Interview Briefing Form**

| | |
|---|---|
| Media Outlet | Name the newspaper, or television or radio station. If the broadcast outlet is an affiliate (e.g., ABC, NBC, CBS, FOX), indicate affiliation. |
| Reporter | Include name and title, if the reporter has one. Reporter Note if the reporter is bringing a photographer or videographer. |
| Date/Time | |
| Location/Contact Information | Be specific about the location (e.g., Main Library Children's Room near the puppet theater). If this is a phone interview, include all call information, including who is placing the call. |
| Focus/Agenda | Briefly state the topic for the interview. |
| Materials Received (Attached to briefing) | List all of the materials (e.g., press release budget) that you have sent to the reporter. Attach the materials to the briefing document so that the spokesperson has them at hand. |
| Possible Questions | Provide a bulleted list of the questions that the reporter indicated he or she will ask. Include the questions that you think he or she might ask. Don't forget to include the worst possible question you think he or she might ask. |
| Data Points | Provide a bulleted list of the data and other information that the spokesperson should have handy. You may want to develop this list in collaboration with the spokesperson depending on the interview topic. |
| Background on Reporter | Be as detailed (and honest) as possible about your relationship with the reporter and his or her interest in the topic. Also, if he or she has any relevant specific interests, include them. While a bio from a newspaper or television station's Web site might be helpful here, don't simply cut and paste it. This section should be a brief description of the reporter and your library's history/relationship with him or her. |
| Background on Media Outlet | Include audience reach/circulation and tone of the media outlet. If other reporters have covered your library in the past, include any relevant information about that. If they sponsor your summer reading program, don't forget to mention it. |
| Previous Coverage | Include any previous coverage from this reporter or media outlet as an attachment. If it was broadcast coverage, review the tape with the spokesperson prior to the interview. |

## TIPS FOR AN EFFECTIVE INTERVIEW

Your spokesperson is briefed and has the necessary information handy. The reporter has arrived or is on the phone and, of course, your spokesperson has participated in media training. The following tips will help ensure that this media opportunity produces positive results.

Be ready to greet the reporter. If he or she is coming to your school, let the office know, or—if your schedule allows—be near the office with a visitor's badge ready. If the reporter is coming to your public library, tell the front desk—especially if a camera crew is coming too. If you haven't already talked about where the reporter would like to do the interview, that should be your first question, especially if it is a broadcast interview. If it is a print interview, you might say, "We would like to do this interview in the library director's office."

When you get to the interview location, introduce the spokesperson. But, remember, you will want to stay nearby during the interview. If it is a print interview, without a photograph, you can simply sit unobtrusively with the reporter and your spokesperson. If it is a broadcast interview, stay nearby where you can hear, but out of camera range. You are there as a resource—to assist, to run and get a document that the spokesperson might need, and to analyze the effectiveness of the interview. Try to take some quick notes on the questions asked, any surprise issues that arise, and any great or not-so-great answers that the spokesperson gives. This information will help you evaluate the success of the interview, determine any follow-up, and plan for future opportunities.

Occasionally there may be a time when an interview strays too far from the original direction and you need to intervene. If you have scheduled a children's librarian to do an interview on summer reading and the television reporter sees a broken window in the library and wants to ask questions about the deterioration of the library building instead, you may need to interject, "Laura is really not the best person to talk with you about that, but I would be happy to set up a time for you to talk with the library director. Laura is here to talk about summer reading." Hopefully, your spokesperson will do this herself, but if not—or if she tries to answer such questions—a pleasant but firm interjection should direct the reporter back to the interview topic.

Once the interview starts, each question should be analyzed carefully. It never hurts to pause for a second and think about the question—even when there is a television camera in your face. The production editor will just edit out the pause.

There are really only three ways to answer a question:

1. Answer directly.
2. Suggest that someone else is more appropriate to answer the question.
3. Tell the reporter that you aren't in a position to answer the question at this time, but will get back to him or her when you have the information and/or are in a position to comment.

### Three Key Interview Techniques: Bridging, Hooking and Flagging

Public relations professionals have identified three techniques for answering questions in a media interview: bridging, hooking, and flagging. Learning these techniques will help your spokespeople ace any interview, and they are easy to practice in daily life. You can use them when dealing with your children or chatting at a cocktail party. Each technique is described below with interview question-and-answer examples.

### *BRIDGING*

Bridging is switching the subject to one that you want to talk about. It helps you get your message across even when the reporter asks a question that you don't want to answer. Following are examples of two ways to "bridge" an answer.

*Example: Bridging*
**Reporter:** Why weren't these libraries included in the city's new buildings bond issue ten years ago?
**Library Director:** I don't have the information to answer that question, but I can tell you that we are seeing support for our new building plan across all segments of the community.

*Example: Bridging*
**Reporter:** Don't you think that the city should provide more ongoing funding for libraries?
**Library Director:** We have our challenges, but I am confident that the community will support the bond issue for new libraries.

### *HOOKING*

Hooking is prompting the next question by placing an interesting premise in the answer to a previous question.

*Example: Hooking*

**Reporter:** If libraries spend more money on technology and online resources, won't books become obsolete?

**Library Director:** Your question points out an interesting misconception. But actually, circulation of books has increased in our community and because of the economies that come with purchasing online reference materials, we have been able to reallocate funds to increase our investment in our print fiction and nonfiction collection.

## FLAGGING

Flagging is prioritizing your comments for the reporter or editor. This is a great way to ensure that a reporter hears what you are saying and actually gives him or her a guide for taking notes. You can say, "The three most important things are . . ." or "The most important issue is . . ." or "Our top two funding priorities for next year are . . ." Watch as the reporter takes notes. If you indicate three items, a reporter will often write "1, 2, 3" down the side of the notepad. It must be a throwback to elementary school, but it is a great strategy for getting your point heard.

*Example: Flagging*

**Reporter:** As the new library director, what are your goals?

**Library Director:** My top goal is to provide the community with the highest quality library service. We will achieve this in three ways. First, we will invest more in books and other resources. Second, we will extend the hours at our branches. Third, we will work with the community to develop a plan for the future of our library system.

*Example: Flagging*

**Reporter:** Why do you need more funding for your school library?

**School Principal:** The most important thing that we can teach our children is to read and love reading. By providing a strong school library as the hub of our school, we are showing them the high value that we place on reading and the critical role that it plays in helping them to be successful in school and in life.

## Answering Challenging Questions

Some types of questions are challenging to answer. It is critical to think carefully before answering any interview questions, but especially hypothetical questions and ranking questions.

### HYPOTHETICAL QUESTIONS

When a reporter starts a question with "What if," tread carefully. These answers can often be included in an interview report as if they were in response to a real—not a hypothetical—situation. Be sure that your answer quickly acknowledges that the situation does not exist.

> *Example: Hypothetical Questions*
> **Reporter:** What if your bond issue fails?
> **Library Director:** We know that with the support of the community we will pass this bond issue.

> *Example: Hypothetical Questions*
> **Reporter:** If authorities came to your library and requested patron records, what would you do?
> **Library Director:** No one has ever requested our patron records. We have a policy in place that we would follow if that situation occurs. I would be happy to share it with you.

### RANKING QUESTIONS

Reporters will often use ranking or choice questions when they are trying to get a more specific answer to a question than what you have previously given them. Don't let them corner you into making a choice that you aren't ready or in a position to make.

> *Example: Ranking Questions*
> **Reporter:** If you only get partial funding, which of the new library buildings would you build?
> **Library Director:** All areas of our community are an important part of our new building plan. We are confident that we will get full funding.

> *Example: Ranking Questions*
> **Reporter:** If you had to choose between buying a print or an online encyclopedia which would you buy?
> **School Librarian:** We make our purchasing decisions based on criteria that are based on providing students with the best possible resources for learning.

## SPEECHES—NOT QUESTIONS

Reporters have opinions and sometimes they will share them with you during an interview by making a short speech. They will tell you all about a negative experience that they had at the library or how poorly they think the school board or the city council is behaving. If there isn't a question at the end of the speech, don't say anything. Smile. If the pause gets to be too long, bring up a topic that you want to discuss. Sometimes they are baiting you; other times they are just passionate. But just in case, don't take the bait.

> *Example: Speeches—Not Questions*
> **Reporter:** Well, the library in my neighborhood is a mess. It is just falling down and there is no space. And no parking. I just don't see a way that the community can't fund this bond issue. It is a deplorable situation.
> **Library Director:** <SMILE> <PAUSE> Would you like to see the plans that we have for each of our new library buildings?

> *Example: Speeches—Not Questions*
> **Reporter:** When I went to school, our library had so many books and encyclopedias. I loved to read the encyclopedia. Today it seems like all the school board wants to do is buy computers. There are no books in the school library. Kids need books,
> **School Librarian:** <SMILE> <PAUSE> Let me show you our new reading area where students can come during their free periods and read or study.

## DON'T BE AFRAID TO SAY "I DON'T KNOW"

Be forthright, honest, and helpful, and make "I don't know, but I'll find out and call you" an important part of your vocabulary—even when you are interviewed for radio or television. It is preferable that reporters wait for the correct information than that they receive incomplete or erroneous information. Wrong information will diminish your credibility as a source and eventually reporters will stop contacting you or devalue the information that you provide. No one can fault you for saying, "I don't know," and the return phone call to the reporter with the information that you find is another chance to tell your library's story.

## THERE'S NO SUCH THING AS "OFF THE RECORD"

Going "off the record" is dangerous stuff. In novels, in the movies, and on television, sources frequently go off the record with reporters. They share information that they don't want attributed to them or that they don't want included in the story. Sometimes this is done because the interviewee believes that the background is essential to understanding other issues, but, for legal or personal reasons, he or she doesn't want the information published or attributed. The idea is that the reporter is then bound by some moral code to honor the agreement that the information is off the record. The reality is that, particularly for individuals who are novices in working with the media, there is no such thing as "off the record." If you don't want to be quoted or you don't want the information included in a story, don't say it to a reporter. It puts you both in a bad position—you may offer some information that the reporter simply cannot avoid reporting, and you may risk your job for sharing the information. Again, be forthright, honest, and helpful, but don't share "off the record," confidential information with a reporter.

### Recapping the Interview

The interview isn't over when it is over. Obviously the coverage is still pending. But while you nervously await it, there is other work to be done. If possible, immediately debrief with the spokesperson. Discuss what went well and what didn't go so well, identify any necessary follow—up and decide how it will be handled. Be kind, but be honest. If the spokesperson gave out erroneous information, think about a strategy for getting the correct information to the reporter. The reporter wants his facts to be right. A quick call to say, "We went back and checked the circulation figures and actually they are higher than what we told you in the interview; here are the actual figures," will be appreciated.

Figure 8.5 is an interview recap form that will help guide your debriefing. Keep a completed copy of the document for future reference. This completed form is particularly helpful when preparing for future interviews and as a permanent record of each interview. Provide the spokesperson with a copy of the recap so that he or she can use it to continue to build interview skills and/ or to feel good about a job well done.

---

**FIGURE 8.5  Interview Recap Form**

Date/Time

| | |
|---|---|
| Meeting Overview | Write a brief, narrative overview of the interview. Include high points, low points, and things you would do differently in the future. |
| Sound bites | • Provide a bulleted list of the great sound bites that your spokesperson shared during the interview.<br>• This is a good positive reinforcement for the spokesperson and a great resource for other spokespeople. |
| Coverage Anticipated | When and what kind of story do you anticipate? |
| Questions Asked and Answered | • Include a bulleted list of the reporter's questions.<br>• It may be difficult to record all of these questions during the interview, but try to include the highlights. |
| Follow-Up | • List anything that you still need to send the reporter or information that you need to send.<br>• Be sure to note who is responsible for completing each follow-up item. Include status, so you will know when it is done. |

---

# DEVELOPING A RELATIONSHIP WITH THE MEDIA

In many ways, the professions of journalism and librarianship share similar values, particularly in the areas of intellectual freedom and freedom of information. Libraries also have a variety of resources that can support reporters in their work. Use these resources to develop a strong relationship with members of the media. When a reporter drops by to do a story on preschool storytime, but mentions a business story he is working on, tell him about the new resources in your business section. Take every opportunity to tell reporters about areas other than the one you are discussing. If a reporter is doing a story on the lack of parking near your library, provide the information and then tell him or her about the drive-through window service that you have started. Turn every topic into a win-win situation for your library and the reporter!

When a reporter calls, return the call promptly. If you have been dissatisfied with the quality or quantity of past news coverage, and if encouraging more accurate coverage is a priority for your library, returning reporters' calls in a timely fashion could be a key to changing the coverage in the future. The next time a library story comes up, the reporters may remember you were helpful.

When you have a photo opportunity at your library, call the newspaper photo editor or a photographer that you have worked with in the past. It may just be the day they need some stand-alone art for the front page. On the other hand, you may spend hours compiling information and setting up interviews or a reporter on what you think is a terrific story, and that may be turn out to be the day that the mayor resigns or there is a terrible traffic accident. Don't give up! Be friendly, but be persistent. The reporter will remember the work you did and your investment will pay off down the road!

Listen carefully anytime you talk with a reporter. For example, you may be walking together after a library board meeting and the reporter may tell you that he is a Civil War history enthusiast. Jot that information in your Rolodex or electronic contacts list. Then when your library buys new books on the Civil War, you can send him an e-mail calling his attention to the new resources. This gives you an excuse to contact him, and remind him that your library is there. It will be a positive experience for both of you—people are always flattered when others take note of their interests, and your follow-up will provide him with a positive feeling about both you and your library.

Some of the things mentioned above may seem time-consuming. However, if you build relationships over time with reporters in your community, it will eventually pay off. If media representatives like and trust you, you will have more straightforward and pleasant dealings in the future. Ultimately, building strong relationships with reporters, without compromising their integrity or yours, will result in positive, honest news coverage for your library. The story may not always be the one that you want told, but you will have the opportunity to share your side of things.

## GETTING YOUR STORY COVERED

While it may often seem that getting your library's story covered by the local media is a matter of luck, strategically targeting various media outlets, being aware of the story possibilities at your library, and building relationships with reporters, producers, and editors will help increase your chances for coverage. Most importantly, don't give up. If you spend three days providing a reporter with background and interviews for a story and then there is a national or local crisis, you have every right to be disappointed if your story is dropped, but your efforts have not been in vain. If you carefully select the media outlet for your story and then develop your message especially for the selected outlet, however, you have a better chance of success.

Chapter 9 focuses on print tools for garnering media coverage, but there are some other media relations tools that you may wish to use when appropriate. They offer ways to handle breaking news, promote special programs, and meet the ultimate goal of telling your library's story.

## NEWS CONFERENCES

Before planning a news conference, decide if what you want to announce is really breaking news. Don't let the Junior League talk you into holding a news conference to announce its recent book donation if you don't think your local media will be interested in covering it. If, for political reasons, you need to hold a news conference that the media might not be interested, turn it into a special event. Invite staff and library supporters, have a speaker, and serve refreshments. That way, if the press doesn't show, the Junior League members present won't be disappointed. You are still celebrating their donation! Just don't strong-arm reporters into attending this event—let them know that you understand their priorities.

If you do have something of high news value to announce, such as the appointment of a new library director, a news conference may be the best tool for making the announcement. Choose a time and location convenient for the members of the press to attend. For example, don't schedule a news conference one hour before deadline at the daily paper and expect an article to appear that day, or at 5 p.m. and expect the story to be on the six o'clock news. Be sure there is parking available for the press at the location you choose and plenty of outlets in the room for the videographers to plug in their lights. Also, try not to have the news conference in a bland conference or meeting room. If you can accommodate it, consider holding it in the reading room of the library or some other location that will tell viewers—even if they aren't listening to the story—that this news is about the library. Reporters, photographers, and videographers will appreciate this extra touch because it gives their story more interest.

Announce your news conference as far in advance as possible. A media alert often works best for announcing a news conference. Media alerts should be one- page long and have a "just the facts" format. Remember to include the details, but save the "news" for the news conference. For example, tell them that you are going to announce the appointment of the new library director, but save the "who." A sample media alert is included in Chapter 9.

Rehearse your news conference. Have each participant show up an hour early and walk through how you will conduct the conference. If you are holding the news conference in a public place, you may have to rehearse elsewhere so you don't give away the news. Ask participants a few of the questions you anticipate being asked at the news conference so that they can begin to think through their answers.

After the news conference, different media outlets may want varied angles on the story. Think about this possibility before the news conference. Identify staff to work with reporters from different stations and newspapers. Take camera crews to different areas in the library so that each media outlet gets a unique angle on the same story.

Use news conferences sparingly! Libraries aren't police departments. They shouldn't have many stories that demand news conferences. If you do have something "hot" to announce, such as the outcome of a censorship challenge, schedule a news conference. For other news and information, use such tools as news releases, public service announcements, and newsletters. Don't demand that the press show up at a specific time and place if the "news" doesn't warrant it. You'll get a reputation as the "PR person who cried wolf" and the media response will dwindle. Use other times when the media might already be in attendance (for example, library board meetings, city council meetings, and special events) for such activities as accepting donations from generous community groups.

## STORIES IN THE DRAWER

Libraries have many stories. However, many library-related stories are not time-sensitive. The fact that your school library media center has a parenting collection and that parents visit after school and share books with their children might make a wonderful feature story on the 11 o'clock news, but it isn't going to preempt a plane crash. There are, however, always slow news days. So, part of your job is to develop a list of stories to keep in your desk drawer—"stories in the drawer"—for such occasions. Draft a couple of notes about the angle for your story, who should be interviewed, and so forth. As you build a relationship with various reporters, hint that you keep a file of potential stories. Tell them a little bit about one or two of them. Eventually you will get a call from a reporter who is looking for news and you'll be able to say, "I have the following stories that you might be interested in using. What can I do to help you?"

If you are a school library media specialist or an academic librarian, you might want to use this technique to sell stories to your district, college, or university communications office. Draft your ideas and send them to the communications office on a regular basis. Let them know that something newsworthy is always happening in your library.

Keeping stories in the drawer is an excellent way to get feature coverage, and once a reporter knows that you can come through in a pinch with a good feature, you will get more calls from both the reporter and his or her editor—when they are struggling to fill the six o'clock news or the features page of the newspaper.

## OTHER OPPORTUNITIES FOR WORKING WITH THE LOCAL MEDIA

There may be other opportunities for working with your local newspaper, television stations, and radio stations. They probably all have public affairs divisions that produce programs and projects that your school, public, or academic library could support. For example, when you see an advertisement for an upcoming public affairs television program on alcoholism, call the station and ask to speak to the public affairs director. Say that your library would be willing to prepare a book list on alcoholism and post it on your Web site. Then they can mention the link during the program. The station is able to point its viewers to more information and your library gets publicity and reaches more users.

The broadcast media offer coverage opportunities that don't exist in the print world. Television talk shows and radio call-in shows are wonderful chances to tell your library's story. If your local television station has a regular talk show, you might try to schedule library staff or individuals who are presenting programs at the library to appear on the show. This is a great chance to tell the library's story in more than a 30-second sound bite. Be sure that the people you send are confident and articulate, and brief them on what they will be discussing before they arrive in the studio. Radio call-in shows can also be a great tool for spreading your message if you carefully select the person who represents your library. Make sure that the library representative knows and understands the discussion topic and can think on his or her feet.

If it is your representative's first experience with such an interview, consider rehearsing together beforehand and have him or her listen to the show several times before the appearance. Listening to the show will indicate what the interviewer is like and what kind of people call with questions.

Many newspapers have a Newspapers in Education program and might like to work with school and public librarians as they develop their materials for distribution to teachers and students. Such a program is also part of relationship building with the media and can help you promote your services and resources.

# CABLE-ACCESS PROGRAMS

Developing cable-access programming for your library may not really be media coverage, but it is an opportunity to share your library's story using television—and with the ability to shape the message yourself rather than having a reporter put a specific "spin" on it. Most school, public, and academic libraries have opportunities to produce and air cable-access programs. In fact, many school districts, cities, and universities have their own cable channels and are often desperately seeking quality programming.

Developing and producing your own cable-access program is a time-consuming task. Even if the production expenses are provided by the cable channel, you need to think about focus, talent, and script. A program with an amateur appearance may communicate the wrong message about your library and be worse than not having any cable television presence. Finding quality talent for your program may also be a challenge. Some libraries, however, have been successful at developing a talk-show format that focuses on their programs and services. If you have the time and energy and can find the talent to do this, it can be a wonderful way to disseminate accurate information about your library.

Another option is to produce one or two programs on an annual basis that provide an overview of your library or focus on a couple of services. You can put resources into developing these "feature" programs and then ask the channel to air them on a revolving basis. If you choose this option, be sure not to include any time-sensitive information in your programs, so that they can have a relatively long life. For example, if you produce a program on your school library's services and resources, you can mention that you host parents' nights on a regular basis, but don't mention dates.

The least time-intensive option for producing cable-access programming is taping and airing library programs (for example, a preschool storytime or an adult program). You provide the public with a preview of what they could take advantage of if they visited your library, and yet you don't have to plan, cast, or script each program. Be careful to select programs that would air well on television. For example, a book discussion group may not be the best choice because participants might be nervous and there may be lags in the discussion. Presentation programs, such as a reading by a local author, are probably better options. Remember, however, that you may have no control over when these programs air—you may find preschool storytime is being shown at 2 a.m. on occasion!

Cable access can be an inexpensive and effective way to tell your library's story, particularly if you have free access to production facilities and staff. Best of all, your programs will probably air over and over again. Granted, sometimes it will be in the middle of the night, but a program about your library may be a viable alternative for insomniacs whose only other television choices are "infomercials."

# KEEPING TRACK OF MEDIA COVERAGE

You've worked hard to get the local media to cover your library's activities and you have been successful. But your work is far from over! First, you must work to maintain the relationships you have developed. Second, it is important to keep track of and analyze the coverage you have received.

Make a regular practice of scanning all local print publications for articles mentioning your library. Clip them and store them, by topic, in a file or a scrapbook. Take note of who the reporter is, which library staff are quoted, the length of the articles, and so forth. In addition, monitor radio and television broadcasts, and make videotapes and audiotapes of coverage of your library. Mark the tapes with the date, topic, and station for each story, and store them in one place—so you review them when you create your next public relations/communications plan or when you assess the progress of achieving the goal in your current plan.

You are creating an archive of the media coverage of your library. This archive will be an invaluable resource when you audit your communications efforts, consider future communications efforts, or need to show your library board that your library is, in fact, getting lots of coverage from the local media.

# CONCLUSION

In spite of the bum rap that they sometimes receive, reporters are typically great people. They are dedicated to their jobs and focused on reporting accurate, balanced, fair stories. As in any profession, there may be a few bad apples with a hidden agenda, but, in general, if you follow the tips in this chapter, you will like the reporters that you work with and be successful in your media relations efforts.

However, while public relations may have gained more credibility with the public over the past ten years, the proliferation of organizations clamoring for media attention has increased the media's skepticism about public relations and public relations professionals. And today's technology gives reporters great tools for screening out contacts from PR professionals. It is easier to check the caller ID on the telephone or hit the big "X" on an e-mail message and delete it without even opening it.

Remember that every time you pick up the phone to call reporters you are confronting their negative opinions about PR people—even if you are calling from their community school or public library. Your challenge is to rise to the top of the heap. Be the well-informed, helpful, and smart PR person who helps them do their jobs. Good PR people help reporters do their jobs; bad ones can't even get reporters to answer their calls or read their e-mails.

In my opinion, media relations is the best part of public relations work. When you do your research, your media targets, and pitch your targets as an informed PR pro, you will see a terrific return on your investment in media relations.

# 9 PREPARING PRESS MATERIALS THAT GET ATTENTION

You have developed a PR plan, thinking carefully about your messages and audience. You have begun to think about who your media targets are and to develop targeted media lists and intelligence on your media contacts. Now you are ready to begin developing tools to support the media relations portion of your PR program.

While the media environment has changed over the past ten years and technology has become an incredibly integral part of all businesses, the basic tools for media relations have remained the same. Tried and true, well-written, news-driven press releases and other press materials are still the best way to get the word out and build relationships with the media. What has changed is the way that we deliver these materials to the media and some of the tools that we use to develop them.

In addition, news conferences, print and e-mail pitch letters, guest op-ed columns, and letters to the editor are also great media relations tools. It is important to consider what tool you will use based on the type of coverage that you want, the time frame for the coverage, and how complicated the story might be. Libraries of all types should also consider expense. It is important to have accurate, attractive, and, at times, clever materials to sell a story that you want covered, but you must always take into consideration the fact that the public is paying the bill. For example, using a press kit complete with confetti and party horns to announce the opening of a new branch library might initially seem like a great idea, but if this is the first new library opened in your city in 45 years, do you really need to spend so much money to encourage the coverage? What if a reporter decides to do a story on how much money you spent on those press kits and how many more books the cost of the press kits could have bought for the new branch?

With the press, you constantly walk the fine line between developing effective, interesting materials and developing materials that might become targets of criticism. A good rule of thumb with the media is to focus on providing accurate, concise information; save the clever gimmicks for publicity projects.

# CORE PRESS MATERIALS

In addition to press releases that announce library news, you need to develop some core press materials to support your media relations activities. The basic items are a library backgrounder and fact sheet. You may also want to develop a leadership biographies document, with background on the library's leadership team and/or board members. These materials are tools for putting library background information at reporters' fingertips when they are working on a story or when you are trying to pitch them on a particular story.

## BACKGROUNDER

Your library's backgrounder should be no longer than two pages and include your mission statement; a top-line overview of your programs, services and facilities; a list of the names and titles of your leadership; and, of course, press contact information. The backgrounder descriptions of programs and services are the foundation for how you talk about them in all other press materials. Ultimately, the backgrounder serves as a reference document for you as well as the media. A backgrounder template appears in Figure 9.1.

## FACT SHEET

A fact sheet is just that—the facts! No more than one page in length, this document includes your mission statement, a list of locations, a list of major programs and services, a list of leadership team/board members, and contact information. Reporters who cover the library on a regular basis can use this document as a reference tool to ensure that they spell names correctly and have your phone number at their fingertips. A fact sheet template appears in Figure 9.2.

## LEADERSHIP BIOGRAPHIES

A list of leadership biographies is optional for your press kit. If you want to promote the backgrounds of your library director, top leaders, or board members, however, this is a great tool for doing that. Plus, once you develop the comprehensive document the biographies will be available when you need them—like when the board chairman receives an award and you need to do a press release. These biographies should be short (50–100 words each) and include only information that is relevant to the individual's position at the library. Don't include personal information or the

---

**FIGURE 9.1 Backgrounder Template**

### [YOUR LIBRARY NAME] Backgrounder

**Overview**

Include your library's mission, a short history of the library, and any key goals or high-level projects. If you are in a school or academic library, include a description of the institution and the library's mission and role.

**Programs and Services**

Often a bulleted format works best for this section. Write an introductory paragraph describing the philosophy or guiding principles behind your programs and/or services and then list the individual services, along with a one-sentence description and a Web link if available.

**Facilities**

List all of your facilities and street addresses.

**Library Leadership**

List the names and titles of your library's leadership in hierarchical order. You may want to include an introductory paragraph that describes how your library is governed and funded.

**For more information, press only:**
Name, title, phone, and e-mail for your PR contact.

---

names of their pets. Such detail may seem warm and clever, but it is extraneous information that reporters aren't interested in digging through. Do include academic degrees, other community involvement, and perhaps number of years of service if significant.

List the biographies in hierarchical order. For example, in a public library system, it would typically be board chair, vice-chair, and members (in alphabetical order), and then the library director. As for press materials, be sure to include your press contact's information.

You may want to have photos taken of your library leadership and board members. You can post them on your Web site, and also have them available in print and electronically in case you get a request from the media for a photo. Sometimes a photo

---

**FIGURE 9.2 Fact Sheet Template**

### [YOUR LIBRARY NAME] Fact Sheet

**Mission:** Include your library's mission statement. If you are at a school library or an academic library, you might want to start with the institution's mission and then finish with the library's mission.

**Locations:** Just list the names of your libraries and their street addresses. To save space, do this in a paragraph format with appropriate punctuation. Or if there are too many libraries to list, include a Web link to the list. If you are in a school or academic library or a public library with only one location, don't include this portion of the fact sheet. It is covered below.

**Leadership:** If you are in a public library, you might want to call this "Library Board" instead. No matter what type of library, just include the name and title of each individual in hierarchical order.

**Address:** Main or central library complete street address

**Web site:** Main Web site URL

**Phone:** Main phone number—not the press contact's private line

**Press contact:** Name, title, phone, and e-mail for your library's press contact

---

increases the profile of your coverage—particularly when you announce an award or the election of board officers.

# NEWS RELEASES

News releases are a way to communicate information as simple as an upcoming holiday closure and information as complicated as the conversion to your new circulation system. You can use a news release to announce a new program or service, a special event, or a new policy. "News release" and "press release" are interchangeable terms, and they will be used that way throughout this book. However, to develop successful releases, remember just one word—news. There must always be news in a release—whether you call it a "press release" or a "news release," it must have NEWS!

Before you even think about starting to write a press release, get a copy of the *Associated Press Stylebook and Libel Manual*. Referred to by *American Bookseller* as "the Bible of the newspaper industry," this book must be at your fingertips whenever you are writing press materials. It defines the word usage, grammar, and spelling that journalists use. It also has guidelines for how to write photo captions and proofread text. Your library may have a copy in its collection, but buy your own office copy of *AP Stylebook*. The book costs under $20, and with your library's discounts, the price will be even less. It will be one of the most important investments that you make in the media relations portion of your PR program. Even after working in the PR business for more than 20 years and writing countless news articles and press releases, I still keep a copy on my desk and refer to it every day.

A news release is short and to the point—one or two pages is best. A good release is written in an inverted pyramid format, with the most important information first and the least important last. The information in a news release answers the standard news questions: who, what, when, where, and why. Sometimes it is helpful to draft the answers to these questions before you begin writing your release—then you have an easy way to check that everything is included. As newspaperman Joseph Pulitzer used to say about news, the three most important things are "Accuracy, Accuracy, Accuracy."

The news release can be written on plain paper or on library letterhead; it should always include the name, address, and phone number of your library. There should always be a contact person listed with his or her personal contact information, including direct phone line and e-mail address. The last thing you want is an interested reporter who cannot track down the PR person.

Also, it is important to include a release date so it is clear when the information can be published or announced. The release date is especially important now that press releases are being distributed via e-mail. Since a reporter might not read unsolicited e-mail on a daily basis, you may want to include the release date in the subject line when you send a press release by e-mail.

A news release should be double-spaced or spaced one and one half. It was once recommended that, for the reporters' convenience, releases be printed only on one side of the paper, but with today's focus on saving paper (and money), it is now acceptable to print press materials on both sides of the paper. If your release continues beyond one page, type MORE at the bottom of the page. Multiple pages should be stapled together in the upper left corner. Type ### or –30– at the end of your release (to indicate to the editor or reporter the end of the news item or article).

Write a boilerplate about your library to include at the bottom of every news release. The boilerplate is a paragraph (about 50 words) that describes your library, its mission, and services and includes your Web address. This information provides the reporter

---

**FIGURE 9.3  Sample News Release: Smithville Public Library**

### JANE WEAVER JOINS SMITHVILLE PUBLIC LIBRARY AS DIRECTOR

**Library Board Selects Weaver for Fundraising, Planning Skills**

SMITHVILLE, Mass.—Feb. 24, 2004—The Smithville Public Library Board Trustees today announced the appointment of Jane Weaver as library director. Weaver will assume her post on March 7.

"We are excited that Ms. Weaver has agreed to lead the Smithville Public Library," said Linda Workman, chair of the library board of trustees. "Her strong background in fundraising and building planning is exactly what our library needs at this time."

Weaver is currently the director of Johnsonville Public Library, a post she has held for six years. She has more than 15 years of public library experience as a library director, reference librarian, and children's librarian.

"There are going to be so many wonderful new challenges at Smithville Public Library," said Weaver. "It will be wonderful to work with the dedicated staff, board, and supportive community."

A complete biography of Weaver is available on the library's Web site at *www.smithville library.gov/newdirectorweaver.* Weaver replaces Brenda Bixler who retired in September 2003 after 10 years as library director.

**About Smithville Public Library**
Smithville Public Library (*www.smithvillelibrary.gov*) serves the Massachusetts communities of Smithville, Jonesville, and Thomasville. Founded in 1898, the library system has eight branches and a main library located in downtown Smithville. The library system is dedicated to providing community members of all ages with the highest quality library resources and services.

**For more information, press only:**
Jim Smith, Reference Librarian, Smithville Public Library, 555-999-9999, jsmith@ smithvillelibrary.gov

---

with quick information about the library in every release, but removes it from the "news" body of the release. See Figures 9.3–9.5 for some sample news releases.

**FIGURE 9.4 Sample News Release: Johnsonville Elementary School**

### JOHNSONVILLE ELEMENTARY THIRD-GRADERS DEBUT WEB PROJECTS

**Parents, Community Members Attend High-Tech, Open House at School Library**

**JOHNSONVILLE, Ill.—March 5, 2004—**Third graders at Johnsonville Elementary School debuted their personal Web sites at today's high-tech open house in the school library. More than 250 parents and community members attended on-site, and the students' 130 Internet pen pals from around the world attended virtually.

"I am so impressed with the ways that these young students are using technology to learn," said Frank Bradley, principal, Johnsonville Elementary School. "Our faculty members in collaboration with school librarian Sue Roberts really know how to harness the power of the Internet to help students understand the world around them and build a new excitement learning."

The students from the school's six third-grade classes selected a research topic related to the country where their Internet pen pals live, conducted Internet research on the topic, and then reported their findings on a Web site. They conducted primary-source research by interviewing their pen pals on their topics.

"My pen pal is from Frankfurt, Germany, and my research topic was food in Germany," said Jason, a third-grader in Joanne Tinseth's class. "It was great to learn about the German food he likes, but he also told me that he liked McDonald's like I do."

The projects are on display at *www.johnsonvilleelem.k12.il.us/thirdgraderesearch.* To protect the students' privacy, they are identified only by first name on the Internet.

**About Johnsonville Elementary School**
Johnsonville Elementary School (*www.johnsonvilleelem.k12.il.us*) is one of three elementary schools in the Johnsonville, Illinois, School District. The school serves 800 students in grades K–6 with a curriculum that uses technology as a tool for teaching and learning. The school library is at the center of the school—both physically and philosophically.

**For more information, contact:**
Sue Roberts, School Librarian, Johnsonville Elementary School, 555-555-5555, sroberts@ johnsonvilleelem.ki12.il.us

**FIGURE 9.5  Sample News Release: Moorefield College Library**

### MOOREFIELD COLLEGE LIBRARY OPENS DOORS TO THE COMMUNITY

**HELLERTOWN, Iowa—March 6, 2004—**Moorefield College Library is opening its doors to all members of the Hellertown community. Beginning April 1, residents can apply for free library cards, get e-mail accounts and use the Internet at the college's state-of-the-art library.

"Hellertown offered our college a great deal of support and we think that offering access to our new library is one way that Moorefield College can give back to the community," said Joseph Kavanaugh, college president. "Our library staff and students are excited about seeing more residents on campus and in the library."

The college library has also extended its night and weekend hours to better serve both students and the Hellertown community. The library is now open from 8 a.m. to midnight, seven days each week.

"We want to work in collaboration with the public library to ensure that Hellertown's residents have access to the information and services that they want and need," said Marge Moore, college library director. "By working together, we can maximize the investment in library resources for everyone's benefit."

**About Moorefield College**
Founded in 1878, Moorefield College (*www.moorefield.edu*) is a private, liberal arts college. More than 2,000 students attend classes on its three-acre downtown Hellertown campus.

**For more information, press only:**
Marge Moore, Library Director, Moorefield College, 222-555-5555, margemoore@moorefield.edu

The press release dos and don'ts listed in the sidebar on the next page are based on mistakes I have made—and have seen others make—over the past 20 years. Once you start developing your own press releases, you will likely have tips to add to the list.

---

**Call 'Em "Press Releases" or Call 'Em "News Releases":
Before You Send Out a Release, Follow These Dos and Don'ts for Success**

**Dos:**
- Always remember that your goal is to get a reporter to read your release and use it.
- Start writing a release as soon as you decide that there is news. Sit down at the computer and hammer out a first draft. Save it and come back to it the next day and make revisions. Do this again if there is time. You will be amazed at how the quality and conciseness of your writing improves with each draft. There may not always be time to do several drafts, but when there is, take advantage of it. Editing and revising your own work improves the overall quality of your writing.
- Keep it simple and short. In the words of *Dragnet*'s Joe Friday, "Just the facts."
- Check your facts and figures. If you are publicizing an event, be sure the date, time, and location are correct. If there are budget figures or other numbers in your release, be sure they are accurate. Run the budget numbers past your finance officer. Check the circulation numbers with the manager of circulation services. These extra steps will pay off in both accuracy and peace of mind when you distribute your release.
- Be sure that the release has been reviewed by all appropriate parties. In particular, if you include a quote in the release, make sure the words and turns of phrase sound like the person to whom the quote is attributed. Then, make sure that person approves his or her quote. Taking such care will improve the quality of your release. Plus, it is just common courtesy.
- Include information or quotes from individuals outside your library. If your release is about the more than 200 percent increase in circulation at a branch library, include a quote from the branch manager, but also try to find an avid branch library user who is willing to comment on the services there.
- Once you think your release is complete, use your spell-check on it.
- Proofread it online.
- Print it out and proofread it again. For some reason, errors that aren't obvious on the computer screen will pop out when you look at a printed copy.
- Ask a colleague to proofread it for you. We all sometimes get too close to our own writing, and our mind cleverly inserts a missing word or corrects a spelling because we know how it was "supposed" to be.

**Don'ts:**
- Don't use a smaller type size to pack a lot of information into a press release. Your copy should always use 11-point type or larger. Reporters shouldn't get eyestrain trying to read your release. In fact, they won't—if it is hard to read, they'll just hit that dreaded "Delete" key.
- Don't try to write the great American novel. It is a press release. The information needs to be concise, clear, accurate, and compelling, but it will also have a very short shelf life. Focus on clean writing, rather than on crafting the perfect sentence.
- Don't be too clever! Reporters want the details, the information. Focus on getting your

---

**Call 'Em "Press Releases" or Call 'Em "News Releases" (*continued*)**

message out. Don't write complicated sentences filled with "marketingese" or literary devices, such as alliteration.

- Don't put too much news in one release. While every press release needs news, putting two or three disparate items in one release will only confuse reporters and make targeting the appropriate reporters almost impossible. For example, don't announce your new hours at the main library, the appointment of a new children's coordinator, and the opening of a new kiosk at a local mall in a single release. Write three short, separate releases and distribute them over several weeks. You will reach the reporters that you want with each piece of news (because of your targeted media lists) and each release gives you an excuse to make pitching calls. By using e-mail to distribute your release, the only added cost is your time.
- Don't clutter up a release with fancy art, clever fonts, or graphics. These devices don't add to your news, they make it harder to understand, and, if you are e-mailing your release to reporters, they make the file larger and harder to download. Obviously, if the artwork (such as a new library logo) is the news then ignore this "don't," but still be sensitive to the size of your e-mail and send the artwork in the smallest possible file format.

---

## PRESS RELEASE DISTRIBUTION

The way we distribute press releases has changed a lot over the past ten years. When I started out in public relations, we spent a lot of time at the photocopier, copying press materials. Then we had to put mailing labels on envelopes and stuff and send them out. Today most PR professionals use e-mail to distribute press releases; your library must adopt this strategy as well. Most reporters rely heavily on the Web and e-mail, and you can use this to your advantage. But, first a few words of warning.

While you want to remind the press regularly that your library exists, you don't want them to think that you are personally trying to crash their e-mail servers by sending out as many news releases as possible. For example, if you want to promote the new preschool storytime schedule at your six branch libraries, try to get all of the information in one release. Don't send the major media separate releases for each branch. If you are targeting neighborhood newspapers, however, you might want to customize a special release for each newspaper, focusing on the schedule at their neighborhood's branch. This may seem like a lot of extra work, but it was much harder only 15 years ago when we used typewriters to customize press materials. The net rewards will be worth the investment. Your news will be covered and the reporters will know that you understand them and what they cover. And we have already learned how important that is!

Typically, it is best to send news releases to your local media at least two weeks prior to the event or program that you are announcing. Some publications may have calendars or columns that require even more lead time. Find out. Often such a requirement is stated on a newspaper and broadcast organization's Web site. (Find those Web sites and save them in your browser's "Favorites" file so you can link to them any time you need to do a bit of research on a particular outlet.)

Of course, there will be times when you have breaking news, such as the appointment of a new library director. The great thing about e-mail is that you can distribute those releases quickly—with the press of the "Send" button, the reporter will have the release in seconds. Just be sure that your subject line indicates the importance of the information in the release and make your follow-up calls immediately after sending the release.

Other important things to remember when e-mailing releases include the following:

- Ask a reporter first if he prefers to receive releases via e-mail. Most reporters do, but it is only polite to ask.
- Send e-mail as a plain text file.
- Do not send the press release as an attachment. With today's fear of computer viruses, if you send an unsolicited release as an attachment, a reporter will probably hit the "Delete" button. (That is not to mention the long download times for attachments, if the reporter happens to be using a dial-up connection.)
- Don't e-mail an entire press kit. If you have one available, mention it in your pitch. Then you can send it to reporters who ask for it. You can also post the materials on your Web site and provide a link in your pitch e-mail.
- Write a concise, clear subject line. You might always start your subject line with something like "ANYTOWN PUBLIC LIBRARY NEWS" followed by the title of the news release. Make sure your subject line says something. And don't use clever or deceitful subject lines to try to get the reporter to open your e-mails; chances are that such messages will be deleted by a spam filter.
- Write an e-mail that is short and to the point. If possible, write a personalized e-mail, but limit it to just a few sentences, please. Don't rewrite the press release, but tell the reporter what it is about in the first sentence of your e-mail, and why he or she should be interested. Then ask

for the kind of coverage that you want—such as inclusion in a calendar or a feature story on new library services. Finally, close politely, telling the reporter that you will be in touch in the next few days.

- Send press releases from your library or school system e-mail account—not Hotmail, Yahoo, or AOL account. The other addresses look unprofessional and also scream "SPAM" to the filters.
- Don't put READ or DELETE receipts on your e-mails to reporters. It is a pain the neck for them to take the extra step to deal with these and may only work against your story and relationship with the reporter.
- Always include a full signature file (including contact information) at the bottom of the e-mail.
- If you are sending one e-mail message to your entire press list, use the BCC (blind copy) so that reporters can't see who else received the press release. Or better yet, send individual e-mails to each reporter. This approach may take more time, but it will yield more positive results. If you have a big media list, break it into "tier one" and "tier two" for your top and secondary targets and send personalized e-mails to the reporters on your "tier one" list.

Ensuring that reporters—or their e-mail filters—don't view your e-mail as spam is not only important in terms of garnering news coverage, it may be a legal issue as well. The CAN-SPAM Act took effect on January 1, 2004. A summary of the law states:

> The Controlling the Assault of Non-Solicited Pornography and Marketing Act requires unsolicited commercial e-mail messages to be labeled (though not by a standard method) and to include opt-out instructions and the sender's physical address. It prohibits the use of deceptive subject lines and false headers in such messages. The FTC is authorized (but not required) to establish a "do-not-email" registry. State laws that require labels on unsolicited commercial e-mail or prohibit such messages entirely are pre-empted, although provisions merely addressing falsity and deception would remain in place. (The complete law is available at www.spamlaws.com/federal/108s877.html.)

Obviously, you will want to check with your legal counsel before you interpret this law, but PR and marketing organizations are quickly learning how it will impact their activities. There are financial penalties if your e-mail is determined to be spam. There has been a lot of discussion about whether this law applies to PR as well as marketing, but, as we discussed earlier, that is a fine line, and there are some things you can do to try to comply with the law.

Most PR and marketing professionals recommend that PR follow the same rules for e-mail communications as marketing and advertising. Remember, however, that this is not legal advice; you need to get that from your library's legal counsel.

In her article, "You and CAN-SPAM," published in the January 23, 2004, issue of *Marketing Technology*, Kristin Zhivago provides the following summary of dos and don'ts for compliance.

### What CAN-SPAM Says You Must *NOT* Do (Kristin's Comments or Suggestions Appear in *Italic*):

- Don't knowingly access a protected computer without authorization and intentionally initiate the transmission of multiple commercial e-mail messages from or through such a computer.
  *Always send your e-mails through your company's own outbound e-mail server or the outbound e-mail server of a third-party service that you have hired to send mail for you.*
- Don't use a computer to relay or retransmit multiple commercial e-mail messages with the intent to deceive or mislead recipients, or any Internet access service, as to the origin of those messages.
  *Be absolutely straightforward about who you are and what you're selling.*
- Don't falsify header information in multiple commercial mail messages and transmit those messages.
  *Same as above. Say who you are and what you're selling.*
- Don't register using false information. You must not falsify the identity of the actual registrant, for five or more e-mail accounts or online user accounts or two or more domain names, and then intentionally initiate the transmission of multiple commercial electronic e-mail messages from any combination of such accounts or domain names.
  *These are classic spammer ploys. They try to hide their identity. You are a legitimate marketer selling a legitimate product. There is no reason to hide your identity. So don't.*
- Don't falsely represent yourself to be the registrant or legitimate successor in interest to the registrant of five or

more Internet Protocol addresses, and then intentionally initiate the transmission of multiple commercial e-mail messages from such an address.

*Are you starting to see the theme here? This law is mostly about being deceptive, in the way you send messages and the way you represent your identity and the contents of the message. So if you want to separate yourself from a spammer—and stay out of trouble—be very, very clear about who you are and what you're selling.*

- Don't harvest e-mail addresses, randomly generate e-mail addresses, or send e-mail addresses that use false domain registration information.

  *If you are going to use an outside list house, know how they obtained the addresses. You will want PROOF.*

- Don't use headers that falsify the origin of the message.

  *See above. No lying.*

- Don't use "From" lines that are false.

  *Again, no lying.*

- Don't send messages through someone else's computer without their knowledge.

  *You wouldn't do this knowingly, but you better make sure that no one you're using to send messages for you is doing it.*

- Don't use subject lines that are misleading.

  *Deja vu, anyone?*

- Don't send sexual e-mail that is not labeled as such (not later than 120 days after this law is enacted, the FTC will prescribe clearly identifiable marks or notices to be included with commercial e-mail that carries sexually oriented material, so it can be filtered by recipients).

  *You aren't selling sexual products anyway, so no problem here.*

- Don't allow others to transmit misleading messages to their customers, without stopping the transmission and/or reporting it to the FTC. You will be held responsible if you know—or should have known—and/or if you received or expected to receive an economic benefit from the promotion.

  *It's time to pay very strict attention to all of your affiliate programs. If you are partnering with companies that are sending out commercial messages on your behalf, you must review and authorize everything they are sending. And, if the message is selling something you offer, the subject line and content should be very clear about who is sending the message and what it contains.*

**What You Must Do:**

The law focuses primarily on the clear identification of who you are and what you're selling. For example, every commercial e-mail has to have the company's physical (snail mail) address at the end of it. Here are some other general guidelines. Again, this is not legal advice. Talk to your lawyer.

1. All recipients of your commercial messages should have double-opted-in, and their permission should be filed in a safe place, with redundant storage systems set up. It should be easy to retrieve proof of permission, when required.

   "Double-opt-in" (which some people call "confirmed opt-in") means that the following steps take place:
   - John signs up for your newsletter on your website.
   - You—or your automatic double-opt-in system—sends an e-mail to John's address. The e-mail says: "Thanks for signing up for [our newsletter]. Just to confirm that you just signed up, place an X between the brackets below." Give them two choices:
     - [ ] Yes, I signed up for [your newsletter].
     - [ ] No, that wasn't me.

2. All of your e-mails should allow the recipient to opt-out of e-mails on that subject and/or ANY e-mails from your company.

3. You have **10 business days** to unsubscribe a person after they ask to be unsubscribed.

4. Subject lines should always either mention your company name or the product name, so there is no doubt as to the origin and content of the e-mail.

5. NEVER send an e-mail that says one thing in the subject line and then conveys a different meaning/message in the body of the message.

6. Seriously consider never using rented lists, and only sending to people who have "double-opted-in" to your [electronic] mailings, as described above. We expect that list companies will find ways to be able to prove to you that their recipients have opted in, and that they have not obtained addresses by harvesting them from websites. But the law is very clear about "not using harvested e-mail addresses," so don't take this lightly.

7. All of your e-mails should provide a way for the recipient to contact a real human being, or at least report problems/concerns via an address that will be read and answered by a human being.

8. You must investigate the e-mail practices of your divisions, partners, and affiliates, and create a strict e-mail policy for

those companies. You should sign up for mailings so you can experience their processes first hand, and you should make sure you can opt out successfully.

9. If you make a change to any e-mail address used for unsubscribing—let's say you change "unsubscribe@ MyCompany.com" to "unsubscribe@MyCompanyInc.com" —you need to leave the old unsubscribe address active for 30 days after the last message sent which included that address.

10. All messages must include a "valid physical postal address of the sender" (your company).

11. If someone asks to be unsubscribed from one of your mailings, but continues to receive other mailings from your company, you could get into trouble. You absolutely need to know who is sending what to whom, and get it all under control. You absolutely need to develop a website form that people can click to, via an e-mail, that allows them to pick and choose the mailings they want to receive. Someone needs to "own" this, or it will not be handled properly. (Reprinted from *Marketing Technology*, January 23, 2004, with permission)

Don't fax press releases to reporters. Six years ago that was a cost-effective way to reach reporters, particularly with breaking news. Today it is nothing but an annoyance and, frankly, faxes cost media outlets money—for paper and toner. And I bet if you asked a lot of reporters what happens to most faxes, they would point to the circular file on the floor beside their desks. Unless the reporter is expecting something from you, fax is no longer an effective distribution method for press materials.

## WIRE DISTRIBUTION

Depending on the geographic area that your library serves, you may want to consider wire distribution for some of your press releases. Services such as Business Wire and PR Newswire distribute your materials electronically to the type of reporters that you identify in a geographic region. While national distribution can be costly, both services offer state and local metropolitan market distribution at a significantly lower cost. This may be a good strategy if you want to reach reporters throughout your state and your human resources are limited. (Interestingly, you often can get the same national pickup using the less-expensive state and regional wires as the more expensive national wire.) You should still e-mail the release to your key targets, however, and follow up with telephone pitches. Another benefit of putting a press release out over one of these wire services is that they often get picked up by Web sites and other distribution sources, such as Yahoo news or AOL news.

If you have a particularly unique project or success (like a big bond issue win) and your goals include building a national profile for your library, then using wire distribution is a good strategy. However, in most instances your press releases will be locally focused and wire distribution is not appropriate.

For more information about wire distribution, check-out Business Wire at *www.businesswire.com* or PR NewsWire at *www.prnewswire.com.*

The sidebar points out the big snags that you can run into when developing and distributing press releases. The author, Joan Stewart, is a media relations consultant and professional speaker from Wisconsin; she publishes a free electronic newsletter, *The Publicity Hound's Tips of the Week.* Stewart's insights come from her experiences on both sides of PR—as a publicist and a journalist.

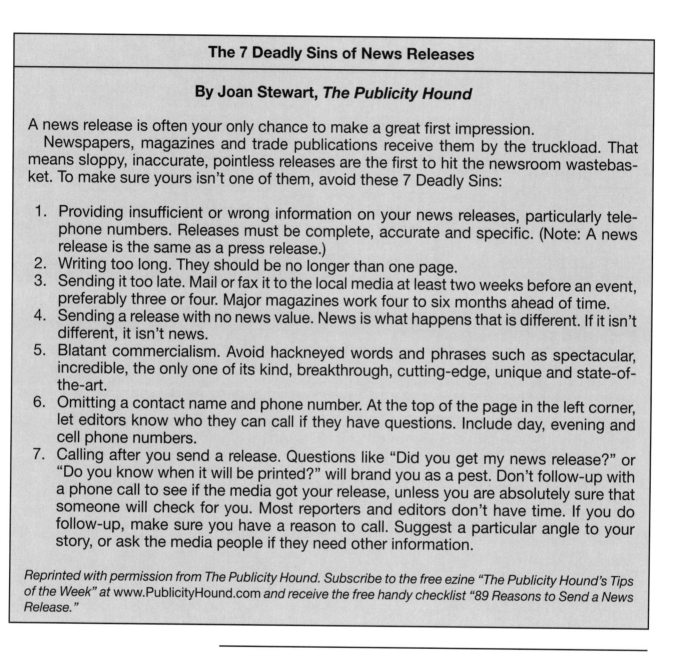

### The 7 Deadly Sins of News Releases

#### By Joan Stewart, *The Publicity Hound*

A news release is often your only chance to make a great first impression.

Newspapers, magazines and trade publications receive them by the truckload. That means sloppy, inaccurate, pointless releases are the first to hit the newsroom wastebasket. To make sure yours isn't one of them, avoid these 7 Deadly Sins:

1. Providing insufficient or wrong information on your news releases, particularly telephone numbers. Releases must be complete, accurate and specific. (Note: A news release is the same as a press release.)
2. Writing too long. They should be no longer than one page.
3. Sending it too late. Mail or fax it to the local media at least two weeks before an event, preferably three or four. Major magazines work four to six months ahead of time.
4. Sending a release with no news value. News is what happens that is different. If it isn't different, it isn't news.
5. Blatant commercialism. Avoid hackneyed words and phrases such as spectacular, incredible, the only one of its kind, breakthrough, cutting-edge, unique and state-of-the-art.
6. Omitting a contact name and phone number. At the top of the page in the left corner, let editors know who they can call if they have questions. Include day, evening and cell phone numbers.
7. Calling after you send a release. Questions like "Did you get my news release?" or "Do you know when it will be printed?" will brand you as a pest. Don't follow-up with a phone call to see if the media got your release, unless you are absolutely sure that someone will check for you. Most reporters and editors don't have time. If you do follow-up, make sure you have a reason to call. Suggest a particular angle to your story, or ask the media people if they need other information.

*Reprinted with permission from The Publicity Hound. Subscribe to the free ezine "The Publicity Hound's Tips of the Week" at www.PublicityHound.com and receive the free handy checklist "89 Reasons to Send a News Release."*

## MEDIA ALERT

When you are hosting a special event or a press conference and want to drive media attendance, it often makes more sense to do a one-page media alert than a press release. A media alert does what it says—it alerts the media to your event. Media alerts follow a "who, what, where, when" format, with all of the details needed to cover the happening. A template for a media alert appears in Figure 9.6.

---

**FIGURE 9.6 Media Alert Template**

**Media Alert**
**RELEASE DATE**

**SHORT HEADLINE, NO LONGER THAN TWO LINES**
**TRY TO INCLUDE LIBRARY NAME**

What:   Description of the event that you are announcing. Be sure to tell reporters what will be happening, particularly in terms of visuals for broadcast media and news-paper photographers.

Why:   Tell them why you are having the event—for example, opening a new library, announcing the decision on an intellectual freedom challenge, celebrating the launch of summer reading.

Where:  Complete address of the location of the event. Plus, if it is in a specific location in the library, indicate that—for example, Main Library Reading Room, Second Floor.

Who:   Who are you targeting for the event? This information is particularly important if you are hoping for coverage prior to the event to drive attendance.

How:   This section is optional. Use it if you are trying to drive attendance to the event. Include registration information or a Web address for more information.

**For more information, press only:**
Name, title, phone, and e-mail for your PR contact.

---

You may announce the event with a media alert and then have a press release available following or at the event. For example, if you are cutting the ribbon on your library's new computer/study room, you would issue a media alert announcing the ceremony and then issue a press release describing the event. Of course, you will want to issue this release right after the ceremony, so it should be developed in advance and ready to go after the ribbon cutting. This strategy drives media to your event because they don't get the whole story in advance, but then the release provides another opportunity for coverage from media outlets that weren't able to attend the event. If you take digital photos of the ceremony, tell reporters when you send the press release that these are available; this is yet another way to encourage coverage, particularly by small or weekly newspapers.

# PRESS KITS

A core press kit for your library is a tool that will help with both proactive and reactive media relations. An informative press kit includes a backgrounder about your library, a fact sheet, and your most recent press releases. When you have a special event or series of events to promote, or when you need to communicate a lot of information about a complex issue, you may want to develop a customized press kit. But every press kit should include the backgrounder and fact sheet, so that reporters always have that information at their fingertips

When reporters come to a news conference or even visit the library for an interview, they usually like to receive a printed press kit. Have them ready for distribution and offer them to the reporters. Some may request that you e-mail the materials, but others will take them and flip through them while waiting for the press conference or interview to begin. Put the materials in a nice, two-pocket folder with your library logo on it if possible. If printing folders is out of your budget, you may be able to create a colorful sticker with your library's logo to paste on a plain folder. Do something distinctive so that the reporter recognizes your library's press kit when he is digging for it on his desk.

You may also want to add promotional materials to your press kit. For example, if the kit is promoting summer reading, include your core summer reading materials. Just don't go overboard—keep it simple.

Include your business cards in your press kits. Your contact information is on all of the press materials as well, but you want to give the reporters as many ways to find you as possible.

It is easy to burn a CD press kit on a computer, and some reporters may like getting the information that way. For a meeting or press conference, however, I recommend print kits that they can refer to and even take notes on.

Your press kit materials should also be posted on the press room of your library's Web site. But more on that later.

## PRESS KIT FORMATS

Some organizations use formats other than folders in the hopes that their press kits will stand out in a reporter's pile of mail. The warning earlier in this chapter about spending too much money developing clever formats for press kits is worth repeating. If you do decide, however, to develop a special format for your press kit, consider asking your Friends of the Library or the Parent

Teachers Organization to fund the project. Be sure to give them full credit on the materials ("This packet printed courtesy of . . . ") to avoid any accusations of "frittering away taxpayer dollars." Whatever format you choose for your press kit, don't get so caught up in being clever and creative that you accidentally end up distributing information that isn't accurate, clear, and easy to use.

My recommendation is that if extra funds are available for media relations, you should use them to customize your pitches and build relationships with reporters. Choosing this option will yield a much greater return on your investment than, for example, than choosing to send a reporter a press kit that announces your new branch opening and also spills confetti all over his desk.

# LETTERS TO THE EDITOR

If you receive news coverage and the facts are blatantly wrong, if you have a story that you can't seem to get covered, or if you must receive mention in the newspaper, you can write a letter to the editor. For instance, if you have trouble getting the newspaper to announce the Junior League's recent donation, a thank-you letter to the editor might be a solution. Or if the paper publishes an article stating that your library director's salary is $20,000 more than it really is and then refuses to run a correction, the letter to the editor might be the way to get the correct information published. This is another tool you should use sparingly, however, to avoid being perceived as a "whiner." Also, if you only submit a letter on an occasional basis, you have a better chance of the newspaper publishing it.

The first thing to decide is who the letter should be from. Perhaps it is better that the letter be signed by your library board chair, the principal, or the library director. Draft it under that person's name and then be sure to get approval before submitting it to the newspaper.

Most newspapers publish specific guidelines for letters to the editor. Follow them carefully. Again, your letter has a better chance of being published if it doesn't require a lot of editing or a follow-up phone call for more information. Some media outlets also provide opportunities for community members to write (or record) opinion-editorial articles. You may wish to explore this option for your principal, library director, or a board member when you want to tell the community more about a particular issue, such as intellectual freedom. See the next page for great tips.

## Writing Letters to the Editor

### By David M. Freedman

**It's a respectable way to express your point of view and gain exposure in the marketplace.**

Writing a letter to the editor is a great way to (1) correct a mistake, misquote, or distortion in a recent news story; (2) illuminate one or both sides of a controversy involving your profession; or (3) comment on how proposed regulations or policies may affect your clients.

There is no guarantee that your letter will be printed, of course, but you'll have a better chance of seeing it published if you follow these guidelines:

**Write concisely, clearly, and to-the-point.** Newspapers commonly recommend a length of 200 words or less, which translates to about 20 lines of text. However, they often publish letters that are much longer, if they're well written and well reasoned (or if you're a friend of the publisher).

**Try to discuss controversial issues as objectively as possible.** Your own bias may be apparent, but it's usually best to show respect for both sides of the issue. If you are responding to a published article, refer to the title, author, page number, and date of publication.

**Use facts and examples to support your argument or point of view.** If you are correcting a reporting error, be good-natured about it. Don't alienate the reporter or editor.

**Sign your name.** As a general rule, don't ask that your name be withheld for privacy reasons or any other reason. For one thing, you'd lose the publicity benefit. For another thing, anonymous opinions are often perceived as the mark of a coward. If you're not proud of your viewpoint, reconsider it.

**Leverage the exposure.** Once your letter is published, make photocopies of it and send them to clients with a brief cover letter explaining how the issue affects their interests. That'll ensure that the people who didn't read the publication still get to see your letter, which confers a measure of third-party credibility upon your message.

David M. Freedman is a Chicago-based writer, editor, and media relations consultant *www.dmfreedman.com*. Reprinted with permission.

# SPECIAL TOOLS TO ENCOURAGE TELEVISION AND RADIO COVERAGE

In most cases, the tools described above will work to encourage both print and broadcast coverage of your library. But some other tools, such as public service announcements and video news releases, can be used specifically to target broadcast media attention.

## PUBLIC SERVICE ANNOUNCEMENTS

Public service announcements (PSAs) are written statements to be read on the radio or on television. You may wish to develop public service announcements for your local radio or television stations to use to spread your library's message. Before you put time and energy into developing a PSA, contact your target media outlet and find out what they are most likely to use. In many instances, radio and television reporters prefer to take your regular news release and adapt it for their use. In some cases, they may want it written as a public service announcement, and, in still other instances, they may be interested in broadcasting a prerecorded or videotaped version of your announcement.

A public service announcement should be typed in all capital letters and triple-spaced. You should write several versions that take different amounts of time to read. A good guide for estimating the time for a public service announcement is 2.5 words per second. Figures 9.7–9.8 are examples of public service announcements of different lengths.

If you have a special message to relay and if your local radio stations will air prerecorded PSAs, you might want local celebrities, such as the mayor or a professional athlete from your hometown, to record your PSAs. Special celebrations like National Library Week or Children's Book Week are good times to produce PSAs that talk about the role that libraries play in your community. If you keep the message in your prerecorded PSA generic, it can be used over a longer period of time.

Video public service announcements for television are expensive to produce; before developing them be sure that the local television stations are willing to air them. A television station in your community might be more interested in producing a public service announcement for you using some of its on-air news talent. Having the anchor from the six o'clock news appear in a public service announcements for the local public library is a win-win opportunity for both your library and the television station—

---

**FIGURE 9.7 Sample Public Service Announcement: Smithville Public Library**

---

PUBLIC SERVICE ANNOUNCEMENT

SMITHVILLE PUBLIC LIBRARY

<u>FOR IMMEDIATE RELEASE</u>

Contact:    Jim Smith
            Reference Librarian
            jsmith@smithvillelib.gov
            (608) 999-9999

                    LOG ON TO THE SMITHVILLE LIBRARY

                                                    20 SECONDS
                                                    KILL: March 2005


YOU CAN VISIT THE SMITHVILLE PUBLIC LIBRARY AND NEVER LEAVE HOME . . .

JUST VISIT OUR WEB SITE AT *W-W-W-DOT-SMITHVILLELIB-DOT-GOV*
AND DO RESEARCH, RESERVE BOOKS, AND MORE . . .

LOG ON TO YOUR LIBRARY TODAY.

---

the television station gets a unique public service announcement that says something positive about their on-air talent and your library gets its message out. Radio stations may also be interested in producing prerecorded PSAs using their on-air personalities.

## VIDEO NEWS RELEASES

A video news release (VNR) is exactly what you would expect—a video version of a news release. Some VNRs are so sophisticated in their production quality that they look as if they were produced by a television news team. They are expensive to produce and rarely aired. For a quality VNR, production costs start at about $35,000 and go up from there. Before considering producing a video news release, check with your local television stations and find out whether they would use them.

You might seriously consider producing a VNR when you have something visual that you really want the media to see because it sells your story. For example, if you are putting a bond issue for new library buildings on the ballot and you want the media to

**FIGURE 9.8 Sample Public Service Announcement: Wellsville Public Library**

**PUBLIC SERVICE ANNOUNCEMENT**
**WELLSVILLE PUBLIC LIBRARY**

**FOR IMMEDIATE RELEASE**
Contact:  Bill Wells
Public Information Officer
(212) 666-6666
bwells@wellsville.lib.il.us

30 SECONDS
KILL: July 15, 2005

**SOLVE A MYSTERY AT THE LIBRARY THIS SUMMER**

ADULTS, CHILDREN, AND TEENS . . .

GRAB YOUR MAGNIFYING GLASSES AND RUN TO WELLSVILLE PUBLIC LIBRARY . . .

HELP SOLVE A MYSTERY BY PARTICIPATING IN THE FREE MYSTERIOUS SUMMER READING PROGRAM . . .

ATTEND PROGRAMS, READ GREAT BOOKS, AND WIN GREAT PRIZES . . .

ANYONE CAN READ TEN BOOKS AND EARN A TICKET TO MAGICIAN DAVID COPPERFIELD'S AUGUST TWELFTH WELLSVILLE PERFORMANCE . . .

FOR MORE INFORMATION VISIT THE LIBRARY WEB SITE AT *WWW.WELLSVILLE. LIB.IL.US* OR CALL THREE-NINE-SEVEN-EIGHT-ONE-FOUR-NINE.

see your main library building's crumbling foundation, a VNR may be the best way to get their attention. Think carefully, however, before you invest the time and money required to produce a quality VNR.

# CONCLUSION

As you have learned, many different tools are available for reaching the media and encouraging coverage of your library and its programs and services. Your challenge will be to select the appropriate tool for each instance and to target the right reporters with the right stories. Press materials and media relations are at the very core of public relations and many individuals will measure the success of your public relations program based on your media relations success. However, some other strategies are also an important part of any successful public relations program, and they should be part of your overall public relations/communications plan. In the next few chapters, you will learn more about these other PR strategies and how you might make them part of your library's PR plan.

# 10 USING TECHNOLOGY AS A PR TOOL

When the first edition of this book was written, libraries—and the business and government communities as a whole—were just beginning to use the Internet as a tool for communications. Sure, in the mid-1990s we had computers on our desks and were realizing the benefits of word processing, presentation software (such as Microsoft PowerPoint), and, in some instances, internal e-mail systems. Some of us had ventured into online worlds (such as America Online and CompuServe). But, in general, e-mail and the Web were novelties and we were all just beginning to explore their potential.

Less than 10 years later, the Internet and e-mail are ubiquitous. They are critical tools for communicating, doing business, and, in many cases, delivering services and buying merchandise. While waiting in the airport, everyone is on a cell phone or typing madly into a BlackBerry or other handheld Internet device. People of all ages have e-mail addresses, and home computers have become as common as televisions.

Libraries have been pioneers in the technology revolution. Some naysayer predicted that the proliferation of the Internet and online resources would make libraries obsolete. Instead libraries have been at the forefront of helping to close the digital divide. Can't afford a computer? You can use one at your library. Don't have Internet access or an e-mail address? Many public, school, and academic libraries can provide you with both. Need computer or Internet training? Again, many libraries of all types offer free workshops. And like the business community, libraries are offering home users everything from virtual reference services to online resources.

So where does technology fit in a library's public relations and communications strategy? Simply put, as another tool. Rather than offering a different way of doing PR, technology just offers us a new tool for accomplishing traditional communications activities in more effective and efficient ways. Because of that, the use of technology as a PR tool is dealt with throughout this book. For example, online media relations is covered in Chapter 8 and distributing press materials online is covered in Chapter 9.

Just like any other organization, libraries should use their Web sites to communicate with their customers. Ten years ago, communication was often the only purpose for the handful of libraries that had Web pages, and managing the Web site was usually part of the PR or communications person's job description. But today that task may be relegated to an overall library Webmaster or perhaps the Manager of Virtual Library Services. In many ways, the library's Web site is another branch or location, or part of an overall Web presence for a college, university, or school district. This chapter talks about the role that PR can play in that "branch library."

## WHO USES THE INTERNET?

Before you invest time and energy in developing an online PR presence for your library, let's answer this question. Who uses the Internet? And where do they use it?

First, let's talk about library users. According to a 2000 study by the Urban Libraries Council, 75.2 percent of Internet users also used the library and 60.3 percent of library users also used the Internet. Forty percent of the survey population used both the library and the Internet. That tells us that we can reach library users on the Internet and that we can also reach library nonusers that way.

Now, how about reporters? Research finds that reporters are using the Internet in large numbers and for many hours a week. The article reprinted on Page 148, "How Journalists Use the Net," by Michael Pastore, offers highlights from the 2004 study "Media in Cyberspace." His data tells us that both library users and reporters are using the Internet; thus the data and support using the Internet as a way to reach them. Now let's talk about ways to do that.

## BUILDING AND, MORE IMPORTANT, MAINTAINING AN ONLINE NEWSROOM

If your library is going to develop and distribute press materials, then it makes great sense to create an online newsroom for the Web site. In fact, reporters will expect you to have a newsroom available online, with such information as archived releases and background information on your library. In her "PR Tactics" article, Joanna Schroeder reports:

recent research shows that 30 percent of study respondents visit company online pressrooms every day, 41 percent visit once a week and 22 percent visit at least once a month.

Moreover, 39 percent said that online pressrooms are very important and 31 percent said they were important to them when writing a news story.[2] With that kind of empirical support, it would seem that an online newsroom is a critical part of any PR strategy that includes media relations.

The online newsroom is a place to offer electronic copies of all of your press kit materials, including the most recent press releases. You may also want to provide a downloadable version of your library's logo, some photos that are available for the media to use, and a list of library staff and their areas of expertise. Links to recent coverage of your library and/or of libraries in the national news is another nice addition to an online newsroom. (Just remember to get the proper permissions to link to these stories.)

Be sure your online newsroom has a "guest book" so that reporters can register to automatically receive future press releases. If you are in a small community, you may think this feature is unnecessary because you know all of the reporters—but you also might be surprised to find out who is visiting your site and interested in your library. Keep the form short and sweet—just name, outlet, phone, fax, and e-mail—to encourage visitors to take the time to complete it.

Prominently display the contact information for the library's media spokesperson on the first page of your online newsroom and include a link to his or her e-mail address. You may want this e-mail to go to a "PR alias" so that it gets checked daily even when the PR person or spokesperson is on vacation or out on sick leave. You don't want to miss a contacts or opportunities. You may also want to include links from your online newsroom to other library news sites, such as the American Library Association or your state library association. Links to your Friends of the Library Web page or your library foundation should be included here as well. These additional resources help reporters put your library's story into a larger community and national perspective.

The sidebar provides lots of helpful tips for creating and managing an effective newsroom on your library's Web site. Two additional pieces of advice (well, the first is a reiteration of the first tip in the sidebar): KEEP THE NEWS UP TO DATE! The minute your newsroom starts to look dated, reporters will stop visiting it; it no longer is a valuable resource to them. And worse yet, if

## How Journalists Use the Net

### By Michael Pastore

The Internet has joined pens, notebooks, laptops, and tape recorders in the reporter's toolbox, and every year Associate Professor Steven Ross of the Columbia University Graduate School of Journalism and Don Middleburg, founder and CEO of the communications firm of Middleberg + Associates survey journalists on their use of the Internet.

This year marked the sixth annual Middleberg/Ross "Media in Cyberspace Study" which tracks the growth of online publishing techniques for developing stories, how reporters work with sources online, the reporting of online rumors, the use of wireless devices, and instant messaging.

Questionable ethical practices are also expanding along with journalists' use of the internet. Reporters find the Web to be lacking in credibility, yet they admit to publishing rumors, as well as using online sources. When asked to rank Web sites based on credibility, only trade associations were found to be more credible than non-credible, the survey found. Message boards and chat groups were judged the least credible. But lack of credibility would not keep journalists from using Web postings, especially if the information is confirmed by another source. Seventeen percent said they would consider doing so in the future, even if it is not confirmed elsewhere.

More than half (60 percent) of respondents said they would consider reporting an Internet rumor if confirmed by an independent source, while only 12 percent said they would not, and three percent admitted to already having done so. Nineteen percent said they would if the rumor came from a "reliable" professional news site.

Other findings from the 2000 Media in Cyberspace Study include:

- Weekly, journalists spend on average, 4.7 hours online at home and 8.7 hours at the office.
- The most popular use of the Internet is article research, which has displaced e-mail. Internet use for finding images almost doubled to 52 percent; in the previous four years it had been 21, 23, 25 and 29 percent, respectively.
- Half of the respondents reported using the Internet in the development of story ideas and pitches, compared with 30 percent of the past three years.
- Journalists are reading publications online more frequently, with almost two-thirds of respondents reporting they do so. In previous years, this never rose above 50 percent.
- Even though 25 percent of respondents use instant messaging, only six percent use it daily.
- Journalists say that responding to readers is part of the job. More than half say they regularly participate in dialogues with readers via e-mail, at least occasionally. One out of every seven newspaper respondents say they do so daily and almost one-third do so at least weekly.

The survey was sent to more than 4,000 magazine and newspaper editors throughout the country. The response rate was approximately 10 percent.[1]

## Tips for an Effective Online Newsroom

### By Steve Momorella and Ibrey Woodall

Every organization can use an online newsroom to provide documents, graphics and press kits to the media. Below are tips that can help any PR professional create and manage an effective newsroom that provides a return on investment.

**Be Timely**. Post news immediately or schedule its release.

**Take Control**. Use dedicated content management software to make changes. Don't wait on your IT department to get to it.

**Categorize News Releases**. Create sections such as financial, legal, and product news. Journalists will be able to find what they need quickly.

**Add New Sections**. Ensure that you can quickly add a new section to accommodate breaking news or crisis management.

**Feature Important Releases**. Promote releases in a pleasing layout. Don't let important information get lost in a chronological listing.

**Post Release Dates**. Show timelines—place publish date next to the title of the news release.

**Extend Information Availability**. Automatically place a link to related articles on each press release.

**Extend Information Availability**. Automatically place a link to related articles on each press release.

**Offer Exclusive Information**. Create a password-protected area specifically for registered journalists.

**Provide Work Space**. Offer registered journalists a virtual personal folder or briefcase for document storage.

**Extend Information Distribution**. Enable journalists to email a release, along with an appended message, to a colleague.

**Design Intuitive Navigation**. Clearly display direct links to various product lines. Group news by product line.

**Follow Usability Guidelines**. Keep important information above the fold, use a readable color scheme and reduce the need for scrolling as much as possible.

**Link Up**. Provide a link to your corporate Web site and other partner sites, if applicable.

**And Vice Versa**. Provide a link from your corporate Web site to your online newsroom.

**Offer Downloadable Graphics.** Supporting, high-resolution pictures and logos increase the chance of press coverage. Offer audio and video. Provide streaming video and audio on demand.

---

### Tips for an Effective Online Newsroom (*continued*)

**Embrace Web Technology**. Utilize online chat and videoconferencing technology to minimize the cost and expand the availability of press conferences. Provide access to archived conferences.

**Offer Convenience**. Provide real-time access of releases. Don't force a journalist to download a Microsoft Word document or Adobe Acrobat PDF file.

**Retain Corporate Branding**. Use company logos, colors and styles to assure journalists that the online newsroom is an official company site.

**Package Content Efficiently**. Simultaneously display the same content on both the newsroom as well as the corporate home page—each with its own design—without extra effort. Reduce duplication of work.

**Provide Universal Search**. The ability to search the site should be available on each page.

**Expand Search Capabilities**. Offer an advanced search so journalists can search on specific archived date ranges, topics and product lines.

**Post PR Contact List**. Clearly display names, phone numbers, e-mails and areas of responsibility.

**Provide PR Contact Search**. Enable journalists to get to the correct person, for the correct information, quickly.

**Promote Events**. Publish a calendar of events, such as trade shows, product releases, and executive appearances.

**Celebrate Executive Personalities**. Promote executive biographies, pictures, and appearances.

**Show History**. Publish a corporate timeline that outlines the growth and milestones of the company.

**Display Financials**. Create a section containing earnings releases, stock information, investor relations, and other financial data.

**Supply Technical Data.** Include white papers, technical documents, product features and specifications.

**Provide Pricing**. Update price sheets as quickly as possible.

**Prepare for Crisis**. Store prepared crisis information. In the event of a crisis, immediately switch it to live status. Reduce the stress of preparing information during a panic.

**Publish E-mail Alerts**. Send out tailored news to journalists. Allow them to select the type of news they wish to receive.

**Target News Distribution**. Maintain separate distribution lists to target key messages to certain groups (e.g., geographic regions, automotive industry reporters)

**Manage Media**. Create and maintain a database of media contacts. Record the requests of individual journalists and use that knowledge to provide appropriate information, pitch stories effectively and monitor publications.

**Gather Information**. Generate online surveys and polls for feedback.

**Go Beyond Keyword Search**. Analyze what journalists want from your site. Use that knowledge to promote the content you want them to review.

**Know Your Visitors**. Access site reports to see how often a journalist visits the site and what information is being reviewed.

**Track Releases**. Know which journalist reads which release.

**Show Return on Investment.** Reduce overhead and shipping costs by providing press-kit downloads.

**Track Downloads**. Count press-kit downloads to quantify return on investment and identify the most popular content. Be reliable. Host on a world-class Tier 1 backbone for heavy traffic spurts.

**Provide Global Access**. Utilize an online publishing system that provides global administration.

**Standardize Procedures**. Utilize database-driven templates to increase productivity while maintaining a consistent design.

**Standardize Workflow**. Utilize a built-in approval process so that administrators can interact with the system from any location.

**Reduce Staff Expense**. Use an easy-to-learn content management system that doesn't require a technical staff.

**Be Print Friendly**. Provide a printable version of each release for those who prefer a hard copy. Include only text, contact information and logo on the printable version.

**Go Wireless**. Provide wireless distribution to mobile devices such as personal digital assistants and cell phones. Be international. Handle multiple languages with the storage of translated documents.

**Increase Security**. Assign different levels of authorization to a variety of administrative staff.

**Provide Universal Formatting**. Ensure that newsroom content can be extracted into XML format so that it may be easily reused across the organization and between suppliers, partners, and distributors.

Steve Momorella and Ibrey Woodall are members of TEKgroup International Inc., providers of Internet software solutions for professionals. They can be reached at 954-351-5554 or *www.tekgroup.com.*

they were relying on it for information and then there is nothing new there, they may think your activity level is down and not contact you. The result? Missed opportunities. It sounds drastic, but if because of budget or staff cuts you can no longer maintain and update your online newsroom, take it down and direct reporters to an e-mail contact for the library spokesperson. There is nothing worse than a Web page that goes up looking ready for business and then quickly appears stagnant and not helpful.

Second, don't hide your online newsroom on your library's Web site. Often when you visit a Web site, you have to go on a treasure hunt to find the online newsroom—clicking first on "About the Library," then on "Administration," then on "News." At times the path isn't even that intuitive. If a reporter is only mildly interested in writing about the library, do you think he will spend time digging for information on your site? Not likely. I recommend putting a direct link to the online newsroom on the library's home page and also featuring selected news flashes on the homepage. Sure, it means that the public will also visit your newsroom—but that is just one more way to reach them with your news, right? Samples 10.1–10.3 illustrate some great online library newsrooms.

**SAMPLE 10.1  Cleveland Public Library Online Press Room**

# CLEVELAND PUBLIC LIBRARY

THE LIBRARY CATALOG

DATABASES & LINKS LIBRARY

LOCATIONS & INFORMATION

THE EVENTS CALENDAR

THE READING ROOM

THE EXHIBIT HALL

Text Only Version

Read the CPL Strategic Plan

**Search the Site**

## YOUR LIBRARY ONLINE

**My Account**
Renew your items, review fines & requests.

**KnowItNow24x7**
Ask a librarian or MetroHealth Line nurse anything, anytime.

**ReadThisNow**
Librarians *always* available with information about books and reading.

**HomeworkNow**
Get live help with your homework from a librarian or tutor.

**paginas.cpl.org**
La Biblioteca de Cleveland, sus colecciones, programas y servicios en español.

**North Coast SeniorsConnect.org**
A web site designed exclusively for older adults.

**eBooks**
Borrow eBooks from the CLEVNET Digital Library Connection.

**NetNotice**
Sign up for email notification services.

**YRead?**
Youth unite through books!

**The Necrology File**
Search Cleveland death notices online.

**Ohio Center for the Book**
An affiliate of Library of Congress, a website to promote books, reading, libraries, and literacy in Ohio.

MYACCOUNT
*Renew*
What do I have checked out on my card?
Check Your Fines
*Cancel Requests*

## LIBRARY NEWS & EVENTS

**Quick Links**
Contact Information

**Cuyahoga County's Polling Location Finder** makes it easy to find out where you should go to vote. Click here to

Reprinted with permission. Cleveland Public Library.

## SAMPLE 10.2  Halifax Public Libraries Online Press Room

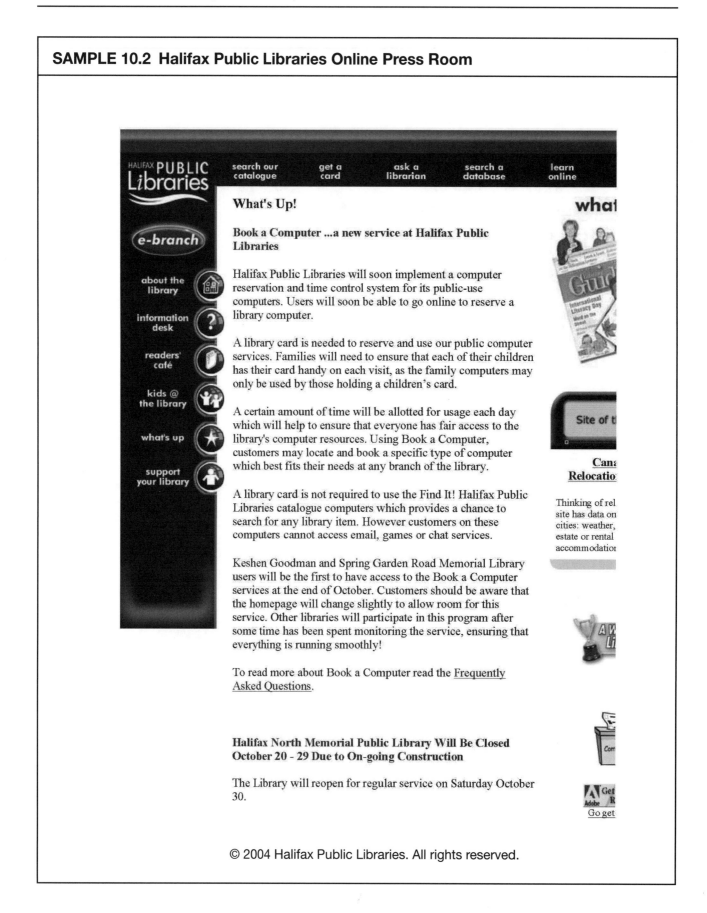

**What's Up!**

**Book a Computer ...a new service at Halifax Public Libraries**

Halifax Public Libraries will soon implement a computer reservation and time control system for its public-use computers. Users will soon be able to go online to reserve a library computer.

A library card is needed to reserve and use our public computer services. Families will need to ensure that each of their children has their card handy on each visit, as the family computers may only be used by those holding a children's card.

A certain amount of time will be allotted for usage each day which will help to ensure that everyone has fair access to the library's computer resources. Using Book a Computer, customers may locate and book a specific type of computer which best fits their needs at any branch of the library.

A library card is not required to use the Find It! Halifax Public Libraries catalogue computers which provides a chance to search for any library item. However customers on these computers cannot access email, games or chat services.

Keshen Goodman and Spring Garden Road Memorial Library users will be the first to have access to the Book a Computer services at the end of October. Customers should be aware that the homepage will change slightly to allow room for this service. Other libraries will participate in this program after some time has been spent monitoring the service, ensuring that everything is running smoothly!

To read more about Book a Computer read the Frequently Asked Questions.

**Halifax North Memorial Public Library Will Be Closed October 20 - 29 Due to On-going Construction**

The Library will reopen for regular service on Saturday October 30.

## SAMPLE 10.3  University of Virginia Library Online Press Room

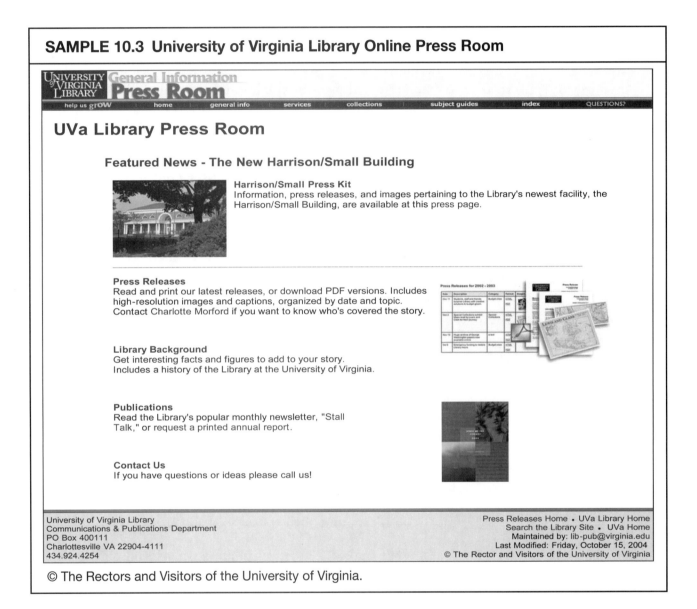

UNIVERSITY *of* VIRGINIA LIBRARY | General Information **Press Room**

| help us grOW | home | general info | services | collections | subject guides | index | QUESTIONS? |

# UVa Library Press Room

## Featured News - The New Harrison/Small Building

**Harrison/Small Press Kit**
Information, press releases, and images pertaining to the Library's newest facility, the Harrison/Small Building, are available at this press page.

**Press Releases**
Read and print our latest releases, or download PDF versions. Includes high-resolution images and captions, organized by date and topic.
Contact Charlotte Morford if you want to know who's covered the story.

**Library Background**
Get interesting facts and figures to add to your story.
Includes a history of the Library at the University of Virginia.

**Publications**
Read the Library's popular monthly newsletter, "Stall Talk," or request a printed annual report.

**Contact Us**
If you have questions or ideas please call us!

University of Virginia Library
Communications & Publications Department
PO Box 400111
Charlottesville VA 22904-4111
434.924.4254

Press Releases Home . UVa Library Home
Search the Library Site . UVa Home
Maintained by: lib-pub@virginia.edu
Last Modified: Friday, October 15, 2004
© The Rector and Visitors of the University of Virginia

© The Rectors and Visitors of the University of Virginia.

## REACHING THE PUBLIC OVER THE WEB

As mentioned above, today's libraries use the Web for service delivery as well as for communication. In most cases, then, the overall responsibility for managing the development of the Web site has moved out of the PR office and into either IT or another library department. PR people are usually expected to be Jacks-of-all-trades, so it is a good thing that the time-consuming task of Web development has found a new home in most organizations. However, PR people do have expertise in communications and design and should consult on the development of the Web presence from that perspective. If you do find the development of the Web site on your list of already overwhelming duties, there are tools and resources available, such as Microsoft FrontPage, to help you; also, a small Web development shop could help you set up design templates and update pages. A great printed resource is *Building Better Web Sites: A How-To-Do-It Manual for Librarians*, by Yuwu Song (Neal-Schuman, 2003).

However, let's hope you end up consulting on the Web design from a PR and communications perspective. Messages and design should be consistent. Copy should be well-written, clear and short, and to the point. Be sure that the copy and images target the audience you are trying to reach. In my opinion, the best Web sites are clean, load easily on my computer—even when I am using dial-up—and are easy to navigate. Users are typically frustrated by a lot of fancy flash animation and other bells and whistles when they are trying to find information. Or, as content management consultant and author Gerry McGovern says:

> "What makes a great Web site is focus and clarity of purpose. A great Web site is unpretentious. It doesn't pretend to be what it is not. It never wastes your time, because it always gets to the point. A great Web site helps you to act."[3]

### ONLINE NEWSLETTERS

You may want to consider publishing an online newsletter to reach your library users with news and information on an ongoing basis. If you are already publishing a printed newsletter, an online newsletter will save you money for printing and mailing. However, you may need to continue to publish both a printed and an online newsletter for a while, as not to leave in the lurch those subscribers who don't have Internet access.

If you think an online newsletter would be a cost-effective and efficient way to reach a large number of your library users, then you will need to decide which type of online newsletter is most appropriate for your audience. Each has its own strengths and weaknesses and software requirements for viewing. You will have to make the decision based on the level of technology and Internet access of your target audience.

You have four options for your electronic newsletter—plain text, HTML, Web, or PDF. A plain-text e-mail newsletter can be read by anyone who has an e-mail account, but you can't use any color or graphics in this format. An HTML e-mail newsletter looks like a Web page with color, photos, and graphics. Recipients need an HTML-capable browser to view this type of newsletter. A Web newsletter lives on a Web site and can have full graphics just like a Web site. Readers need to link to it, but you can distribute an e-mail with the link. A PDF newsletter can be sent out as an e-mail attachment or posted on the Web site. Readers must have Adobe Acrobat Reader, available for free from the Adobe.com Web site, installed on their computers to view this newsletter. To create a PDF newsletter, you just make an Adobe file of your print newsletter.

If you are making the change from a printed to an online newsletter, you will want to have a carefully thought-out plan for making the transition. Many of your library's newsletter readers (such as senior citizens or others living on a fixed income) will not have access to a computer or the Internet. Of course, they can always come to the library to use the computer—but that kind of flies in the face of using the newsletter as a communication tool for encouraging library use.

Perhaps you could first take a poll of your current readers. Find out how many have Internet access and would like to receive the newsletter online. In the introduction to your survey, carefully explain the advantages of publishing the newsletter online—especially in terms of cost savings. If you have a high level of response from readers who would like to receive an online newsletter that way, then you have a difficult decision to make. Do you continue to incur the expense of publishing in both formats, or do you just accept that will lose some readers and proceed to publish online only?

If your response is about 50–50 or less, you will likely want to continue publishing the printed newsletter. But perhaps you could offer an incentive for switching from the printed to the online newsletter. For example, you could waive $10 in library fees for any library user who decides to make the switch. The important things to emphasize in all of your communications about the changes are the significant cost savings and the fact that the newsletters will reach readers in a much more timely fashion.

# TECHNOLOGY IS A MEANS, NOT THE END

There are many other creative ways that technology can be used as tool for public relations. Technology allows cost-effective, efficient communication with library users, the community as a whole, and the media. However, none of these uses of technology—an online newsletter, a Web site, an online newsroom—is PR. These are simply methods of delivering your message, getting the word out there. The basic principles of good PR and communications apply to these delivery techniques as much as any other tool. Remember, when it comes to your PR program, technology is a means—a way of sharing your story—but definitely not the end.

# NOTES

1. Michael Pastore, How Journalists Use the Net, *www.internetprguide.com/pr_insight.*
2. Joanna Schroeder, "Keep Journalists Coming Back To Your Online Pressroom." *PR Tactics*, Public Relations Society of America, Feb, 13, 2004. *www.prsa.org/_Publications/magazines/1102hands1.asp*
3. Gerry McGovern, "What Makes for a Great Web Site?" Marketing Profs.com, Feb. 17, 2004, Marketing Profs.com, *www.marketprofs.com/4/mcgovern23.asp*

# 11 TRANSFORMING VOLUNTEERS INTO LIBRARY ADVOCATES

In the words of Children's Defense League Leader Marian Wright Edelman, "Service is the rent we pay for living." And, in spite of our increasingly overscheduled lives, Americans continue to volunteer in large numbers. According to the Independent Sector's 2001 Giving and Volunteering Survey, 83.9 million American adults over age 21 volunteered 3.6 hours in 2000—the equivalent of more than nine million full-time employees. The total assigned dollar value of U.S. volunteer time—$239 billion.[1]

How can your library benefit from that investment in volunteering? What are the challenges and is there a PR benefit?

Before you get scared off by the challenges of including a volunteer program as part of your library's public relations communications strategy, let's talk first about the PR benefits. People are always the best PR tool available, and using volunteers can help you to both get the job done and spread the word about your library's value. In fact, there is no better way to tell your story than to ask people to become a part of it! But you have to recruit, train, and reward volunteers before they will be a positive public relations tool for your library. As with all communications tools, managing volunteers requires both human and fiscal resources. Furthermore, they are not handled thoughtfully and carefully, they can do more harm than good in terms of creating a public perception of your library. A professionally managed volunteer program, however, will attract high-quality volunteers who will become advocates for your library.

The key to using volunteers successfully is to treat them like paid employees. In *The Pursuit of WOW!* Tom Peters says, "Never treat a temp like a temp!" The same goes for volunteers. To paraphrase Peters, treat volunteers just as you would paid employees—welcome them into your library, show them respect and trust, give them real responsibilities, and hold them to the same high standards.[2]

You have to run your volunteer selection and management program just like any other personnel activity in your library. Keep in mind that retention of high-performing volunteers is the key to your success. In fact, a 1998 study by the UPS Foundation concluded:

The primary reasons for no longer volunteering—demands on time and no longer involved—are beyond the control of most volunteer groups. What concerned us, however, was the number of people leaving because of poor management practices: two out of five volunteers stopped volunteering for one or more of these reasons (i.e. not good use of time; poor use of talents, tasks not clearly defined, not thanked). The best way to build the number of volunteers and their hours is to be careful managers of the time already being volunteered.[3]

Obviously, developing and implementing a volunteer program for any type of library goes beyond its role as part of PR for the library. You will need to do research and consult experts beyond the scope of this book. The sidebar lists a variety of resources dealing with volunteer management. This chapter offers an overview of working with volunteers from a public relations perspective and points you in the direction of other great resources on volunteerism, particularly in libraries and nonprofit organizations.

# DEVELOPING YOUR VOLUNTEER PROGRAM

Volunteers can provide additional human resources for your library and they can also be terrific advocates in the community. Those who want to volunteer obviously already think that your library and services are valuable enough for them to contribute time and energy. That commitment communicates a great deal even before they tell their friends and relatives about the library's programs and services. The effectiveness of your library's volunteers as spokespersons for your library, however, is dependent upon the effective management of your volunteer program. In addition, remember that a well-managed volunteer program communicates to the community—even to those who never have the time or the inclination to volunteer—that your library is well-managed.

Whether your library needs one volunteer or several hundred, you will want to develop a volunteer program that includes job descriptions, recruitment strategies, training, and opportunities to recognize and reward your volunteers. In many ways, volunteers should be treated as "unpaid employees." They should be as involved in the life of your library as your paid employees, and you should put as much time and energy into their selection and training as you do for your paid employees. In the end, the time that you invest in your library's volunteers will pay off with well-trained, committed, unpaid employees and wonderful community advocates for your library. Sally Reed's *Library Volunteers: Worth the Effort* (McFarland, 1994) addresses all of these issues.

## MAKE SURE THERE IS WORK

Before you decide to recruit volunteers for your library, make sure you have something for them to do. If you are in a school library, volunteers may be able to help with shelving or processing books or with cutting out figures for your library's bulletin boards. In a public library, you may want volunteers to serve as docents and give tours of your library or to train patrons to use the online catalog or the Internet. Perhaps your library has a literacy program and needs volunteers to teach reading.

Once you decide that there are jobs for volunteers, write volunteer job descriptions just as you would for paid positions. For each job, include a description of the work, who the position reports to, a work schedule, and the type of training, education, or skills that the job requires. Decide how many positions you have open in each job description area. These descriptions will help you recruit volunteers. When someone calls and asks about the volunteer opportunity you are promoting, you will be able to give them specific details about the position. Do not start recruiting volunteers until you have job descriptions—otherwise your recruits will not have a positive experience and that would be a negative public relations move for your library.

It is also a good idea to determine a minimum amount of time that a volunteer must commit to the position. Training volunteers takes library resources, so you want volunteers to stay long enough for your investment to pay off. For example, you may want at least a two-year commitment of five hours per week from your docents. In contrast, you may need only a short commitment from the parent who is helping with your bulletin boards. You may also have some project-based volunteer opportunities. For example, you might need a group of volunteers to run your library's annual book sale—to come in for a specific period of time, do their work, and go away until the next sale.

With the number of extremely talented senior citizens available to volunteer today, it is important to structure some volunteer jobs to meet their unique needs. For example, you might have a number of "snow birds" in your community—retirees who spend only the summer there and go to warmer climates in the winter. Think about the types of jobs that they can do during the summer, such as support summer reading, so that you can take advantage of their talents while they are in town.

## MAKE SURE THE WORK IS MEANINGFUL

After you read the job description, think about whether you would consider volunteering your time for this position. Is the work meaningful? Will it make the volunteer feel that he or she is truly contributing something to the library? Recruiting volunteers to come into the library every week and do nothing more than put pockets in new books might not be an easy task. You might want to incorporate such a job into a broader job description that includes opportunities for working with other library staff or volunteers or that includes some other interaction with people. For example, parent volunteers at the school library might find helping to process books more bearable if they occasionally could use their creativity to help with bulletin boards.

If you advertise higher-level tasks, you will recruit higher-level volunteers. Many retired people with high levels of education and excellent skills are looking for meaningful volunteer opportunities. Think about those things your library would do if you could only afford it, and then match those tasks with qualified and interested volunteers!

Recruiting and placing volunteers is different from hiring paid employees because you have more flexibility with your job descriptions for volunteers. You might receive an application from a volunteer who is best suited to do activities from several job descriptions in a different configuration from what you had originally planned. If reconfiguring the job descriptions works for your overall volunteer program, do it. You will end up with more satisfied, committed volunteers.

One note: If you are in a library with a union, you may want to confirm that you are not recruiting volunteers for negotiated tasks. Often, union leaders are willing to approve recruitment of volunteers particularly for tasks that library staff don't want to do or don't have time to do. Unions can be understanding about fiscal restraints and the importance of using volunteers in libraries, but checking first is the best strategy.

## RECRUITING AND RETAINING VOLUNTEERS

As for other parts of your public relations/communications program, one person will need to be responsible for coordinating the recruitment, training, and management of your volunteer staff. This doesn't mean that person has to do all the work, but one person should coordinate your library's efforts so that no enthusiastic and willing volunteer falls between the cracks.

Once your volunteer job descriptions are written, you are ready to recruit volunteers to fill the positions. You have a variety of options for promoting the opportunities. You may want to run a notice in your newsletter. If you are in a school, you could send a notice home with students or ask the PTO president if he or she knows of any parents who might be interested. You can distribute the volunteer job descriptions to community volunteer centers or maybe post them (under volunteer programs) on your Web site. A local training program for women reentering the workforce as well as the senior center might be good places to recruit volunteers. Maybe the local government television station will run your announcement along with the paid positions that they regularly advertise. You may also want to write a news release announcing the positions and distribute it via the local media. Just as with a paid position, consider specifying an application deadline for your volunteer positions, to facilitate scheduling interviews.

## The Challenge of Recruiting Volunteers Today

There are challenges to recruiting volunteers today! The economic necessity for two-income households has put into the paid workforce many individuals who would otherwise have spent their time as volunteers. Evening and weekend hours that might be spent on volunteer work are dedicated to errands and other family duties that don't get done during the hectic work week. This is another reason that it is critical that volunteer work be meaningful and valued.

The opportunity to volunteer in your school library may provide parents with the chance to give something back to the school and also to observe what is happening where their children spend much of their time. Today some schools even require that parents volunteer a certain number of hours per year in their children's schools. The school library media center is a great place for them to meet that commitment.

At a public library, a grandmother who misses her grandchildren in another city might be thrilled to help with preschool storytime. Helping patrons use your special history collections might provide the stressed-out banker with a chance to use his undergraduate history degree and a distraction from his daily grind of numbers and balance sheets.

The example of the banker above expresses an important point. When recruiting volunteers for your library, don't assume that people will want to do the same thing in your library that they do every day for pay or that retired people did in their careers.

The public relations person from the local hospital may not want or be able to help your library with its public relations efforts, but that person might enjoy serving as a docent or helping to process books. In general, people who have full-time jobs volunteer for relaxation rather than as an extension of their work day. In addition, for conflict of interest reasons, they may not be able to help your library in their area of expertise. Don't assume automatically that a lawyer will want to volunteer legal services, that a banker will offer financial advice, or that a public relations person will assist with your library's public relations. Ask them about their interests and you may find they have much to offer in other areas.

Susan J. Ellis, president of Energize, Inc., a volunteerism training and publishing firm, and author of *The Volunteer Recruitment Book*, offers five simple recruitment tips to en-"treat" volunteers without "tricking" them:

- Don't just ask for "help" or "volunteers." This vague approach leaves everything up to the prospective volunteer's imagination . . . and YOU ought to be frightened at that! Design a different recruitment message for each specific assignment you need to fill—including an appealing job title. Give potential recruits enough information to be able to say "that's for me." Challenge people and they'll rise to the occasion.

- Specify up front how many hours a week or month a volunteer assignment requires—and for how long you hope the volunteer will remain in the position. Be honest! Then someone who applies to become a volunteer already knows what you expect. (Besides, you may surprise some people by being reasonable and flexible!)

- Be perceptive about what someone might fear about your work and address these things in your recruitment message. Is personal safety a concern? Note the well-lighted adjacent parking lot or the buddy system you can use. Are there unknowns about how your facility looks? Add lots of photos showing bright spaces and smiling faces. Might there be some out-of-pocket costs? Explain your reimbursement policy.

- Talk about the training that you give all newcomers, so that no one has to worry about not being skilled enough or unprepared. Assure prospects that they'll be supported while learning how to be good volunteers and even after.

- Show that volunteering can be fun! It's okay to enjoy community service activities . . . or other participants . . . or the experience itself. If people are going to choose volunteering for you in their spare time, it ought to sound like something they wouldn't want to miss."[4]

## Applications and Interviews

If volunteers have to apply for your positions, they will know that you are serious about the jobs that need to be done and the kind of people you need to do them. Set up a formal application and interview process for volunteer positions, just like the process for a paid position. Ask careful questions and then choose the volunteer who is best for the job.

Possible volunteer interview questions might include:

- Why did you apply for this volunteer position at our library?
- Tell me about your other volunteer experiences.
- Do you have any questions about the job description?
- Can you work the schedule outlined in the job description?
- Are you willing to make the time commitment described in the job description?

Be sure to ask specific questions about the applicant's skills, education, and experience in the areas specified in the job description. Do this just as if you were hiring a paid employee:

- Tell me about your experience working with computers and the Internet.
- What special skills, experiences, or education do you have that would help you serve as a docent for our library?

It is also important to ask questions that inquire into the applicant's philosophical views about the library. It's touchy, but this is when you can discover if an applicant wants to change some important library policy or service and thinks that the way to do it is from within. Your questions might reveal, for example, a community member who thinks that only "certain" kinds of books should be in your collection or thinks that all library fines should be waived. You don't want such conflicts in philosophy and it is good to find out about them before you place someone in a volunteer position. Your library likely already has a set of questions along those lines that it uses with paid employees and you may want to modify them slightly for interviewing volunteers.

## Training and Supervision

Like any library employee, a volunteer requires training and supervision. Be sure that a supervisor is assigned to any volunteer who works in your library; the volunteer then has someone to go to with questions or problems and the supervisor can monitor the volunteer's work and make sure that the volunteer is having a positive experience at your library.

Volunteers should also receive training and orientation similar to that provided for paid employees. In addition to training in the specific tasks of the volunteer position, a tour of the library, the opportunity to meet all of the employees and see all of the service areas, and a review of the library's policies and procedures should be part of each volunteer's orientation and training. If you are recruiting a corps of volunteers or several volunteers for one task, you may want to offer monthly orientation and/or training for volunteers. Alternatively, you could include volunteers in part of your regularly scheduled employee orientation sessions. The important thing is to provide your volunteers with all of the information they need to complete their tasks successfully and to feel as if they are a part of your library's staff.

## Time Sheets

Volunteers should complete and file time sheets just like paid employees. In some cases, you will be required to carry liability insurance (similar to Workers' Compensation) for volunteers who work in your library and you will need these records to compute your rates. In addition, these records provide helpful information when you want, for example, to reward your volunteers for their hours of service or when you need to counsel a volunteer who consistently does not show up for the scheduled hours.

## Personnel Files

You should keep a file, similar to the personnel file you keep for paid employees, for each of your volunteers. You will find it valuable to have this information organized and readily available. Include the volunteer's application, the job description for the volunteer position, and copies of all time sheets. Also remember to keep emergency contact information, in case a volunteer is injured on the job or doesn't show up for work and can't be reached at home. This information is particularly important for senior volunteers. This file is also the place to keep copies of any official documents, such as insurance release forms, that your organization requires your volunteers to sign.

Finally, this file is a good place to put copies of letters of recognition that you have sent to the volunteer and notes about things that you want to praise the volunteer for, such as the wonderful way that she helped a small child find his mother when he was lost after storytime.

## Reviews

Be sure to schedule regular review sessions with each volunteer. These sessions should be held by you or each volunteer's supervisor every three or six months. They are a formal opportunity for the volunteer to share questions or problems and for the supervisor to provide the volunteer with positive feedback and constructive criticism.

Telling volunteers that they can improve the way they complete their duties does not have to be a negative experience. First of all, such feedback tells a volunteer that someone cares about what he or she is doing. Second, if the supervisor uses positive language and talks about improvement, the suggestion will be viewed as positive. However, if it is clear that the job assigned is not the best place for the volunteer, it may be the supervisor's responsibility to counsel the volunteer about finding a new assignment in the library. While volunteers should be treated like paid employees in many ways, you often have more freedom to change the job assignments for volunteers than for paid employees.

Consider the volunteer who has been gluing pockets in books, but the pockets are crooked because she doesn't have the manual dexterity to complete the task. The supervisor may have noticed that she has a wonderful relationship with the small children who visit the library. So, perhaps a better assignment for her is as an assistant at preschool storytime. Chances are that both the library staff and the volunteer will be happier if this change is made.

## Recognition and Rewards

Buy your volunteers name badges like those the paid staff wear. In addition to the name, add the title *"Volunteer."* Invite volunteers to your staff parties, staff meetings, and special events. Once a volunteer comes on board, he or she is part of your internal audience.

Remember, however, that volunteers are donating their time to your library. Recognition is the only reward they get. Publish their names in your newsletter often. Hold an annual "Volunteer Recognition Ceremony" to recognize the number of hours they have donated. Such a ceremony is a great opportunity for a media event—you might calculate the value of the hours that they have donated and put it in a press release. Send your volunteers to your state library association conference so they can network with other library volunteers. Be sure they get several thank-you letters each year. When you walk through the library, remember to stop by volunteers' workstations and say "thanks." Encourage the library director, building principal, or board chair to do the same. Volunteers are contributing something very special to your library. If they know how much you appreciate their contribution, you can be sure they'll tell their friends and neighbors what a special place your library is and how important it is to the community.

## CHILDREN AND TEENS AS VOLUNTEERS

Children and teenagers can be dedicated, hardworking volunteers. They want to help, learn, and feel that they are contributing. Just as for adult volunteers, it is important that you identify appropriate and meaningful tasks for these volunteers.

Teenagers are volunteering in big numbers. In fact, a 2003 study by the National Center for Education Statistics reports that 44 percent of young adults volunteer during high school. But, as with adult volunteers, you will be competing for their time. A 2003 study by the Gallup Organization reveals that 22 percent of teens volunteer for church or church-related activities, 11 percent volunteer for youth organizations with community centers, 10 percent volunteer for neighborhood or social action associations, and 9 percent volunteer for educational organizations.

So how do you ensure that your library gets the attention of teen volunteers? The Young Adult Library Services Association (YALSA), a division of the American Library Association, advocates meaningful opportunities for youths to volunteer. In its manual, *Youth Participation in School and Public Libraries: It Works*, YALSA provides guidelines for youth volunteerism or "youth participation" in libraries. Youth participation is defined as the "involvement of young adults in responsible action and significant decision-making which affects the design and delivery of library and information services for their peers and their communities."[5] The result of this participation is, according to YALSA, "more responsible and effective library and information services for this age group" and enhanced "learning, personal development, citizenship and transition to adulthood" for the teenagers.[6]

In addition, YALSA suggests that projects involving youths should have the following characteristics:

- be centered on issues of real interest and concern to youth
- have the potential to benefit people other than those directly involved

- allow for youth input from the planning stage forward
- focus on some specific, doable tasks
- receive adult support and guidance, but avoid adult domination
- allow for learning and development of leadership and group work skills
- contain opportunities for training and for discussion of progress made and problems encountered
- give evidence of youth decisions being implemented
- avoid exploitation of youth for work that benefits the agency rather than the young adults
- seek to recruit new participants on a regular basis
- plan for such issues as staff time, funds, administrative support, and transportation before launching project
- show promise of becoming an ongoing, long-term activity.[7]

While many of these characteristics are the same as those recommended for adult volunteer opportunities, the list also includes special consideration for the needs of youths. Above all, YALSA reminds us that youth volunteers should both contribute to and benefit from their volunteer work. They should not be exploited simply as "free labor," but should be respected, listened to, and have opportunities for learning on the job.

Today many high schools have courses that require students to complete a certain number of community service/volunteer hours. You may wish to collaborate with the teachers of those classes in your community to recruit volunteers for your library.

## PARENT VOLUNTEERS IN SCHOOL LIBRARIES

If you are in a school library, you may have access to your building or district's corps of volunteers. You may only need to develop job descriptions and submit them to the volunteer coordinator to find the help you are seeking. Schools also have a wonderful pool of potential volunteers in the parents, guardians, and grandparents of their students. Often these individuals want to be involved in the life of their child's school, and volunteering in the library is an excellent way for them to do this.

Best of all, parents who volunteer in the school library media center will learn about what happens there and the value of the program. They can become advocates for the program. Showing people something is a good way to communicate your message—involving them in it is the best way!

A school librarian may also have tasks that a parent can do at home, such as preparing art for the bulletin board or using desktop publishing to create bookmarks or flyers for the students. Such tasks allow parents to contribute without having to rearrange their work schedules to be at school during the day.

Parent organizations, such as PTAs and PTOs, are excellent sources of volunteers for school libraries. Often the parents involved in such groups are looking for opportunities to contribute to the school on a regular or project basis. When you determine your volunteer needs, approach your school's parent organization and ask for their help. They may offer, for example, to come in on a Saturday as a large group to help move your library, rather than have you recruit two people to do it over a period of two weeks. Seek their assistance in getting the job done and you'll be amazed at the end result!

## VOLUNTEER SPEAKERS BUREAUS

Perhaps one of the strategies in your public relations/communications plan is to make presentations about your library and its services to a variety of community groups. When you are ready to implement this strategy, however, you may discover that library staff aren't available to leave the library to make these presentations. Developing a volunteer speakers bureau may be the way to get started.

A speakers bureau is an excellent way to spread the word about your library—and who could be better to go out and tell the story than community members? You may wish to train a group of volunteers to be a part of your library's speakers bureau. For example, the mother of a handicapped child who has used your resources since the child's birth might tell you that she would love to volunteer, but she simply can't adhere to a regular schedule. She would be a wonderful member of the speakers bureau, telling your library's story from her own point of view; after the initial training she could schedule speaking engagements as they fit into her schedule. Best of all, you have a wonderful strong advocate telling your story and you don't have to leave a library service desk unattended.

You will want to provide speakers bureau volunteers with a draft presentation script and lots of resources, such as handouts. It also might be a good idea to offer to videotape a rehearsal of their presentations for a critique of their style—perhaps a speech professor from a local college or university would be willing to review these tapes for your volunteers. You will probably also want to coordinate scheduling the speakers through your library so that you can make good matches. For example, the retired small businessman who can talk about how your library's business collection helped him build his business is probably the best speaker for the Chamber of Commerce's business forum. By having requests come to the library, you can contact your speakers and make the matches.

So, consider using volunteers as part of a speakers bureau. It will give you the opportunity to recruit volunteers who are willing to donate their time, but who have difficulty adhering to a regular schedule. It also offers you a way to answer those requests for a Rotary Club speaker without having to rearrange staff schedules or close a service desk.

## REAL-LIFE EXAMPLE: PHOENIX PUBLIC LIBRARY

The Phoenix (Ariz.) Public Library is a great example of a library system that offers community members a variety of volunteer opportunities, ranging from assisting with programs to mending and shelving books. Two special volunteer programs are the Teen Summer Volunteer Program, which recruits teen volunteers to assist library staff and the public during summer months, and the Friday Club, which greets patrons and provides tours at one of the branch libraries. In addition, the library has a foundation and a Friends group; both groups offer other opportunities for volunteers. Visit the library's Web site at *www.phoenixpubliclibrary.org* for more details.

## FRIENDS OF THE LIBRARY

All libraries need "friends"! Friends groups began in the 1920s and 1930s at libraries at such universities as Yale, Harvard, Princeton, and Columbia, and moved into public libraries as they were established.[8] A Friends group can complement your volunteer program. Members of the Friends of the Library are not only volunteers, they are advocates for your library and for library service.

Friends of the Library groups serve libraries in several primary ways. They assist in the planning, funding, and promotion of library programming, and they are library fundraisers. Traditionally, most Friends fundraising activities have centered on used-book sales, but today innovative Friends organizations around the country have developed all kinds of creative fundraising programs that engage community members in the library while feeding its coffers.

Friends must have a separate corporate structure from the library, by incorporating as a nonprofit organization. They have their own officers and bylaws, and, working with a library liaison, they make their own decisions. Friends may have more discretion about how they spend their money than the library. For example, you may not be able to spend money from your library's

**SAMPLE 11.1 Phoenix Public Library Volunteer Web Page**

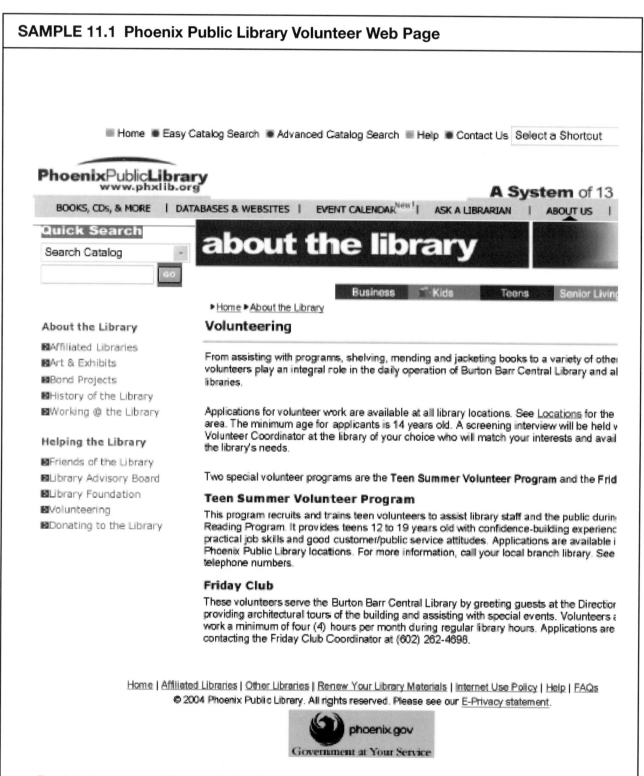

Reprinted courtesy of Phoenix Public Library.

budget to hold a reception during National Library Week, but the Friends can spend their money to plan and host a reception. The reception is an opportunity for the Friends to promote membership in their organization and to invite city leaders to enjoy the refreshments and learn more about the valuable services the library provides in your community. You can hold the reception in the library and promote it together. One event helps both you and the Friends achieve your respective goals.

Having an active Friends of the Library group is important on a day-to-day basis, but it becomes critical when your library is campaigning for a bond issue or a levy increase or when you face a serious intellectual freedom challenge. The Friends become your citizen advocates—they are spokespeople for your cause without the vested interest that some people might attribute to library staff.

When you develop your library's public relations plan, you should consider whether you need Friends of the Library to reach your goal. Ask such questions as:

- What parts of our public relations plan will be difficult to achieve without assistance from individuals outside the library staff? Could a Friends group provide this assistance?
- What components of our public relations plan require advocacy in the community? Could members of a Friends of the Library group play that role in the community?

Once you formulate answers to these questions, your next step will be to identify someone in your community to organize a Friends group. Think about approaching a library trustee or dedicated volunteer and proposing the idea. These individuals already have an understanding of the goals and objectives of your library, and they are also probably well connected in your community. As with any part of your public relations program, don't wait until you are in a crisis situation to decide you need "friends."

## Friends of Libraries USA (FOLUSA)

Like any other aspect of your volunteer program, creating a Friends of the Libraries organization is a complex process and, to be successful, will require more resources than this book provides. Friends of Libraries USA (FOLUSA), the national organization that supports local Friends groups across the country, can provide you with support and information as you work with your community to start a Friends group. The organization just celebrated its 25th anniversary and assists Friends organizations in all types of libraries—public, academic, school.

Sally Gardner Reed is the executive director of FOLUSA. In addition to leading the national organization, she speaks nationwide about the critical role Friends play in ensuring that libraries are fully funded in the community and on campus. In an interview, Reed talked about the role of Friends and FOLUSA today.

**Q: What is the primary role of a Friends of the Library organization? How is it different today from what it was 25 years ago?**

**Reed:** Generally Friends exist to support the library. How they do this should be broad and varied. Traditionally Friends groups primarily worked to raise funds for libraries, which is critically important, but today they are much more outspoken advocates for libraries.

Fundraising can supplement, but not supplant a library's budget. In today's tough economic times, libraries are in deep trouble and Friends speaking out as advocates is the best defense they have against declining budgets.

Friends also help libraries with public awareness. Librarians are often focused internally and Friends are focused externally. They spread the word about libraries at doctor's offices, grocery stores—throughout the community. Even more importantly, Friends groups are now working with their libraries to develop sophisticated advocacy and public awareness campaigns.

Finally, Friends are often volunteers at the library. They provide the library with a cache of volunteers that it can rely on.

**Q: What are the big challenges facing Friends today?**

**Reed:** The biggest challenge is keeping membership high. For many Friends groups, the majority of their funds come from membership dues. The second biggest challenge is keeping active Friends involved in the organization. They need Friends to move books for book sales, run the advocacy campaigns, help with membership drives, etc. It can be hard for working people to find the time needed for this volunteer commitment, and often they are drawn to investing their limited volunteer hours at the school that their children, school or church. Friends groups need energetic people who can do the hands-on, day-to-day work.

**Q: What are the big opportunities for Friends today?**

**Reed:** There are some really fun new opportunities for Friends today. A lot has to do with technology. Friends have Web sites, so they need Webmasters. Or they need volunteers who are tech-savvy and can handle assignments like selling book-sale books on eBay. Many Friends groups are doing direct-mail membership campaigns, and so they need volunteers who are experienced in targeting audiences, securing mailing lists, etc. The new jobs in Friends groups require more intellectual than physical investments. The good news is that today Friends members include a lot of women who have retired from the business world, and so they bring a whole new set of skills to the organizations.

**Q: How does FOLUSA support Friends? Has the organization changed over the last 25 years?**

**Reed:** The way FOLUSA has changed mirrors the way that Friends have changed. We consult with Friends groups and serve as a network for them to talk to one another. In most cases, Friends work in isolation. They don't travel to conferences. They want to talk to other groups about getting new members, successful fundraising, and advocacy campaigns. In isolation, they have to come up with their own ideas. We connect groups across the country so they can share good ideas. Our newsletter is considered our most valued member benefit. We also have an idea-sharing listserv that is very popular. People go online and pose questions, get lots of answers, share happy events and not-so-successful ones. It is a fascinating list to watch. Our core role is really to be the center of a network to connect Friends groups and ideas around the country.

We also provide Friends groups with expertise in marketing, development issues, and advocacy. We do a lot of consulting on the state, regional, and national level.

Our publications help Friends groups do what they are already doing better, and they are very inexpensive. We offer a successful turnkey "Books for Babies" program so local groups don't have to develop their own packets. It is highly affordable and available in mass quantities.

**Q: What is the most important piece of advice that you can offer a community member or library staff member who is beginning to start a Friends group?**

**Reed:** The service and support that Friends provide is incalculable. Working hand-in-hand with Friends can make the difference between a library being good and being great in its community.

The most important thing is to work hand-in-hand with Friends. Any negative calls that I get are when Friends and libraries are not working well together. Start together; create an operating agreement. Define how you will work together in a positive way. By doing that you will build a culture that will succeed you. Once you are on the right foot, you will stay there.

Perservere—it is worth it!

## TIPS FOR STARTING A FRIENDS ORGANIZATION

Among the many resources that FOLUSA provides Friends groups is a variety of fact sheets. One fact sheet covers creating a Friends group to support your particular type of library. FOLUSA also offers established Friends group access to "big ideas" from other organizations around the country. In addition, Reed recently authored *101+ Great Ideas for Libraries and Friends* (Neal-Schuman, 2004)—a must-have for any successful Friends group.

The following fact sheets offer tips for starting a Friends organization in a public, school, or academic library. For more resources from FOLUSA, visit the Web site at *www.folusa.org,* or call toll-free 1-800-9FOLUSA (1-800-936-5873).

**FIGURE 11.1  Friends of Libraries USA (FOLUSA) Fact Sheet 1: HOW TO ORGANIZE A FRIENDS GROUP**

Every library needs Friends! Whether you are a community member or librarian—congratulations, by starting a Friends group you'll be giving an important gift to the community.

1. If you are a librarian, reach out to some of your most faithful and energetic volunteers or a few of your most devout patrons to start a small steering committee. If you are a library lover who wants to start a group, contact your librarian and share your plans. It is critical to the success of the group that the librarian and the Friends steering committee work closely together.
2. The steering committee should reflect the community. Again, it should include the librarian and a small core of active volunteers and/or patrons. It is important to have access to an attorney, PR and advertising talent, and high profile leaders.
3. Determine the group's purpose and mission so that you can plan an organizational structure to accomplish them. This structure will include the types of standing committees you'll need to carry out your work.
4. Work on federal and state tax-exempt status with lawyer's help, so that when you collect dues they will be deductible. At the same time, work on developing the group's constitution and by-laws. Contact FOLUSA for materials that will provide you with sample by-laws and assistance for writing your constitution.
5. Determine what your dues structure will be. Consider a structure that will optimize both the number of members who will join and your ability to raise funds through dues. Starting with a low student or retired rate and increasing the dues incrementally for "higher" categories of giving should accomplish both objectives.
6. Once you have developed an organizational structure and have 501(c)(3) tax-exempt status, you will want to embark on a membership drive. This will probably include a direct mailing and a membership brochure to hand out at the library, the doctor's office, the grocery stores, and other places where members might be recruited.
7. Design a professional looking brochure for the membership drive. The brochure doesn't have to be expensive but it does have to look professional. Be sure that you include a space for new members to become active participants and volunteers in the organization. Be sure to involve those who sign up right away!
8. Hold your first "all member" meeting following the membership drive. This meeting should include a program component to attract a high attendance. At this program/meeting, elect officers and committee chairs to set and accomplish the group's goals.
9. Develop a long-range plan for Friends that includes participation from library staff so that your group's goals can stay in alignment with the library's vision and goals.
10. Join FOLUSA to get access to our special toolkit for members only on how to start and re-energize Friends groups and a host of other materials and advice to help you do what you do even better!

Reprinted with permission. Friends of Libraries USA (FOLUSA).

---

**FIGURE 11.2 Friends of Libraries USA (FOLUSA) Fact Sheet 6: HOW TO ORGANIZE A FRIENDS OF A SCHOOL MEDIA CENTER/LIBRARY**

A Friends group can have a truly positive impact on the school library or media center. Friends can provide a source of volunteers, a source of additional funding, and can be an effective pressure group when the library or media center's funding is threatened.

1. If you are an interested parent or faculty member wanting to start the group, be sure to include and get the support of the media specialist before proceeding. The media specialist should be involved in all aspects of the planning process.
2. Determine the primary purpose for starting the group. For example, this might be to create a volunteer core for the library. The primary purpose, however, should not eliminate other avenues of activity such as fundraising, programming, and advocacy. Let your mission help you determine who best to recruit for a steering committee: parents, student leaders, faculty, or all of the above and begin recruiting members who will be active leaders and volunteers of the group.
3. Meet with the school media specialist so he or she can acquaint the group with the basic philosophy and requirements for an effective media program. He or she should also explain school policies and procedures, and pertinent state and national standards.
4. Meet with the school's administration to get their approval of the group and their support.
5. Define the organizational structure for the group. Determine what committees will be needed to accomplish your goals and who best to lead each committee. Develop a schedule so that officers and committee chairs meet on a regular basis.
6. Develop a dues structure that will allow students to participate at a very low level and community business leaders to contribute at a much higher level with incremental levels in between.
7. Embark on a membership campaign. This might include a direct mailing to parents, handouts for student membership in the media center, or a special invitation to join for faculty members. Target community business leaders for a "special" category of membership. Be sure to solicit volunteers for "active" membership and follow up with them.
8. Plan a general membership meeting and program and be sure to invite all those who volunteered to become active members. At this meeting, elect officers and assign members to committees.
9. Keep the group active through regular meetings and fun activities that will benefit the media center and give it high profile within the school and in the community.
10. Join FOLUSA to get access to our special toolkit for members only called, "School Media Center Friends Groups: A Prescription for Success" along with a host of other materials and advice to help you do what you do even better!

Reprinted with permission. Friends of Libraries USA (FOLUSA).

**FIGURE 11.3  Friends of Libraries USA (FOLUSA) Fact Sheet 4: HOW TO ORGANIZE AN ACADEMIC FRIENDS GROUP**

The idea of an academic Friends group is not new. In fact, the first university library Friends organization was founded at Harvard in 1925. Friends in academia can help their library by raising additional revenues for collections, materials, and equipment. They can also help raise the profile of the library on campus through the programs and events they sponsor.

1. Obtain support of the library administration. The group cannot succeed without their "buy-in" and participation.
2. It will also be important to get support and approval from the development office and the administration of the parent institution. There is sometimes a perception that a Friends of the Library on campus will be competing for the same funds as the development office. You will need to outline with the development office the role you will be playing in support of the library and how you will raise funds in a non-competitive manner.
3. Work with the library administration to select a steering committee of concerned persons from the alumni, faculty, student body, and the local community. Include a liaison with the development office. It is important to have access to the institution's attorney, PR and advertising talent, and high-profile leaders.
4. Define the mission to be fulfilled by the Friends, and develop a constitution and by-laws reflecting this mission.
5. Determine and articulate the group's mission so that you can create an organizational structure to accomplish them. This structure will include the types of standing committees you'll need to carry out your work.
6. Develop your group's constitution and by-laws reflecting this mission. Contact FOLUSA for materials that will provide you with sample by-laws and assistance for writing your constitution.
7. Define your dues structure and membership categories based on what you hope to accomplish through membership. If you are using membership primarily as a fundraising tool, levels might be fairly high. If you are trying to achieve high numbers of interested people, the dues might be a bit lower. Consider any member benefits that will be available at different levels and consider a special student membership.
8. Clarify tax status of the *Friends group or of the parent institution* so that when you collect dues they will be deductible *by the member*.
9. Prepare for a membership drive that will include a membership brochure. The brochure should be professional looking. Though it need not be expensive, the brochure will introduce your new group to potential members and should be well done. Determine what avenues you have available for distributing the brochure. This may include a direct mailing to alumni, handouts at parent events, handouts at the library, and/or distribution to faculty and staff through inter-departmental mail.
10. Begin a publicity campaign. Be sure to involve university public relations and development offices, the alumni office, and the local media. Tell why the Friends group has been established and how others can get involved.

---

**FIGURE 11.3 Friends of Libraries USA (FOLUSA) Fact Sheet 4: HOW TO ORGANIZE AN ACADEMIC FRIENDS GROUP** (*continued*)

11. Decide on a tentative schedule of meetings for the first year in order to involve new members in committees as soon as they join.

12. Set a date for an opening Friends membership meeting that includes a popular program component to help get a large audience. Plan the program carefully and include an opportunity to elect officers and committee chairs.

13. Develop a long-range plan for Friends that includes participation from library staff so that your group's goals are developed in alignment with the library's goals. Re-evaluate it periodically.

14. Join FOLUSA to get access to our special toolkit for members only on how to start and re-energize Friends groups and a host of other materials and advice to help you do what you do even better!

Reprinted with permission. Friends of Libraries USA (FOLUSA).

---

## COMMUNITY ORGANIZATIONS

A big project, such as painting the children's room or putting security strips in all of your books, may be the perfect community service project for a local service club like the Rotary Club or Kiwanis. Such projects have a beginning and an end and can usually be accomplished in a matter of days by a large number of people working together. Think about approaching a local service club when you have such a project. Groups like these are always looking for projects that will contribute to the community and increase their public profile.

Involving community groups in library projects will often encourage additional media coverage of your library. The local newspaper will be enthusiastic about running a photograph of the mayor and Rotary Club members painting the children's room. And the Rotary Club may publish an article about the project in its newsletter, spreading the word to another audience.

## VOLUNTEERS FROM COLLEGES AND UNIVERSITIES

When your library has a special project for which you need volunteer help, you might want to recruit volunteers or interns from local colleges or universities. Like high schools, many of today's colleges have a public service requirement built into their curriculum. Managing the promotion for your summer reading program might be the perfect opportunity for a public relations major. Setting up the books for your new Friends of the Library group might be a great special project for an accounting major. Students may choose to work for your library as an internship for college credit.

You may even set up relationships with university faculty that will provide you with student volunteers or interns on a regular basis. By working with the faculty at the university, you can be sure that the volunteers' work will have expert review. You provide students with an opportunity for real work experience in their field and your library gets expert assistance that it otherwise might not be able to afford.

## VOLUNTEERS BECOME ADVOCATES

Your highly valued volunteers will not only contribute to your library in terms of the services they provide; they will also become advocates for your library. As Peter Drucker said of volunteers in *Managing the Nonprofit Organization: Principles and Practices*, "They live in the community and they exemplify the institution's mission. Effective non-profits train their volunteers to represent them in the community."[9]

By developing a comprehensive volunteer program that has a direct relationship to your PR goals, you will develop volunteers who are able to tell your library's story. The result should mirror the experience that Drucker describes, "Again and again when I talk to volunteers in non-profits, I ask, 'Why are you willing to give all this time when you are already working hard in your paid job?' And again and again I get the same answer, 'Because here I know what I am doing. Here I contribute. Here I am a member of the community.' "[10]

## Volunteer Management Resources

In this book, volunteer management is presented as a part of overall library public relations and communications. It is, however, a broad field in its own right with many issues—human resources, legal, and administrative—to consider. Another Neal-Schuman How-To-Do-It Manual *Recruiting and Managing Volunteers in Libraries,* by Bonnie F. McCune and Charleszine Nelson (Neal-Schuman, 1995), is dedicated entirely to this topic.

Supplement this book with the selected resources on volunteer management to develop and launch a successful volunteer program that results in positive PR for your school, public, or academic library.

### Periodicals/Web Sites

Chronicle of Philanthropy
*www.philanthropy.com*

e-Volunteerism: Electronic Journal for the Volunteer Community
*www.e-volunteerism.com*

The Journal of Volunteer Administration
*www.avaintl.org/product/journal.html*

Virtual Volunteering Project, Handbook for Online Volunteers
*www.serviceleader.org/vv/handbook*

Volunteer Today
*www.volunteertoday.com*

### Books

*Better Safe . . . Risk Management in Volunteer Programs and Community Service*, by Linda L. Graff, Linda Graff and Associates, 2003.
*The Care and Feeding of Volunteers*, by Bill Wittich. Knowledge Transfer, 1999.
*Children as Volunteers: Preparing for Community Service*, by Susan J. Ellis, Anne Weisbord, and Katherine H. Noyes. Energize, Inc., 1991.
*From the Top Down: The Executive Role in Volunteer Program Success*, rev. ed., by Susan J. Ellis. Energize, Inc., 1996.
*Handling Problem Volunteers*, by Sue Vineyard and Steve McCurley. Heritage Arts, 2000.
*The (Help!) I-Don't-Have-Enough-Time Guide to Volunteer Management*, by Katherine Noyes Campbell and Susan J. Ellis. Energize, Inc., 1995.

*Leading Volunteers for Results: Building Communities Today*, by Jeanne H. Bradner. Conversation Press, 2000.
*Managing Library Volunteers: A Practical Toolkit*, by Preston Driggers and Eileen Dumas. American Library Association, 2002.
*Managing Volunteer Programs in the Public Sector*, by Jeffrey Brudney. Jossey-Bass, 1990.
*No Surprises: Harmonizing Risk and Reward in Volunteer Management*, 2nd ed., by Melanie L. Herman and Peggy M. Jackson. Nonprofit Risk Management Center, 2001.
*Passionate Volunteerism*, by Jeanne Bradner. Conversation Press, 1993.
*A Roadmap to Managing Volunteer Systems: From Grassroots to National*. National Health Council. By Claudia Kuric, 2000.
*Virtual Volunteering Guidebook*, by Susan J. Ellis and Jayne Cravens. Energize, Inc. 1999.
*The Volunteer Management Handbook*, ed. by Tracy Daniel Connors. John Wiley, 1999.
*The Volunteer Recruitment Book*, 2nd ed., by Susan J. Ellis. Energize, Inc., 1996.

### Organizations

Association for Volunteer Administration
P.O. Box 32092
Richmond, VA 23924
804-672-3353
*www.avaintl.org*

Energize, Inc.
5450 Wissahickon Ave.
Philadelphia, PA 19144
800-395-9800
*www.energizeinc.com*

National Center for Nonprofit Boards
1828 L St. N.W., Ste. 601
Washington, DC 20004
202-347-2080
*www.ncnb.org*

Nonprofit Risk Management Center
1001 Connecticut Ave. N.W., Ste. 410
Washington, DC 20046–5504
202-785-3891
*www.nonprofitrisk.org*

Points of Light Foundation
1737 H St. N.W.
Washington, DC 20006
800-272-8306
*www.pointsoflight.com*

Resource Centre for Voluntary
   Organizations
Grant MacEwan Community College
5-132, 10700-104 Ave.
Edmonton, AB T5J 4S2, Canada
780-497-5616
*www.rcvo.org*

Volunteer Management Associates
320 S. Cedar Brook Rd.
Boulder, CO 80304
800-944-1470
*www.volunteermanagement.com*

Volunteer Vancouver
301 – 3102 Main St.
Vancouver, BC V5T 3G7, Canada
604-875-9144
*www.volunteervancouver.ca*

# NOTES

1. Based on an hourly rate of $15.40.
2. Tom Peters, *The Pursuit of WOW! Every Person's Guide to Topsy-Turvy Times* (New York: Random House, 1994), 67.
3. 1998 Volunteer Survey, UPS Foundation. *www.ups.com/news/1999report.html*
4. Are You Scaring Away Volunteers? 5 Recruitment Tips that Treat, not Trick, Energize Inc., Press Release, October 2001. *www.energizeinc.com/press/01oct.html*
5. Young Adult Library Services Association (YALSA), *Youth Participation in School and Public Libraries: It Works* (Chicago: American Library Association, 1995): 5.
6. Ibid.
7. Ibid.
8. Friends of Libraries USA, *News Update* 18 (spring 1996): 1.
9. Peter F. Drucker, *Managing the Nonprofit Organization: Principles and Practices* (New York: HarperCollins, 1990), 161.
10. Drucker, xvii.

# 12 REACHING OUT TO BRING USERS IN

The best way to get people to walk in the door of your library is for you and your staff to walk out the door. You need to be out there, involved, meeting people—overcoming the stereotype of the librarian behind the desk guarding the books. Yes, community groups like Rotary and Kiwanis are one way to do this, but if, for example, you are an avid runner, you can also reach out into your community through your involvement in running groups. The key is to get out there, do what you love, and spread the word.

Your library is a part of many different communities regardless of what type library you are in. A public library is part of a city or a county. Branch libraries are part of the neighborhood communities in which they are located. School libraries are members of their building and district-level communities and of the overall neighborhood and city or county that the school serves. Academic libraries are part of their university or college community, the neighborhood that they share with local residents, and their town or city. By being involved in those greater communities, you create an indelible image of the library and its role in supporting the community and you build public support for your services. Hey—you are a great person with similar interests, so the library must be a great place, right?

Read the trading card (Sample 12.1) that comes with Seattle librarian Nancy Pearl's action figure. Yes, her "weapon of choice" might be the Dewey Decimal System, but look carefully at this library icon's accomplishments. In addition to being the director of library programming for the Washington Center for the Book at the Seattle Public Library and—even more prominently—the mastermind behind the country's "One-City, One-Book" project, Nancy is an avid bicyclist who has twice completed the Seattle to Portland Bicycle Classic. What do you think those riders thought when the cyclist next to them revealed that she was a librarian? You can bet that they came back from their journey thinking differently about libraries and librarians.

So if public relations is truly about creating a positive public perception, the relationship your library staff builds with other members of the community is the most effective tool for developing such positive perceptions. When an employee of your library goes home in the evening, stands in his backyard, and talks about your library in a positive way to his "neighbor over the fence,"

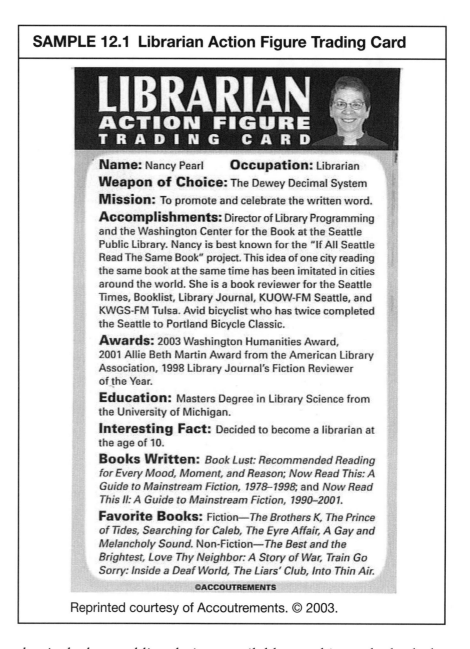

**SAMPLE 12.1  Librarian Action Figure Trading Card**

Reprinted courtesy of Accoutrements. © 2003.

that is the best public relations available—and it can be both the most expensive and inexpensive tool to buy.

Let's face it. If library staff don't speak positively in the community about your library, how can you expect your volunteers to talk about why your library is important? And, ultimately, how can you expect the community to perceive your library as a "community value," if even the people who feed their families by working there are dissatisfied by the services provided?

# LIBRARY STAFF MEMBERS AS COMMUNITY VOLUNTEERS

Just as having community volunteers come into your library helps you achieve your public relations goals, sending library staff out into the community as volunteers will also further your efforts. The library staff person who gets involved as a Little League coach or as a Rotary member or who is in charge of the town's annual fun-run to benefit muscular dystrophy is giving something back to the community. Such a contribution reflects both on the person involved and on the organization he or she works for, especially if the organization—your library—supports the involvement.

Described in the for-profit sector as "corporate social responsibility," providing support for employees' volunteer efforts became more and more widespread in the 1990s. Sometimes this support is provided by "release time"—allowing employees to do community service as part of their regular work day, without losing pay. In cities like Chicago and New York, corporate employees take on such projects as devoting Saturdays to updating the paint in urban schools or weeding flowerbeds in city parks.

The minute libraries think about sending staff into the community, however, red flags about "time off the desk" and "time away from serving the public" go up. But if public relations is truly a priority for your library, you will need to think creatively about staffing and scheduling to accommodate such involvement. One caveat is necessary—while it is important for library staff to be involved in the community in order to spread the word about your library and its services, staff are still needed in the building to serve the public when they show up to partake of those wonderful services you have been promoting.

A library truly committed to supporting staff community involvement might even make it part of the performance appraisal process. In that way, each staff person could work with his or her supervisor to negotiate a way to be involved in the community and for the time to do it. Sometimes the support might be time away from the library; at other times employees might be involved on their own time, but the library might pay all or part of an organizational membership fee. The key is for the involvement to be something that the staff member is interested in and something that will provide the person with the opportunity to tell the library story.

Another way to support staff involvement in outside programs and activities is to provide opportunities for staff to share their interests in such involvement. For example, when I was working in a public library, we had a youth services librarian with a huge interest in environmental issues and one of her big causes was saving bluebirds. So each spring we gave her time and meeting space to do workshops on building feeders for bluebirds. These programs were among our most successful, and our audience reached beyond adult orthonologists to members of local Bluebird troops. In the end, it was a big win for the employee and the library—she got to spread the word about her outside interest and the library got a fantastic, high-interest program.

Your library might even want to develop an application for community involvement support, such as that shown in Figure 12.1. This application helps staff define and articulate the type of support they would like the library to provide, and it gives the library a formal way of deciding about the feasibility of such support. For example, without an application process, a staff person who would like to help deliver Meals On Wheels to the elderly twice per month might not even consider volunteering—she would need an extra 30 minutes added to her lunch hour each delivery day. On the other hand, she knows that a mechanism is in place for asking the library to support her involvement, she is more likely to pursue the opportunity and request support.

It is also important to remember that all library staff members have something to contribute to the community. A master's in library science does not make a person uniquely qualified to tell the library's story in the community; in fact, a support or clerical staff person is sometimes more easily recognized by members of the community than a "professional" librarian, and, therefore, has more recognition value. For example, if your library has a booth at the county fair, community members might be more comfortable approaching the booth if the people working there are the library staff they see on a day-to-day basis (rather than administrative staff whom they never see). In addition, nonusers who visit the library after a positive experience in the booth at the county fair may feel more welcome walking in the door to see the circulation staff member who greeted them at the fair.

There are ways other than release time to encourage library staff to be involved in the community. You might want to designate a staff person to seek out opportunities for community involvement and promote them to your staff. Working the phones for the local public television station during its fund drive is a great opportunity for library staff to volunteer as a team; it is a chance for library staff to volunteer together and for people watching the telethon see them there as a group—giving something back. If your staff cannot volunteer because of scheduling difficulties,

**FIGURE 12.1  Sample Staff Application for Community Involvement Support**

## Middletown Public Library

### Staff Application for Community Involvement Support

Name_____

Position_____

Describe the type of community project/volunteer work that you are involved in:

_____

_____

What type of support are you seeking (e.g., release time, use of library equipment or supplies, permission to solicit contributions from colleagues on site, reimbursement of membership dues)?

_____

_____

For what period of time do you need this support?_____

Why should Middletown Public Library support your involvement?

_____

_____

_____

Signature_____  Date_____

Supervisor's recommendation_____

_____

Supervisor's signature_____  Date_____

Library Director's decision_____

_____

_____

Library Director's signature_____  Date_____

your library could contribute pizza for volunteers to eat or T-shirts for them to wear during the broadcast; the library gets exposure, the staff develops a sense of team spirit, and the community gets needed work done. It makes a lot of sense.

## SENDING LIBRARY STAFF INTO THE COMMUNITY

Once your library's staff is ready and willing to go out into the community and spread the word about your library and its services, there are a wide variety of opportunities to do so. They range from becoming involved as members in such groups as the chamber of commerce and the Rotary to making presentations for community groups to staffing a booth at the county fair. The skills and background necessary for these activities are varied enough that there are opportunities for any library staff member who wants to participate.

### Community Groups

People often become involved in group volunteer activities both for the opportunity to make a contribution and for the social interaction. The staff at your library might be interested in getting involved in the following types of organizations:

- civic groups
- business clubs
- professional societies
- hobby clubs
- fraternities and sororities
- religious organizations
- sports and recreation clubs
- advocacy organizations
- auxiliaries and "friends of" organizations
- amateur performing arts companies

Involvement in these groups allows library staff the chance to build a network of community contacts. For example, when the Kiwanis Club is looking for a service project, your head reference librarian who is also a Kiwanis member might suggest that the library needs its children's room painted. Library staff involvement in these groups helps integrate the library and its resources into the community. For example, the staff person who is involved with community theater might offer to prepare a list of related library materials for the show program or he might arrange a display of library materials for the theater lobby on opening night. This kind of community outreach is extremely valuable and can only be achieved through the support of library staff involvement in community organizations.

## STAFF AS PRESENTERS

Each year, the local Rotary Club appoints a program chair and each year that individual goes crazy trying to plan informative and entertaining programs for the group's weekly meetings. He spends hours on the telephone trying to pin down speakers, tries to talk all of his friends and relatives into presenting at least one program, and when Aunt Minnie refuses to discuss her button collection at the group's next meeting, he wonders why he ever became a Rotarian to begin with. Your library can help make the program chair's experience more pleasurable and can make him admired and envied by his fellow Rotarians. How? By providing the group, on an annual basis, with a list of library staff who are available to make presentations on a wide variety of topics. Best of all, this "speakers bureau" is an excellent way for you to spread the word about your library and its services. The program chair can use this list to schedule your staff to present at his group's meetings throughout the year. (He will also have the list as a backup resource when Uncle Frank has to have gall bladder surgery and can't talk at next week's meeting about his experiences in the Korean War.)

To develop a speakers bureau for your library, think about the people on your staff who have particular areas of expertise. In what subject areas is your business reference librarian really up to date? Can the librarian in your local history collection talk about the architecture of downtown buildings? Does your collection development librarian love mysteries and mystery writers? Approach people and ask them if they would be willing to develop a presentation to be included on your list. You may wish to put out a general call for presenters, but be careful—perhaps not all of your volunteers will be good presenters, but if they volunteer, you may feel obligated to use them. Your business reference librarian may really know a lot about business reference materials, but he could be deadly as a presenter. However, as part of the community involvement component of your library's public relations plan, you might be able to encourage him to be the library's representative to the chamber of commerce; there he could share business resources on a one-to-one basis with his fellow members and come back to the library from each meeting with more information about what is happening in your community.

Ask each presenter to complete a speakers bureau presentation description similar to that in Figure 12.2. This description will

---

**FIGURE 12.2  Speakers Bureau Presentation Description**

Staff person _____

Presentation topic_____

Brief description of presentation_____

_____

_____

_____

_____

Length of presentation_____

Audiovisual equipment required_____

Intended audience (e.g., adults, children, business people, senior citizens)

_____

_____

Days and times presenter is available_____

_____

Additional information _____

_____

---

help you compile your list of presentations and provide you with a reference tool when people call to request a speaker.

Don't forget presentations about books when you develop your speakers bureau. Service clubs and other groups are always looking for booktalks. If you have staff members who are particularly good at talking about books, be sure to include them on your list. You might have staff who can talk about books on a particular subject or genre, such as the Civil War or science fiction, and others who are well suited to talk about the most recent bestsellers. People associate libraries with books, and lots of people are looking for a recommendation for a good book to read. Send your librarians out into the community to do just that!

Once you have a list of presenters and they are ready to go out into the community, promote your speakers bureau. In addition to mailing information to a list of service organizations, you might run an item in your library's newsletter about the available speakers or you might issue a news release describing your new service. Remember that, just as for any service your library provides, groups need to know about your speakers bureau and the speakers available before they can take advantage of it.

# PARTICIPATING IN COMMUNITY EVENTS

Any special event or activity that takes place in your community offers an avenue for your library to become involved. The possibilities are endless—booths at community and county fairs, a float in the local parade, puppet shows for children during the restaurant fair—and they all include a chance to tell the library story.

In addition, most groups that host special events are anxious to have groups such as libraries involved and they will offer booth or display space free or at a reduced rate. Look at your community and think about the possibilities. Could your school library have a booth at the neighborhood's community center festival to exhibit student work? If you are trying to get the people from the neighborhood to use your academic library, handing out magnets listing library hours might be a great outreach tool at the Octoberfest celebration. The key is to determine where the people are that you want to reach—and then to go there to reach them.

If your library has a bookmobile, this can be a great exhibit on wheels. It is easy to transport, it has books on it that people can actually check out, and people love to visit a bookmobile. All you have to do is drive the bookmobile to the event, staff it with a couple of friendly library staff, and wait for the crowd to materialize.

If you are a school librarian, try to find a way to participate in all school events. Be a part of the school community! The library should be open (with students using it) on Parents' Night. If the school has a building-wide festival, be sure that you and the library are a part of it.

Academic libraries should also try to participate in school events and activities. Think carefully about how your library can participate in Homecoming or Parents' Weekend. Can the welcoming reception for parents be held in your library's lounge? Should the library have a float in the homecoming parade? There are lots of possibilities for involvement that can further your library's public relations goals, and your staff might even have fun in the process!

# WHEN YOU WALK OUT THE DOOR, THE LIBRARY USERS WALK IN

The more time your library staff devotes to its community, the more the community will view the library as an integral player. Community involvement for both your library staff, as individuals, and your library, as an organization, is an excellent tool for reaching your public relations goals. Like other public relations tools, community involvement allows you to select your target audience and to participate in activities and events that will reach that audience. It creates a positive public perception of your library as an organization that "gives something back" to the community, and supports its staff in "giving something back," too. And, best of all, you can support the special interests and abilities of your staff members while promoting the library and its services.

# 13 CREATING PRINT COMMUNICATIONS MATERIALS THAT WORK

The topic for this chapter might seem trivial or silly. Organizations are often guilty, however, of investing huge amounts of money in print materials that may be glossy and look professional but that do not communicate what they were designed to communicate. The key to avoiding this mistake is careful planning and development of print—or for that matter all—communications materials.

In the years since the first edition of this manual was published, our society has come to rely heavily on electronic communications. We check the weather or movie showtimes online and even get our news from e-mail lists and Web sites. At the same time, we also have an ingrained reliance on printed communications. Check out anyone's trash can or recycling bin before garbage day and you will see the newspapers, magazines, newsletters, and brochures that we continue to rely on for information. So while electronic tools will, of course, be an important part of your communications strategies, it is critical to remember the tried and true print materials when trying to reach your target audiences.

Before you decide "We need a brochure for that" or "Let's do a newsletter," however, you should think about a variety of things. This chapter will take you through the process of planning, budgeting, and scheduling your library's publications. It will help you think about whether your printing and design can be done in-house or whether they should be contracted out. It also provides tips for working with printers and designers. If you would like step-by-step help with producing print publications, *Creating Newsletters, Brochures and Pamphlets: A How-to-Do-It Manual for School and Public Librarians*, by Barbara Radke Blake and Barbara L. Stein (Neal-Schuman, 1992) is an excellent resource.

# PUBLICATION PLANNING FOR YOUR LIBRARY

There are many options for print publications. You may want to produce a regular newsletter or intermittent promotional flyers. Your library may publish one overall service brochure or a separate brochure for each type of service. The goals and objectives that you detail in your public relations/communications plan should help you make decisions about the type of print publications necessary to meet your overall communications goals.

## EDITORIAL STYLE SHEET

Before you begin to develop any publications—print or electronic—you need to develop an editorial style sheet to guide the content development for all library publications. As part of the development of your library's corporate image, you have already developed a graphic style sheet to guide the design of your publications. An editorial style sheet will help ensure consistency within the content of your library's publications.

You may wish to adhere to one of several editorial style manuals, such as the *Chicago Manual of Style* or the *Associated Press Stylebook*. These guides make many major editing decisions for you. You simply develop a list of editorial standards specific to your library in addition to those published in the manuals you choose to follow. The *Associated Press Stylebook* is the easiest to use, and the style it recommends may be most familiar to your audiences since it is used by most major newspapers. It will help you and your authors decide when to use words or numerals to represent numbers, agree on standard abbreviations for states, and decide when to capitalize certain words and titles.

You will, also, want to develop a customized style sheet for your library. This special guide will include how you want to refer to your library in first and second reference. For example, all first references might be "Anytown Public Library" and second references might be "the Library." By determining the style for these references and publishing and distributing that information, you will help ensure consistency in all of your library's publications. This consistency will contribute to the quality of your overall image.

Developing an editorial style sheet may take a bit of time, but it will be time well spent. You will find that it makes developing the content for any future publication a lot easier and provides any author in your library with guidelines for his or her writing.

You may even want to recommend that staff use the style sheet to guide writing business letters and other corporate communications, in addition to actual publications or Web content.

## PUBLICATION DESCRIPTION

You will want to develop a publication description for each item that you plan to publish. It should be based on the goals and objectives of your public relations/communications plan and ultimately will become a part of that plan. The development of this description also provides another opportunity for you to decide if the printed publication you are considering meets your communications needs. You may get halfway through writing the description and discover that you already have a publication that meets the need. Or, after developing the description, you may compare it to your public relations/communications plan and decide that there is no relationship between the two—the new publication was a nice idea, but it wouldn't further your library's communications goals.

Above all, the publication description will be an important communications tool when you work with writers and designers. It will describe exactly what you want your new newsletter, brochure, or flyer to look like and the goals you want to achieve with it. See Figure 13.1 for an outline of a publication description. Figures 13.3 and 13.4, which appear later in this chapter, are sample outlines for a newsletter and a brochure, but the samples can be customized to suit any type of publication that you are considering.

## BUDGETING FOR PUBLICATIONS

The information in your publication description will help you develop a draft budget for your publication. You can total the number of people in your audience, get some printing quotes, and determine how many people you can realistically afford to reach. You may discover that, while a four-color publication would be great, two ink colors are all you can afford. Once you develop a budget based on this information and decide what you can truly afford, you should update the description to reflect what your publication will really be like. In addition, this information will provide you with a plan for developing the content for your publication and its printing and distribution.

Each publication that you produce should have its own budget, and you should keep careful track of expenditures for that publication. This information will help you measure the effectiveness of your communications efforts based on the resources

---

**FIGURE 13.1  Publication Description Outline**

---

**Purpose:** What is the goal of this publication? What do you want to communicate or promote? Think about how it relates to your library's overall communications goals.

**Description:** This is a physical description of the publication. What size are you thinking about? How many colors of ink would you like to use? Will it include photos or other graphic illustrations?

**Publication Dates:** How often will this publication be published or revised? If it is a newsletter, include a publication schedule. If it is a brochure, you will probably want to include a revision schedule.

**Audience:** Provide a detailed list of your audience, with a ballpark number of members of each group (for example, parents of school-age children in our community—10,000; all members of the Friends of the Library—2,000).

**Number Produced:** Based on your audience, how many copies of this item do you plan to print?

**Cost:** You may not be able to fill in this figure when first developing your description, but you can use the information that you put in this description to determine how much your publication will cost. When you have that information, provide it here, both in terms of total cost and cost per item.

**Content:** What will the content of this publication be? How will it address the audience?

**Distribution:** Merely producing a print publication doesn't communicate anything to your audience. From the very beginning, you need to have a plan for distributing the publication to your target audience. You would have been better off not publishing the item—even if it is spectacular in terms of content and design—if it just sits in boxes under a table in your library's workroom.

**Person Responsible:** As for every item in your public relations/communications plan, you will want to designate one person who is responsible for the publication. That person doesn't have to do all of the work, but he or she does have to coordinate it. That person is responsible for seeing that the publication is reviewed for revision on schedule, that the planned distribution occurs, and that it stays on its publication schedule.

that you have dedicated to them. It is just as important to keep track of the number of staff hours spent on the publication as the actual dollars that have been paid for design, printing, and distribution.

Basically, copywriting, design, photos or other artwork, printing, and distribution will be the basic elements in any publication budget. You'll need to determine which tasks will be done in-house and which will be done by outside professionals. Then you can begin to build a budget based on price quotes from outside professionals and your own estimates of the time for in-house work.

### Copywriting

In many cases, you will probably decide to do at least the preliminary copywriting in-house. You and your staff are the closest to the topic and can pull the information together most quickly. You may, however, want to consider employing an outside editor to review your copy. Editing is particularly important for items that you expect to have a long life, such as service brochures. Freelance copywriters can edit your copy based on your style sheet, correct any grammatical errors, and catch any professional jargon that might have found its way into your copy. In addition, they might be able to put a little "flavor" or "spin" into copy.

### DESIGN

With the prevalence of easy desktop publishing programs and computers, you have many choices about how to manage the design of your publications. If you have a large budget, using an outside designer is your best choice. No matter how good someone becomes at desktop publishing, if he or she isn't a trained professional designer, certain skills will be lacking. A professional designer will also help to maintain consistency of your corporate image. If you are fortunate enough to be in a library, university, or school district with an in-house professional designer, you have a terrific option for the design of your publications. Talk with the designer to see if he or she can handle the additional work and what the production time will be.

If you don't have an in-house designer or the budget to contract someone to do all of your design work, the best option is to have desktop publishing templates designed as part of your corporate identity package. Then you can use your desktop publishing skills to create different publications based on those templates—you will maintain your corporate identity and produce quality publications. If you use these templates, you may want to build in a fee for having the designer review publications produced with the templates on an annual basis. Your designer may even do this for free—it will be a chance to share tips for using the templates in the best graphic fashion.

In many cases, you will start with a lump sum available for your publication and then work backwards in terms of what you spend on each area. If you are working with an outside designer, you may want to tell the designer what you can spend and share your publication description with him or her. The designer can then either come back with a proposal for a publication that will meet your goal, staying within your budget, or tell you that what you are trying to do is unrealistic for the amount of money you have to spend. At that time, you can get a second opinion, alter parts of your plan, or go back to your library director, building principal, or library board for additional funding.

## Photos or Other Illustrations

If you plan to use photographs or to purchase illustrations for use in your publication, it is important to build this into your budget. Both can be quite expensive, and, if they are important to you, you must determine how much you can afford to spend on them. Get a quote from a photographer, an illustrator, or a stock photography or illustration company, and include that figure in your budget.

Digital photography offers a less-expensive option. Your library can purchase a high-quality digital camera for less than $700 and use it to shoot photos for both your printed and electronic communications. One of the best things about a digital camera is that you can preview each photo immediately to determine if the shot meets your needs. In addition, you can electronically transmit the photo to your designer without the added time and expense of photo processing.

## Printing

Once you have your design and know how many copies you want to print, you can approach printers for quotes. You can adjust your quantity, number of ink colors, or type of paper to stay within your budget. It is important to get a preliminary quote from a printer before you proceed with design on a project. You don't want to end up with a beautifully designed publication that you cannot afford to print.

## Distribution

If you plan to distribute this publication in your library, the distribution budget line item might actually be zero. If you plan to mail the publication by itself, however, or stuff it into someone else's mailing, you want to include those costs.

Bulk mailing is a viable option for most libraries because they can apply for nonprofit status. Schools, colleges, and universities may already have a bulk nonprofit permit that the library can use. Remember to include in your budget both the postage for mailing the item and the cost of preparing the mailing. You can either learn how to prepare bulk mail yourself or hire an outside mailing service to do it for you. Often, hiring an outside mailing service is the best option; such a service is very knowledgeable about postal regulations and can sort your mail for the best possible postal rate. If you are going to prepare the mailing yourself, your local post office may offer a course or at least have a video-tape that you can watch to learn how to prepare mailings. It will be important to refresh your knowledge on an annual basis as postal regulations are constantly changing.

If you will be mailing your publication nonprofit bulk rate or first class, take a mock-up of it to your post office or your mailing service and have it reviewed for mailing before you go to press. For instance, you may find out that, because your publication is an unusual size, it will be expensive to mail. Then you will have to decide between the uniqueness of your design or format and its impact on your distribution budget.

If you are including your publication as an insert in another mailing, such as the water department's bills, you may be asked to pay for part of the process of stuffing these inserts. At the time you agree to insert your materials, find out what costs you will be required to cover—it might still be a bargain compared to paying for separate preparation and postage.

Another option to consider for distributing your publication is having it stitched or inserted in another publication, such as the school district newsletter or the local newspaper. Investigate the costs of such distribution and think carefully about the kind of perception it will create. If you insert your public library's newsletter in the local newspaper will you be reaching your constituency or a much wider group? What will the costs be, compared to mailing it separately to all of your cardholders?

Another wonderful distribution method is sending things home from school with children. If you are a school librarian, this makes perfect sense. Public library materials may need to be approved by the superintendent of schools or school board before being distributed in this way, but, particularly for summer reading promotional materials, this method might make sense. Experience has shown, however, that there is a direct correlation between the age of the student and whether the item arrives at home. (The

| FIGURE 13.2 Sample Publication Schedule | |
|---|---|
| **Publication Needed** | **May 1** |
| To Printer | April 1 |
| Copy to Designer | March 1 |
| Copy Plan Developed | February 1 |

younger the students, the better the chance your publication will reach their home.)

Of course, in some instances, you may want to skip the printed publication and deliver your information to library users via e-mail. However, in these days of huge amounts of spam, sometimes users hit the "Delete" key quickly when scrolling through their e-mail. A printed publication that arrives via snail mail may have a better chance of grabbing their attention as they shuffle through their daily stack of mail.

## DEVELOPING A PUBLICATION SCHEDULE

The best way to develop a publication schedule is backward! Determine the date that you want the publication to be available and work backward from that date. Determine how long it will take your printer to do the printing. Working backward, you now have the date that you or your designer will need to send your artwork to the printer. Next decide how long it will take to design your publication. How long will it take to write the content? How long will you need between developing the copy plan and having the content written? Eventually, experience will provide you with time frames for these elements of your schedule. From the start, your designer and printer will be able to estimate time for their part of the process. A general guideline, however, is four weeks for each step in the process. A sample publication schedule appears in Figure 13.2.

This may not always be a realistic time schedule. Newsletters will probably need a tighter schedule, because you will want information to be timely when it reaches your readers. But always allow enough time for careful proofreading, editing, and checking of design and layout, and remember that a "rush" schedule may negatively impact your budget. Printers and designers often charge extra for "rush" projects, and rightly so.

# NEWSLETTERS

Newsletters are an effective, if traditional, communications tool, particularly when you are trying to reach a specific target audience. Libraries of all types use monthly, bimonthly, and/or quarterly newsletters to promote their services, programs, and collections. Producing a newsletter on a regular basis can be a burden for library staff, however, and the content often suffers when the editors are overloaded with other work. It is important to consider whether a newsletter is the best tool for communicating your message.

**SAMPLE 13.1** *Focus:* **Friends of Goucher College Library Newsletter**

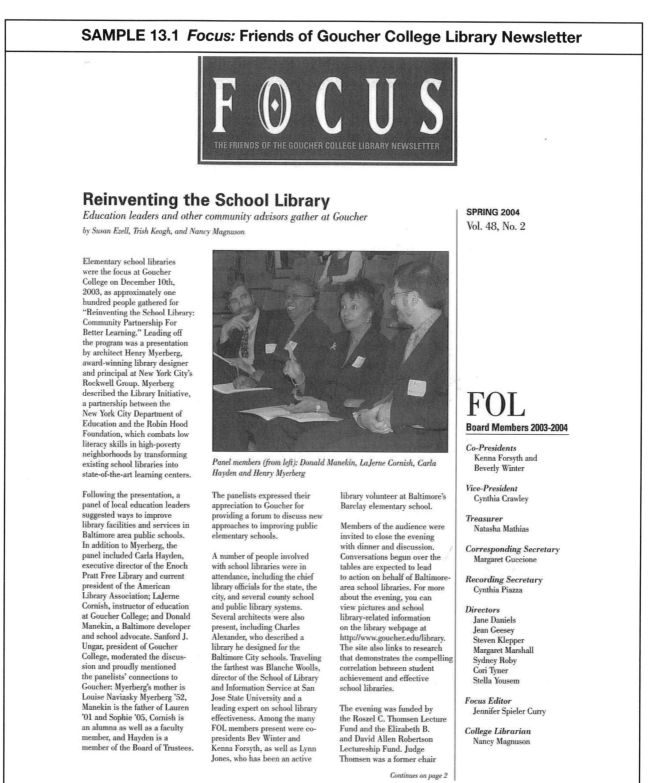

# FOCUS
### THE FRIENDS OF THE GOUCHER COLLEGE LIBRARY NEWSLETTER

## Reinventing the School Library
*Education leaders and other community advisors gather at Goucher*

by Susan Ezell, Trish Keogh, and Nancy Magnuson

**SPRING 2004**
Vol. 48, No. 2

Elementary school libraries were the focus at Goucher College on December 10th, 2003, as approximately one hundred people gathered for "Reinventing the School Library: Community Partnership For Better Learning." Leading off the program was a presentation by architect Henry Myerberg, award-winning library designer and principal at New York City's Rockwell Group. Myerberg described the Library Initiative, a partnership between the New York City Department of Education and the Robin Hood Foundation, which combats low literacy skills in high-poverty neighborhoods by transforming existing school libraries into state-of-the-art learning centers.

Following the presentation, a panel of local education leaders suggested ways to improve library facilities and services in Baltimore area public schools. In addition to Myerberg, the panel included Carla Hayden, executive director of the Enoch Pratt Free Library and current president of the American Library Association; LaJerne Cornish, instructor of education at Goucher College; and Donald Manekin, a Baltimore developer and school advocate. Sanford J. Ungar, president of Goucher College, moderated the discussion and proudly mentioned the panelists' connections to Goucher: Myerberg's mother is Louise Naviasky Myerberg '52, Manekin is the father of Lauren '01 and Sophie '05, Cornish is an alumna as well as a faculty member, and Hayden is a member of the Board of Trustees.

*Panel members (from left): Donald Manekin, LaJerne Cornish, Carla Hayden and Henry Myerberg*

The panelists expressed their appreciation to Goucher for providing a forum to discuss new approaches to improving public elementary schools.

A number of people involved with school libraries were in attendance, including the chief library officials for the state, the city, and several county school and public library systems. Several architects were also present, including Charles Alexander, who described a library he designed for the Baltimore City schools. Traveling the farthest was Blanche Woolls, director of the School of Library and Information Service at San Jose State University and a leading expert on school library effectiveness. Among the many FOL members present were co-presidents Bev Winter and Kenna Forsyth, as well as Lynn Jones, who has been an active

library volunteer at Baltimore's Barclay elementary school.

Members of the audience were invited to close the evening with dinner and discussion. Conversations begun over the tables are expected to lead to action on behalf of Baltimore-area school libraries. For more about the evening, you can view pictures and school library-related information on the library webpage at http://www.goucher.edu/library. The site also links to research that demonstrates the compelling correlation between student achievement and effective school libraries.

The evening was funded by the Roszel C. Thomsen Lecture Fund and the Elizabeth B. and David Allen Robertson Lectureship Fund. Judge Thomsen was a former chair

*Continues on page 2*

**SAMPLE 13.2** *Connections:* The Newsletter of the Plymouth Public Library

## Patriots donate $2,500 to local Literacy Program

The Super Bowl champions are helping The Library tackle illiteracy. The New England Patriots Charitable Foundation made a $2,500 contribution to the Literacy Program at the Plymouth Public Library in honor of local volunteer DonnaLee Williams. A Literacy Program tutor, DonnaLee was a finalist for the 2003 New England

**DonnaLee Williams**

Patriots Community Quarterback Award, which was established by the National Football League and Parade Magazine to recognize individuals who demonstrated outstanding commitment to improving their communities through volunteerism. As a finalist, $2,500 was donated in DonnaLee's name to the Literacy Program at the Plymouth Public Library. She was honored at a special ceremony in February for her "unwavering support and dedication that embodies the spirit of volunteerism and the spirit of the Community Quarterback Award." DonnaLee has been a volunteer tutor for the Literacy Program since 2001. She recently became a member of the Literacy Committee, an advisory group that guides the program.

Members of the Class of 1950 dress in costumes for Freak Day at Plymouth High School.

## Display takes us 'Back to the '50s'

Bobbie-soxers. Studebakers. Ted Williams in his prime. Poodle skirts. Penny loafers. A young Frank Sinatra. Those are just a few of the memories for the Class of 1950, which graduated from Plymouth High School – then located at what is now Nathaniel Morton School.

Those remembrances and many more will be on display at the Main Library during May and June. Called "Back to the '50s," this special exhibit will feature clothing, photos, newspapers, stories and other that show what it was like to graduate from high school in 1950.

This display is the inspiration of Joanne Tassinari, who was a member of that class. She had saved her cheerleader's uniform, gym clothes and many other mementos from that era and thought it would be fun to show today's generation what life was like 54 years ago.

"Things were a lot different back then," Joanne said. "Plymouth had a population of about 10,000 people. For many of us, World War II had taken our fathers and brothers away to fight. It was still the Big Band era. Rock and roll was a few years away. We went to the movies to watch news reels and serials."

"Back to the '50s" will include many of the things Joanne has saved from her high school years, along with items from some of her classmates. The exhibit will be located on the second floor of the Main Library and can be viewed during regular hours.

**New Manomet Branch Library Opens – See Page 4**

Courtesy of the Plymouth Public Library, Plymouth, MA.

**SAMPLE 13.3** *Off the Shelf:* **Wilmette Public Library Newsletter**

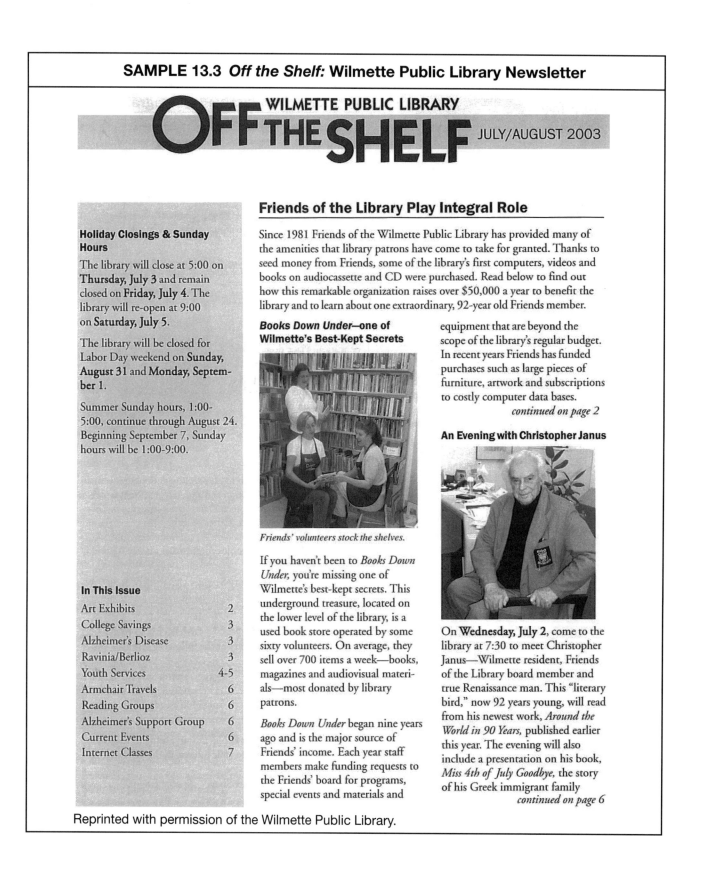

# WILMETTE PUBLIC LIBRARY
# OFF THE SHELF
JULY/AUGUST 2003

## Holiday Closings & Sunday Hours

The library will close at 5:00 on **Thursday, July 3** and remain closed on **Friday, July 4**. The library will re-open at 9:00 on **Saturday, July 5**.

The library will be closed for Labor Day weekend on **Sunday, August 31** and **Monday, September 1**.

Summer Sunday hours, 1:00–5:00, continue through August 24. Beginning September 7, Sunday hours will be 1:00–9:00.

## In This Issue

## Friends of the Library Play Integral Role

Since 1981 Friends of the Wilmette Public Library has provided many of the amenities that library patrons have come to take for granted. Thanks to seed money from Friends, some of the library's first computers, videos and books on audiocassette and CD were purchased. Read below to find out how this remarkable organization raises over $50,000 a year to benefit the library and to learn about one extraordinary, 92-year old Friends member.

### *Books Down Under*—one of Wilmette's Best-Kept Secrets

*Friends' volunteers stock the shelves.*

If you haven't been to *Books Down Under*, you're missing one of Wilmette's best-kept secrets. This underground treasure, located on the lower level of the library, is a used book store operated by some sixty volunteers. On average, they sell over 700 items a week—books, magazines and audiovisual materials—most donated by library patrons.

*Books Down Under* began nine years ago and is the major source of Friends' income. Each year staff members make funding requests to the Friends' board for programs, special events and materials and

equipment that are beyond the scope of the library's regular budget. In recent years Friends has funded purchases such as large pieces of furniture, artwork and subscriptions to costly computer data bases.

*continued on page 2*

### An Evening with Christopher Janus

On **Wednesday, July 2**, come to the library at 7:30 to meet Christopher Janus—Wilmette resident, Friends of the Library board member and true Renaissance man. This "literary bird," now 92 years young, will read from his newest work, *Around the World in 90 Years*, published earlier this year. The evening will also include a presentation on his book, *Miss 4th of July Goodbye*, the story of his Greek immigrant family

*continued on page 6*

Reprinted with permission of the Wilmette Public Library.

## DO YOU NEED ANOTHER NEWSLETTER?

A member of your library board may go to a conference and discover that lots of other public libraries have newsletters. He or she may return and deliver the decree that "Our library needs a newsletter." If that happens, the next questions should be "Why do we need a newsletter, what do we want to communicate, and to whom?"

Often, a new or stand-alone publication is not the best answer. There may be other ways of reaching your audience without incurring the additional expense and work a newsletter entails. For example, a public library might ask to have a monthly column or page in the city newsletter. This option would save both production and distribution costs and also show the public that city agencies are cooperating. If there is no city newsletter, it might be worthwhile asking the parks department director if they have ever considered a newsletter. If the answer is "yes," consider a joint publication. If both the library and the parks department want to reach the parents of school-age children with a bimonthly publication, you can develop a slicker publication and circulate it more widely by pooling your resources. Such a plan has the additional benefit of presenting the positive image of two taxpayer-funded entities working together to save costs. Your Friends of the Library members might want to send your newsletter to its members and thus might help fund the cost.

If you are a school library media specialist, it might be a good idea to request a regular column in the school district or neighborhood newsletter or newspaper. The answer is dependent on the audience that you have selected for your message. If you are trying to reach teachers and the school newsletter is geared to them, that medium is a good choice for your message. If you are trying to communicate with parents, a neighborhood newsletter or newspaper might be ideal. Often these publications are looking for reliable contributors who can produce good copy.

Any library considering developing its own newsletter should ask two questions: Does another existing publication address the same audience that I am trying to reach? Might I be able to obtain regular space in that publication? If the answers are "yes," consider the quality and reputation of the publication before you decide to go in this direction. For instance, if your school district has a newsletter that is considered an important source of information for the parents you are trying to reach, and if parents really do read it, that is definitely where you want to be. On the other hand, if you are a public librarian and your city mails a monthly newsletter to all taxpayers, but it is regularly riddled with errors and ridiculed in the community, publishing your own newsletter is probably a better idea.

You should also think about how much time your target audience has available to read another publication. Young parents might not need another piece of "junk mail" to deal with every month, but senior citizens might welcome an information-filled publication that arrives regularly from the public library. Parents of the children who use your school library media center might appreciate learning about the homework resources available at your library and reading about the interesting projects their children are doing in your library. If you decide that a newsletter is the best communications tool for your audience, thinking about how much time your audience can spend reading it will help you shape content (the subject, length, and style of your articles) and design.

One reason for your library to consider publishing a newsletter is to help create and enhance its public image as part of the development of your corporate identity. A high-quality newsletter—with a distinctive design that is consistent with the library's corporate identity and that includes informative articles—can help create the perception that your library offers quality service and is an important community institution.

## DEVELOPING YOUR NEWSLETTER

Once you decide you are ready to develop a newsletter for your library, you will need to assess the available resources. How much time can someone spend on the writing, editing, and distribution of the newsletter? Who will do the layout and design? Will you hire an outside graphic designer or will you have to produce the newsletter yourself? How much money does your library have to spend on the project? Is there a print shop in your library, school district, or university that can do the printing for free or at a reduced cost? Are there inexpensive ways, such as the campus mail, to distribute the publication?

Writing a publication description for your newsletter will help you determine the resources necessary for your publication. Then you can develop a budget based on what you want and can afford. Figure 13.3 outlines a newsletter publication description.

The next step is to determine, based on your resources, what work will be done in-house and what will be done by outside professionals. Use the information provided in the budgeting for publication section to think carefully about developing your newsletter's budget.

---

**FIGURE 13.3 Publication Description Outline: Newsletter**

**Purpose:** What is the goal of this newsletter? What do you want to communicate or promote? Think about how it relates to your library's overall communications goal.

**Description:** This is a physical description of the newsletter. What size are you thinking about? How many colors of ink would you like to use? How many pages will your newsletter be? Remember, standard formats (11-by-17-inch paper, folded for 4 pages; 8-1/2-by-11-inch, folded for 4 pages) will save you money.

**Publication Dates:** How often will your newsletter be published? If quarterly, indicate publication month.

**Audience:** Provide a detailed list of your audience, with a ballpark number of members of each group (for example, parents of school-age children in our community—10,000; all members of the Friends of the Library—2,000).

**Number Produced:** Based on your audience, how many newsletters do you plan to print?

**Cost:** Use the information that you put in this description to determine how much your newsletter will cost. Then go back to your overall communications budget and see if you can afford what you are planning. If you cannot, you may need to adjust your description to reflect a newsletter that works within your budget.

**Content:** What kind of information do you want to include in your newsletter? How will it address the audience? What regular columns or standing "headlines" will you have? For example, every issue might include a calendar of events and an annotated list of new books.

**Issue Descriptions** (optional): If you plan to publish "theme" issues of your newsletter, list them and the specific issue here (for example, a back-to-school issue in September).

**Distribution:** How will you get your newsletter out to its intended audience? Information racks in your library? Bulk mail? Send it home with students? How timely will the information included in your newsletter be? Will you need a distribution method that will get it there quickly?

**Person Responsible:** Who will be responsible for each task involved in producing and distributing the newsletter?

## NEWSLETTER SCHEDULE

The production schedule for a newsletter may be tighter than for your other print publications, particularly if the newsletter includes a calendar of events or other timely information. The total time frame from copywriting to distribution might only be six weeks. Think about whether and how often you can manage this tight production schedule. You may wish to publish a bimonthly or quarterly newsletter instead of a monthly one—with monthly publications you are constantly in the middle of a production schedule. Or you might want to only publish nine or ten months each year—skipping the summer months when you might not have your audience's attention.

You should also think about newsletter stories that can be produced in advance and used when space is available in an upcoming newsletter. For example, stories about ongoing library services and collections will be interesting to your readers but need not run in a specific issue. This strategy gives you content that is already prepared for each issue, and frees up time closer to the publication date to write articles on timely topics (such as the kick-off of your summer reading program or a new service policy recently passed by the board).

Above all, with a newsletter it is important to stick to your publication schedule. People should know when to expect it and learn to depend on the information they get from it. If you mail it during the first week of the month, be consistent. This isn't always easy to do when you have competing priorities, but it is critical to the success of your newsletter. Samples 13.1–13.3 illustrate some good examples of newsletters from different types of libraries.

## BROCHURES

It seems that every business, every service, and every organization has a brochure. Your library may need one, too, or your library may need several brochures. If you are thinking about developing a brochure for one or more of your library's services, think carefully about the goal of this brochure and which goals or objectives in your public relations/communications plan it supports. Should you produce a variety of brochures for your library's different services and collections, or would investing in one high-quality overall brochure be the best approach? What you decide will depend on how you plan to use the brochure. For example, if you need a printed piece to give to new library cardholders telling them what is available to them, you may want to develop one brochure that describes all of your services and collections. If the head of reference services plans to visit local businesses to promote your library's business collection and services, however, a brochure geared to that audience with information about the business collection and service is the route that you want to go. As with most of your communications planning, you need to base your strategy on your goals and the best use of available resources. The key is to produce effective materials that address your audience, and not to produce materials that are unnecessary, don't have a target audience, or don't further your plan.

Once you determine that you need a brochure and what you need it for, you are ready to think about design, budget, production schedule, and distribution. But, before you develop a publication description for it, think carefully about the elements of an effective brochure.

**SAMPLE 13.4  SIAST Libraries Faculty Brochure and Gift Certificate**

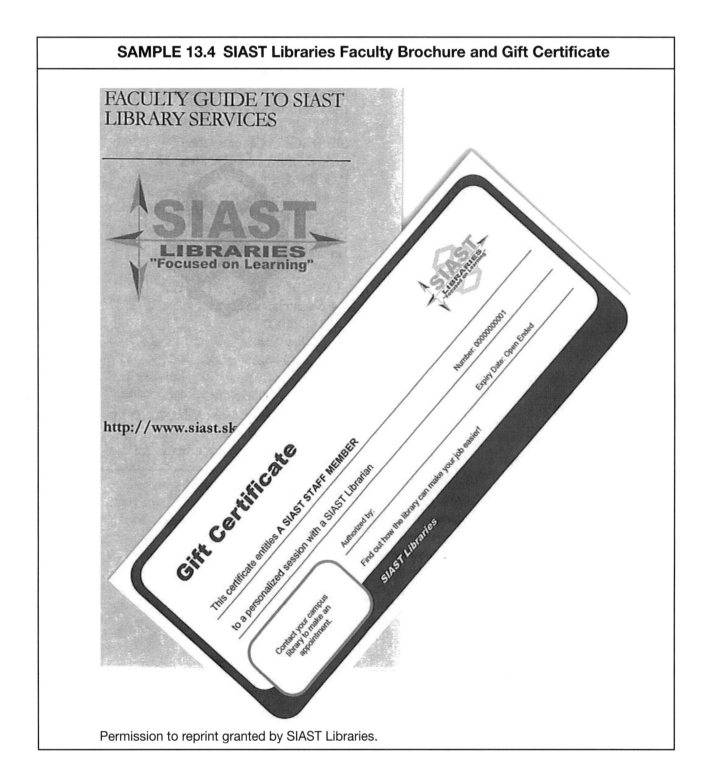

Permission to reprint granted by SIAST Libraries.

**SAMPLE 13.5  Arlington Heights Library Night Owl Reference Brochure**

Used with permission of the Arlington Heights Memorial Library.

**SAMPLE 13.6  Friends of Highland Park Public Library Brochure**

Courtesy of the Highland Park Public Library, Highland Park, Illinois.

### Elements of an Effective Brochure

Think about the brochures that you pick up when you are traveling, visiting a museum, or walking through a shopping mall. Consider the brochures that come as "junk mail" and that you actually pick up and read! What do these brochures have in common? You will probably find that it is the following elements:

- **Eye-catching colors or artwork**
  Colors or artwork make you notice the brochure. The colors don't have to be bright, but they should be attractive to the eye. The artwork should draw you into the brochure's copy and tell you something about the type of information you are going to find in the brochure.
- **Clearly written, enticing copy**
  The copy or text of the brochure should be written clearly so that the person you want to attract will understand it. Don't be clever with words if they will confuse your message. Be succinct. Tell readers exactly what they need to know. For example, if you are developing a brochure to encourage small business owners to use your library's reference collection, the copy should describe the scope and variety of your collection and perhaps list a few exemplary titles—it doesn't need to provide a comprehensive list of titles in your collection.
- **Information about how to act**
  A brochure that describes your library and its services should also include information about how a person can use the services. The address for the library, open hours, and perhaps a brief description of your cardholder requirements are all possibilities for information about "how to act." You won't get the results you want if you simply describe a valuable service or program, but fail to tell people how to take advantage of it.

### Brochure Publication Description

Once you determine that you have a program or service to promote via brochure, you should develop a publication description. This gives you a formal way to consider what you want to achieve with the brochure and how you will achieve it. An outline for a brochure publication description follows in Figure 13.4.

Next you will want to develop a budget and schedule. Use the information provided in the budgeting for publication section to do this. The longer you think the life of your brochure will be, the more money you may want to invest in it. You may want to

---

**FIGURE 13.4 Publication Description Outline: Brochure**

**Purpose:**
What is the goal of this brochure? What do you want to communicate or promote? Think about how it relates to your library's overall communications goals. Are there other services or collections that should be included in this brochure?

**Description:** This should be a physical description of the brochure. What size are you thinking about? How many colors of ink would you like to use? Will it include photos? When determining the format for a brochure, think about how you want to distribute it. If you want to put it in preexisting information racks at your library, make sure the format you choose will display nicely in those racks. If you want to mail it in an envelope, be sure it is the size of a standard envelope. If you want it to be a self-mailer, be sure that a mailing panel is included in the design.

**Publication Dates:** How often will this brochure be reviewed for updating?

**Audience:** Provide a detailed list of your audience, with a ballpark number of members of each group.

**Number Produced:** Based on your audience, planned distribution, and revision schedule, how many copies of this item do you plan to print?

**Cost:** Use the information that you put in this description to determine how much your brochure will cost. Then go back to your overall communications budget and see if you can afford what you are planning. If you cannot, may need to adjust your description to reflect a brochure that works within your budget.

**Content:** What will the content of the brochure be? How will it address the audience?

**Distribution:** Will you place the brochure in information racks? Mail it to a specific audience? Will staff members use it when they make public presentations?

**Person Responsible:** Who is responsible for the production of this brochure? This person is responsible for seeing that the publication is reviewed for revision on schedule, that the planned distribution occurs, and that it stays on its publication schedule. This person must also maintain an inventory of the brochure after it is printed so that you don't run out.

---

make a relatively major investment in the design of your library's overall service brochure because it's the first printed piece a new cardholder gets from you. In contrast, you may want to invest less in the design of the special brochure for your genealogy collection, because it will be used for public presentations only during the month of September and then take its place in your literature racks after that. Samples 13.4–13.6 illustrate high-quality, eye-catching designs.

# ANNUAL REPORTS

Annual reports have traditionally been the way that corporations tell their stockholders the past year's story. An annual report highlights successes and challenges, and shares information about the financial status of the organization. In some states, public libraries are required by law to publish an annual report that includes certain financial information. Some libraries have chosen simply to publish the financial data and make them available to the public on request; others have seen the public relations potential in publishing an annual report that tells the whole story—not just the financial story. Still other libraries don't necessarily have a legal obligation to publish a report but they recognize their responsibility to provide information to the community, and also understand that an annual report is a good public relations tool; they develop and disseminate a report on an annual basis.

The first thing to decide if you plan to publish an annual report is who the audience is for the report. If you will use it primarily with potential donors and sponsors, you will probably develop a different report from the one that you distribute to all of your library users. For example, you might publish a slick, corporate-looking annual report for your fund-raising efforts and you might also publish some brief information (such as data on use and finances, along with bulleted highlights of the last year) on plastic bookbags that you give to library users at checkout. As with any of your printed publications, format should follow function as you determine what type of annual report to develop.

While publishing an elegant annual report can be a rewarding project and can represent your library in a positive light, be sure that your report is consistent with your message. For example, if your financial data and narrative will indicate that it has been a rough budget year for your library, don't publish an annual report that looks expensive. A simple but elegant, one-color publication on attractive paper is probably more appropriate than a slick, four-color book with photographs.

**SAMPLE 13.7  Pioneer Library System Annual Report**

Reprinted with permission.

**SAMPLE 13.8 Toronto Public Library Annual Report**

Reprinted with permission of the Toronto Public Library.

## ELEMENTS OF AN EFFECTIVE ANNUAL REPORT

No matter what format you choose or who your targeted audience is, certain elements are important for any annual report to be effective.

- **Message**
  Your annual report should be developed around a clear message that guided your past year's public relations efforts. This doesn't mean that every library program or service is mentioned in each year's report, but it is the best way to ensure that your annual report supports your communications goals.
- **Design that matches your corporate identity**
  While you may want your annual report to be special or a little different from the materials that your library publishes on a regular basis, it should be designed based on your corporate identity. It may have some enhancements or include some more elegant elements than your monthly newsletter, but someone should be able to glance at your annual report and know that it is a library publication.
- **Letter from the library director**
  This letter summarizes the past year. It includes highlights and challenges and clearly focuses on your overall public relations message. For example, if you have built your public relations plan around the message that "our library is a community center," then the library director's letter should emphasize that message.
- **Narrative of the year-in-review**
  The length of this narrative is dependent on the size and format of your report, but it is important to call attention to highlights from the past year. Be sure that you don't repeat information from the director's letter; this is a chance to focus on other events and activities. For example, if you had a particularly successful summer reading program or series of adult programs, you might want to highlight the actual events here and the library director's letter might call attention to circulation increases that resulted from those programs.
- **Circulation and other use information**
  This information helps the reader see how your library is being used. It should be presented in an easy-to-understand fashion, such as charts or graphs. You may want to consider different ways to present what happened during the past year, depending on the message you wish to convey. For example, you might want to publish circulation

and gate-count information in bar graphs by branch library to show that the branch library you are planning to close next year has limited use in comparison to other libraries. Or you might want to publish your circulation by collection because it demonstrates the high use of your children's collection—and you are about to mount a fund raising campaign for children's books. This doesn't mean that you should skew the information, but you can publish it in a way that supports your library's message and goals.

- **Financial information**
  If your library is mandated by state law to publish financial information, you likely have little flexibility here. If you are able to make your own decisions about what you publish, however, you should think carefully about your audience. If your report is targeted at the general population, simple financial data focusing on broad general areas will get your message across and not confuse people. If you are trying to show the expenses incurred by each library branch, you might want to break the figures out by facility. An annual report published primarily as a fundraising tool should probably include a list of donors and their levels of contribution so that potential donors have that information readily available. The key is to provide just the amount of financial information that your target audience needs—no more, no less. You may want to "test" your annual report copy with a couple of members of your target audience, a supportive corporate sponsor, or your Friends of the Library president to see if you are taking the right approach.

- **Photographs of library board members**
  If you can afford it, including photographs of your library board members in the annual report is a wonderful way to recognize board members and to remind the public that community members are involved in the operation of the library. You may have to invest in portrait photographs, but they should be usable for several years of annual reports as well as for other publications, such as your newsletter or the newspaper.

## DISSEMINATION

When you determine the target audience for your annual report, think carefully about how you will disseminate it. Mailing an annual report may be more costly than mailing a newsletter, but there is no reason to spend money on an annual report that sits on the shelf in your office and doesn't reach its intended audience. The bookbag idea mentioned earlier in this section is a great way to disseminate an annual report targeted at the public. A bookmark might be another format that would facilitate dissemination. If you publish a traditional booklet annual report, you may want to put a few copies in your library's pamphlet rack for the public to pick up. If your annual report targets corporate sponsors, you may want to mail copies to the past year's contributors and then use the report throughout the next year to solicit other contributions.

Another audience for annual reports is the library community. Establishing a mailing list of other libraries in your state or region and mailing a copy of your report to their directors helps you to build a professional network. These libraries will probably include your library on the mailing list for their reports; this exchange will help you to share ideas and strategies and also will keep you abreast of what is happening in other libraries in your area.

### SCHOOL AND ACADEMIC LIBRARIES

While school and academic libraries may not find it necessary or practical to publish their own annual reports, they should work with their organizations' communications offices to be sure that the library is mentioned in an overall annual report. At the time of the year when the annual report is being developed, a note to the communications director reminding him or her of the library's accomplishments during the past year (and perhaps offering to compile copy and photographs illustrating those accomplishments) might be just what an overworked communications director needs. Even if this strategy isn't successful the first time, over time it may prove fruitful and the library and its accomplishments will be a part of the organization's overall communications focus.

# OTHER PRINT COMMUNICATIONS TOOLS

Of course, the printed materials that your library produces will not be limited to newsletters, brochures, and annual reports. You will probably want to develop flyers, posters, bookmarks, booklists, and other types of printed promotional materials. The development process for each of these items should mirror the processes described for newsletters and brochures. The difference for such items as flyers and bookmarks is that they may be more ephemeral—less permanent items than a service brochure that you will use for several years or a newsletter that you publish on a regular basis.

Developing and using a design template for all of your library's program flyers and posters will save you time and help you maintain the corporate identity that you have established. You need only open that template on your computer, key in the copy for an upcoming program, and make the number of copies that you need. You may wish to develop several templates that all have a similar look but that appeal to different age groups.

## MORE ABOUT USING PHOTOGRAPHS

Photographs are often a great enhancement to a publication. With high-quality reproduction techniques, inexpensive digital photography, and widely available scanners, photographs are much less expensive to use than they once were. Even color photos reproduce well in black and white. Including photographs, particularly of people, in newsletters adds to reader interest. It is exciting, for instance, for parents to see their children pictured at storytime in your monthly newsletter.

You may want to think carefully about using photographs of people or places in your brochures. If you plan to update the brochure only once every few years, the photos can quickly become dated. For example, you may produce a brochure for your library's new grants information center and put a photograph of the center's two staff members right smack in the middle of the brochure's cover. If they both resign in the next two months, your brochure is obsolete. On the other hand, a photo of adorable children at storytime in the brochure for your children's services department may never become dated—even when the adorable children are in junior high!

Before using any photographs of people in your publications, however, be sure you have the appropriate signed releases. You may want to check with your legal department or school district or university central office to determine what type of release is required by law. You want to be particularly careful when taking and publishing photographs of minor children. A sample release for using photos of minors is included as Figure 13.5.

---

**FIGURE 13.5  Sample Photo Release for Minors**

---

Note: Use this sample form only as a guide for developing a photo release for your library. Be sure that the final version is reviewed and approved by legal counsel.

As the parent or legal guardian of _____, a minor, I grant permission to the Anytown Public Library to use his/her picture and name (first name only) and to post the attached picture in the library or on the library's Web site. I understand that no further identification of the minor child will be provided by the library or on the library's Web site.

Parent/Guardian Signature_____ Date _____

Library Representative Signature_____Date_____

---

# TIPS FOR CREATING PRINT PUBLICATIONS

Creating effective print publications requires careful planning and close attention to detail. The process also provides an opportunity to get the creative juices flowing and produce materials that are eye-catching and interesting for your audience. The checklists that follow in Figures 13.6 and 13.7 will help you pay attention to detail while developing an interesting publication. They will remind you of every step in the process even when you are working on a rush job. Use them for every project that you develop. You may wish to add other items to each list to reflect your particular publication development process.

The design checklist in Figure 13.6 is the overall checklist for the development of your publication. It will remind you to check each element of design and copy for consistency and accuracy.

The proofing checklist in Figure 13.7 will help guide you through the process of proofreading your publications. Make three copies of the publication mock-up and attach a proofing checklist to each copy. Then, ask three colleagues to proofread the mock-up and complete the checklist. You will be amazed at the errors they find. For some reason, when a person spends many hours working on a publication, his or her eyes play tricks and miss errors when proofreading. Three other sets of eyes will help ensure accuracy of the information in your publication and avoid embarrassing typos. Of course, you should still proofread the publication yourself. There are certain things, such as the spell-

**FIGURE 13.6  Design Checklist**

Project Description_____

Person Responsible for the Project_____

_____ Is the document page size correct for the final document?

_____ Are all of the margins consistent?

_____ Have you run a spell check on the document?

_____ Are all of the headlines, subheads, and text styles consistent throughout the publication?

_____ Is the spacing throughout the publication consistent?

_____ Have you printed out and proofread the hard copy?

_____ Have you asked at least three colleagues to proofread the hard copy?

_____ Have you completed the proofing checklist?

_____ Have you completed the printing specifications checklist?


Signature                                          Date


Date project transmitted to printer_____
_____

ing of people's names, that only you, as the person responsible for the publication, may be in a position to check.

Completing the printing specifications form in Figure 13.8 will help you remember all the important details that you need to provide to the printer. Fill out the form and then make a photocopy for your files. You can send this completed form to several printers when you solicit bids for your job. It will provide them with all of the pertinent information for quoting the job. Your copy of the form will also help you solve any problems with the job, such as the printer using the wrong paper or folding the project the wrong way. It is your proof of the information that you provided to the printer.

**FIGURE 13.7  Proofing Checklist**

Project Description_____

Person Responsible for the Project_____

| Items to Check | Approved | Changes/Comments |
|---|---|---|
| Address numbers and locations | | |
| Postal information (permits, symbols, return addresses, placement, barcodes) | | |
| Names, titles, and affiliations (printing and accuracy) | | |
| Copy in general (word omissions, grammar) | | |
| Photos | | |
| Captions (Is the right caption under the right photo or art? Is the right name under the right person?) | | |
| Page numbers (Is the sequence correct?) | | |
| Sizes (Check all dimensions.) | | |
| **FINAL PROOFING** Have all the revisions noted above been made?_____ _____ | | |

_____

Signature                                    Date

## FIGURE 13.8  Printing Specifications

Person Responsible for the Project_____

Phone Number/E-mail Address _____


**Date Project Is Needed**

**Details**

Size

Folding (if any)

Number of pages

Number of colors


**Art**

Number of photos

Number of illustrations


**Paper Specifications**

Type and weight

**Quantity**

**Delivery Information**

_____

_____

_____


**Printer Used:**

Name_____

Address_____

Phone_____

# SUCCESS STORY: TORONTO PUBLIC LIBRARY

Toronto Public Library in Canada has developed a coordinated and integrated printed communications campaign that ranges from a four-color annual report to a pocket-sized hours-and-locations brochure. The overall look of all of the library's materials is eye-catching and clean. Of particular note is a set of coordinated service brochures that are designed on a similar template but address different topics, such as the library's Internet services and resources and its children's services. The general service brochure includes information on how to get a library card, as well as circulation policies and key library phone numbers; it is published in both a regular and a large-print version to meet the needs of the library system's older users. The library's Web site address is predominantly displayed on all printed materials, and the look and feel of the printed publications coordinates with the Web site.

A simple one-color bookmark promotes the library's Web services and includes a list of suggested Web sites for readers and writers. A similar bookmark, "What can YOU get for $2?" was used to urge library users to support the library during budget cutbacks.

The library's newsletter, *Shelf Life,* is a four-page monthly publication that boasts the same clean design as the system's other materials. The articles are timely news items on library issues, programs, and events. *What's On* is a quarterly, full-color magazine that includes 70-plus pages of news articles, a calendar of events, information from the Toronto Public Library Foundation, and details regarding such issues as the system's strategic planning process and a renovated branch opening.

It is obvious that Toronto Public Library's overall communications program is a well-planned and implemented effort, and that approach is reflected in the quality of its printed—as well as electronic—communications.

**SAMPLE 13.9 Toronto Public Library Magazine—*What's On?***

Reprinted with permission of the Toronto Public Library.

**SAMPLE 13.10   Toronto Public Library Newsletter—*Shelf Life***

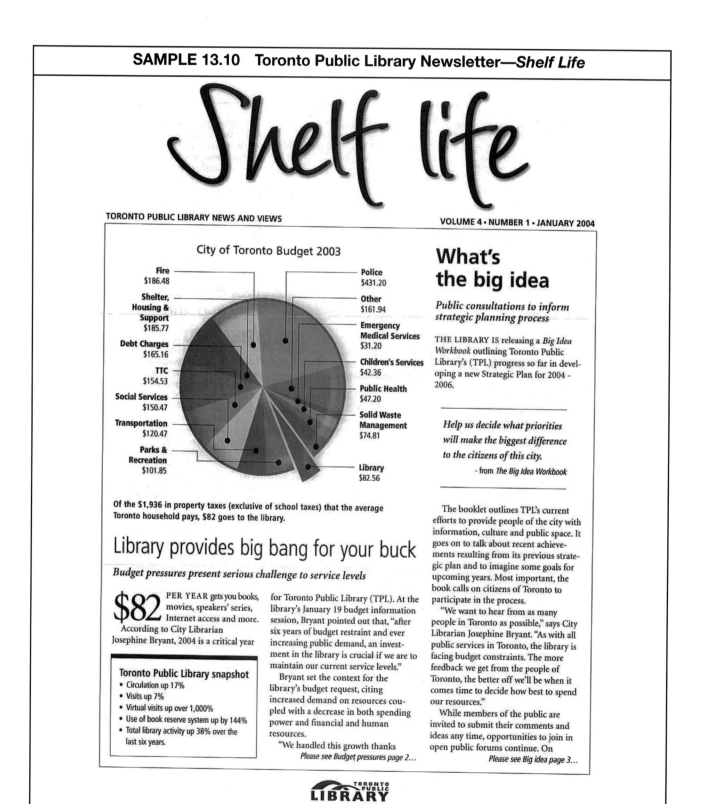

# Shelf life

TORONTO PUBLIC LIBRARY NEWS AND VIEWS

VOLUME 4 · NUMBER 1 · JANUARY 2004

## City of Toronto Budget 2003

Fire $186.48

Shelter, Housing & Support $185.77

Debt Charges $165.16

TTC $154.53

Social Services $150.47

Transportation $120.47

Parks & Recreation $101.85

Police $431.20

Other $161.94

Emergency Medical Services $31.20

Children's Services $42.36

Public Health $47.20

Solid Waste Management $74.81

Library $82.56

Of the $1,936 in property taxes (exclusive of school taxes) that the average Toronto household pays, $82 goes to the library.

## Library provides big bang for your buck

*Budget pressures present serious challenge to service levels*

**$82** PER YEAR gets you books, movies, speakers' series, Internet access and more. According to City Librarian Josephine Bryant, 2004 is a critical year

### Toronto Public Library snapshot
• Circulation up 17%
• Visits up 7%
• Virtual visits up over 1,000%
• Use of book reserve system up by 144%
• Total library activity up 38% over the last six years.

for Toronto Public Library (TPL). At the library's January 19 budget information session, Bryant pointed out that, "after six years of budget restraint and ever increasing public demand, an investment in the library is crucial if we are to maintain our current service levels."

Bryant set the context for the library's budget request, citing increased demand on resources coupled with a decrease in both spending power and financial and human resources.

"We handled this growth thanks

*Please see Budget pressures page 2...*

## What's the big idea

*Public consultations to inform strategic planning process*

THE LIBRARY IS releasing a *Big Idea Workbook* outlining Toronto Public Library's (TPL) progress so far in developing a new Strategic Plan for 2004 - 2006.

*Help us decide what priorities will make the biggest difference to the citizens of this city.*
— from *The Big Idea Workbook*

The booklet outlines TPL's current efforts to provide people of the city with information, culture and public space. It goes on to talk about recent achievements resulting from its previous strategic plan and to imagine some goals for upcoming years. Most important, the book calls on citizens of Toronto to participate in the process.

"We want to hear from as many people in Toronto as possible," says City Librarian Josephine Bryant. "As with all public services in Toronto, the library is facing budget constraints. The more feedback we get from the people of Toronto, the better off we'll be when it comes time to decide how best to spend our resources."

While members of the public are invited to submit their comments and ideas any time, opportunities to join in open public forums continue. On

*Please see Big idea page 3...*

**TORONTO PUBLIC LIBRARY**

Reprinted with permission of the Toronto Public Library.

**SAMPLE 13.11 Toronto Public Library—Your Guide to the Library**

Reprinted with permission of the Toronto Public Library.

**SAMPLE 13.12 Toronto Public Library—Kids Guide to the Library**

Reprinted with permission of the Toronto Public Library.

**SAMPLE 13.13 Toronto Public Library—Question: What's the Difference between your library card and an Internet search engine?**

Reprinted with permission of the Toronto Public Library.

**SAMPLE 13.14 Toronto Public Library—Hours and Locations**

Reprinted with permission of the Toronto Public Library.

**SAMPLE 13.15 Toronto Public Library—What can YOU get for $2? Bookmark.**

# What can YOU get for $2?

- Saturday newspaper
- One ride on the Red Rocket
- Coffee and a muffin
- 60 minutes street parking
- Four stamps

OR $2* will buy you

- **26 days of library service in neigh-bourhood branches AND 53,000 new books**

*on your tax bill

**TORONTO PUBLIC LIBRARY**
www.tpl.toronto.on.ca

Reprinted with permission of the Toronto Public Library.

# SUCCESS STORY: SAINT PAUL PUBLIC LIBRARY AND THE FRIENDS OF THE SAINT PAUL PUBLIC LIBRARY

The Saint Paul Public Library and the Friends of the Saint Paul Public Library launched a multifaceted communications campaign celebrating the reopening of their central library and the simultaneous development of a new library logo and comprehensive identity program. In a truly perfect-world scenario, all of the activities were jointly undertaken by the Saint Paul Public Library and The Friends of the Saint Paul Public Library.

The print materials that were developed to support this campaign and to launch a new identity program are nothing short of stunning. The look of the service brochures—published in languages ranging from English and Spanish to Somali and Hmong—is clean and professional. The four-color glossy brochure on using the central library is first class, but also practical—it includes floor plans for the newly renovated facility, with important locations, such as restrooms, clearly noted.

The materials celebrating the reopening of the Central Library are eye-catching and clean. They incorporate the library's new logo and color scheme into a "Shout it Out!" theme. Examples include a program for the grand opening event, a commemorative booklet on Saint Paul's Central Library (with historical black-and-white photos of the library, a summary of its history, and an acknowledgement of the renewal campaign's donors), and a large button with the library system's new logo and the "Shout it Out" logo. A beautiful poster with a black-and-white photo of the central library in 1920 and a calendar of photos from the history of the Central Library—which is listed on the National Register of Historic Places—are highlights of the celebratory PR materials. Attendees at the celebration took their materials home in a big plastic bookbag imprinted with the two logos and the logos of the campaign's corporate partners.

Finally, a strong kit of press materials was developed to support the campaign. The kit includes press releases and fact sheets on both the rejuvenated Central Library and the new logo.

**SAMPLE 13.16 St. Paul Public Library—Getting the Most from Your Library Brochure**

Courtesy of the Saint Paul Public Library and the Friends of the Saint Paul Public Library.

**SAMPLE 13.17 St. Paul Public Library—Guide to Library Map & Hours**

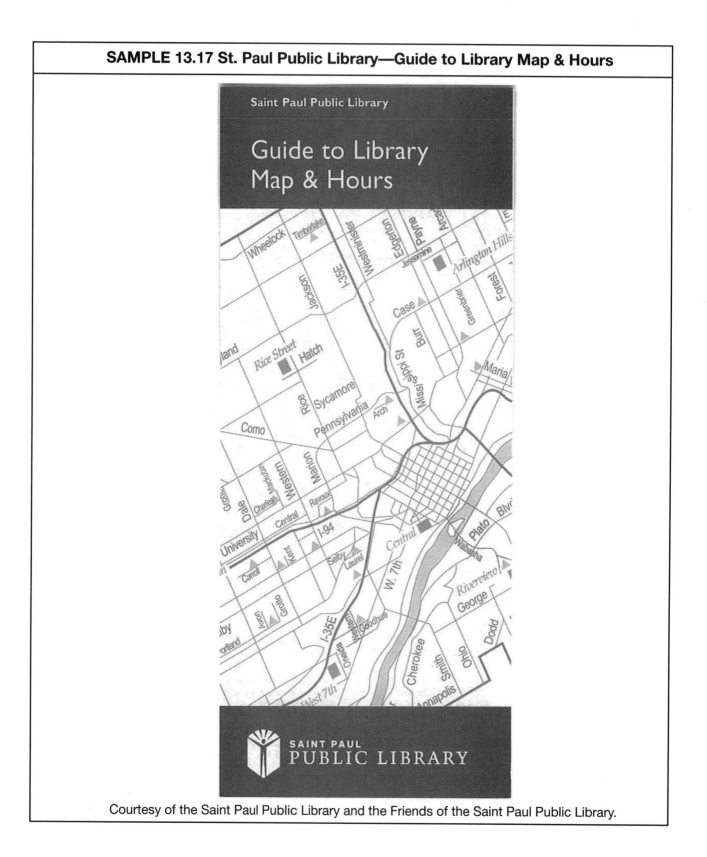

Courtesy of the Saint Paul Public Library and the Friends of the Saint Paul Public Library.

**SAMPLE 13.18 St. Paul Public Library—Using St. Paul's Central Library**

Courtesy of the Saint Paul Public Library and the Friends of the Saint Paul Public Library.

**SAMPLE 13.19 St. Paul Public Library—Threshold: St. Paul Public Library Newsletter**

Courtesy of the Saint Paul Public Library and the Friends of the Saint Paul Public Library.

**SAMPLE 13.20 St. Paul Public Library—Shout it Out! Program from Central Library Reopening Celebration**

# shout it Out!

## Central Library is open!

# WELCOME!

Reopening Ceremony begins at 9:30 am

Emcee: Angela Davis, KSTP-TV anchorperson

Guest Speakers: Mayor Randy Kelly, City Councilmember Chris Coleman, Library Director Carole Williams and Friends President Peter Pearson

Featuring: Highland Park High School Marching Band

**SAINT PAUL
PUBLIC
LIBRARY**

Courtesy of the Saint Paul Public Library and the Friends of the Saint Paul Public Library.

**SAMPLE 13.21  Friends of St. Paul Public Library—Opening New Doors—Annual Report**

Courtesy of the Saint Paul Public Library and the Friends of the Saint Paul Public Library.

# DEVELOP, DESIGN, PRINT, AND DISSEMINATE

Developing, designing, and printing promotional publications is a highly creative process that can be a lot of fun and can help you meet your library's communications goals. Just remember, as you are developing those publications and devoting your library's fiscal and human resources to them, that it is always important to have an effective means of disseminating the publications. The real value of printed promotional materials is only realized when they reach their intended audience. Then you will see the impact of your work as the target audience acts on the compelling promotional information that you have developed.

# 14 OFFERING A WARM, INVITING ENVIRONMENT FOR CUSTOMERS AND STAFF

The key to successful public relations is ensuring that your library's environment supports your communications messages, your mission—your brand! Attention to details, such as customer service and physical image, will help create an environment that will nurture and further your efforts rather than detract from and contradict them.

All the public relations/communications planning and activities in the world will not help you achieve your goal if your library doesn't provide an environment that is conducive to high-quality service and that makes library employees feel valued and trusted. The creation of this environment is driven from the top down in any organization. The library director and board must understand the importance of a positive workplace and devote time and resources to creating it. A school library media specialist must provide an atmosphere of trust for students and faculty members. Academic librarians need to believe that students are their reason for being there—not that an interruption of more important work.

A 2002 American Library Association survey of public library users revealed that 67 percent thought their libraries were "very friendly" and 58 percent thought they were "very comfortable." This is good, but every library's goal should be for 100 percent of all patrons to think the library is a "very friendly" place and "very comfortable."[1]

## VALUE YOUR STAFF

If library staff feel members feel valued by the organization, they will extend that feeling to the library's customers. Providing staff members with the information necessary to do their jobs, rewarding them for doing their jobs well, and supporting them when they make decisions will make your library a place where people want to work and that users want to visit.

## PROVIDE INFORMATION

The most important audience for any organization is its internal audience. Library staff members must know what is happening within the entire organization in order to understand their role in the big picture and to answer questions from the public. It helps to remember that most patrons see every staff member as a "librarian" and think that every staff member is intimately familiar with all of the library's operations. Therefore, it is important that staff understand what is happening in other library departments so that they can make appropriate referrals. There is nothing worse, for example, than calling a library to ask a question and being transferred six times, getting four individuals' voice mail, and then being cut off. If the first person knows where to send the call, this negative experience can be avoided.

You might wish to consider a printed or e-mail internal newsletter to help keep staff informed. An internal newsletter published on a regular basis is an excellent way to share information and provide staff with something to refer to when questions arise. It can also serve as a vehicle for explaining complex issues. If you decide to publish an employee newsletter, have a look at Chapter 10. The information there about electronic newsletters will help you to decide which type of newsletter best meets your internal communications needs.

Regular staff meetings will also help to keep the lines of communication open, particularly if they include an open forum where staff are able to ask questions on any topic. Remember that it is important for library staff to know about anything critical that is happening at your library—before it hits the newspapers.

E-mail now allows instant communication with staff. Consider forwarding all external communications to staff electronically as soon as you release such items to the public. That way your internal audience knows what you have said to the public in your most recent press release or newsletter and isn't caught off guard by comments or questions.

A secure intranet site for staff members is another way to share information internally at your library. If you keep this site constantly fresh and populate it with the important kinds of information that they need to do their jobs, your staff will visit it daily and see it as a valuable resource. Information to post ranges from news about changes in your library's medical insurance to access to an easy-to-navigate calendar of events at all of your libraries. This is also a great location for your internal staff directory.

Providing staff with information via an intranet puts the information at their fingertips when they want to access it. In addition, unlike in the past, you can ensure that they always have the most timely and accurate information—that is, if you have the time and resources to maintain the content.

In fact, timeliness and accuracy are among the biggest challenges of Web communication. Regardless of whether the site is for staff or for the public, if you don't keep the information constantly fresh and up to date, users will not see it as a valuable resource. As a result, what could be one of your library's most effective communications tools very quickly becomes nearly worthless. The lesson here is to consider using Web communication only if you have a plan for refreshing and updating it.

Some libraries implement these internal communications strategies only during times of crisis, such as budget crunches or intellectual freedom challenges. However, just like the tools you use with the public, your internal communications tools will be more effective during times of crisis if they are already a part of day-to-day life in your library.

In the boxes on the next two pages, PR professional Jane Shannon offers great tips for ensuring that your library has a strong internal communications programs. The article, originally published by the Public Relations Society of America, is based on her book *73 Ways to Improve Your Employee Communication Program*.

## PROVIDE REWARDS

Rewarding staff for doing their jobs well is a more complex area. Of course, it would be great if rewards could be in terms of salary increases or bonuses. Often, however, such rewards are not fiscally or organizationally possible, but there are other techniques for rewarding excellence in staff service. Developing and implementing a staff recognition program, such as Employee-of-the-Month, is one way. Recognizing staff and sharing that recognition with library users—through posting a photograph on a bulletin board or adding the employee's name to a plaque—can be a source of great pride for library staff. In addition, allowing staff to explore areas of interest and expertise can often be a reward for exemplary service. If you have a children's librarian who has a particular interest and talent for puppetry, for example, sending her to a puppetry workshop rewards her efforts—and it enhances her skills.

## Seven Simple Ways to Improve Your Employee Communication Program

### By Jane Shannon

Although communicating effectively with employees is a big job, making improvements to your communication program doesn't have to be a big deal. In fact, there are many techniques you can use to enhance your efforts significantly without spending any money or even getting everyone's approval.

In my 30-plus-year career, I've learned that the path to success is often paved with lots of small steps, each of which will help you progress to big goals. Here are seven easy-to-implement ways you can improve your employee communication program, starting now:

### 1. Improve meetings.

Meetings succeed because they're interactive. You're bringing people together to do something they can only do collectively—like solve problems, develop plans, discuss options, and make decisions.

So, send out research ahead of time and include concise summaries. Develop an agenda, and share it. Ask people to come to the meeting with some ideas to share on the meeting topic.

Everyone coming to the meeting should have something valuable to bring. If appropriate, identify what that is in your invitation or when you open the meeting.

And, please, remember the most important rule of all: Meet only when you must.

### 2. Ask what your top managers are reading.

A successful consultant I worked with always knew what business book the president of a client company was reading. She would read the book, and then she made sure that its principles were adhered to in every project she worked on for that client.

She created a brief overview of the book so that anyone who worked for that client could quickly ascend the learning curve.

You can apply this suggestion several ways. Find out what your boss is reading, read it, and give a synopsis to your colleagues. Move up the management food chain, to find out what the boss's boss is reading, and so on. Since knowledge is power, plan to share what you learn as broadly as possible within your company—for example, in a "books in brief" section on your intranet or in your company publication.

### 3. Introduce service journalism into your communications efforts.

In the land of newspapers and magazines (online and print), service journalism is the name of those helpful pieces with titles like, "How to pick the right cell phone for you," or "10 ways you can spend more time with your family" or "Five techniques to avoid the common cold."

In its simplest terms, service journalism means providing a service of value to readers—the writer does all the research and communicates the results to the reader.

Apply this concept to the next press release or article for a company publication or Web site that you write or review. Does the headline say "How to" or Seven Ways to . . . "? If it doesn't, can you rewrite it so it does?

Remember, people read for two reasons, and two reasons only: to get information they believe will be useful and to be entertained. Write a useful piece in an entertaining style, and you're way ahead of the pack.

### 4. Seek inspiration from award winners.

There are times when you look at the award winners in a communication competition, and you think, "Darn, I wish I'd entered my work here — I would have won!"

In any case, you're almost sure to learn something useful by looking at what won and determining why. To do your job well, you need inspiration, and inspiration can come from many sources — magazines, Web sites, movies, and even TV. So, watch, listen, and learn, which leads us ever so nicely to our next suggestion . . .

### 5. Listen to National Public Radio's "All Things Considered."

What's wonderful about this program is that reporters present topics in a way that's interesting, brief, and memorable. (Would that apply to the work you did today?) The show sets a standard you want to strive for.

### 6. Ask great questions.

Here's how: Listen hard to what someone is saying, and then ask the "stupid" questions like: "Why?" "What difference does this make?" "Who wins/who loses?" "Why should we care?" Preface your first question by saying, "This may seem like a basic question, but . . . " and just about every time, you'll receive compliments for asking really good questions.

Smile when you ask a question, so you don't seem confrontational or aggressive. Take notes and ask for clarification or examples if you don't understand an answer. If all else fails, ask, "How would you describe [this topic] to a 12-year-old child?" Experts sometimes know too much to explain things to those of us who aren't as knowledgeable.

### 7. Create opportunities for horizontal communication.

Information flows from the top down in most organizations. Some companies are enlightened enough to want to know what employees think, and then information flows up through the company.

What are you doing to get this information to flow across the organization? E-mail lists and Web sites can help in this process, but face-to-face meetings also represent a great way to help people in similar jobs in different departments or locations share what's working and what's not.

For example, if you host meetings throughout the year to find out how such people are addressing company goals, you could create a great series of articles to help all employees reach company goals and, in the process, show how the work they do helps the company succeed.

Jane Shannon is an independent consultant. This article was based on her new book, *73 Ways to Improve Your Employee Communication Program,* available at *www.davisandco.com*

## PROVIDE SUPPORT

There is a much-repeated story about the returns policy of Nordstrom's, a store praised for its high level of customer service. As the story goes, a customer brought a pair of whitewall tires into a Nordstrom's store to return them. The sales associate accepted the return and gave the customer a refund. However, Nordstrom's is basically an apparel store—they certainly don't carry tires. The story is often told to demonstrate the high level of customer service that Nordstrom's provides, but it also demonstrates the way that the store supports its sales associates' decisions. It is amazing to think that the sales associate felt supported enough to make that decision. Nordstrom's really stands behind the motto, "Use your own best judgment."

Library staff are also often faced with judgment calls: the small child who has $2 in overdue fines and says that his mom is out of work and there is no way he can get the money; the family who comes in to pay for the $500 in library books that were destroyed when their house burned down; the regular patron who insists that he returned two books that show up as overdue on the library's computer. While there needs to be a chain of command for deciding how to handle such situations, the staff members on the front lines also need to be trusted and empowered to make those decisions. And when they do make a decision, they need to be supported—even if you ask them to think about things differently in the future.

The information, rewards, and support that you provide to library staff members will be reflected in their attitude and the quality of their work. They will be willing to go the extra mile—and that "can do" attitude will be consistent with the positive public perception of your library that you are trying to create with your communications efforts.

# CUSTOMER SERVICE

> Smile at your customers. Reserve your best parking spaces for them. Answer the phone before the third ring. These tips come from the American Library Association. They're offered not to patrons who run businesses, but to libraries themselves.[2]

This opening paragraph from a 1995 article in *American Demographics* may hold the key to the survival of libraries as institutions in the age of technology. Let's face it—as technology becomes more and more available and people can access information from their homes, their need for some traditional library services is going to decrease. In addition to providing access to technology, however, librarians help people understand and utilize technology. High-quality customer service is a key to staying relevant.

An essential part of providing high-quality customer service is learning what customers want. Corporations invest large quantities of money in market research to learn what their customers want; then they set out, sometimes successfully, to provide it. Libraries may or may not have the resources to conduct this type of research, but unlike corporate executives who work in an office building far away from their potential customers, librarians have the advantage of being in direct contact with their customers on a daily basis. In addition, as members of an overall community, librarians have constant contact with potential customers in other parts of their lives.

## SPECIAL PEOPLE

Library staff may ask for photographs of "special people," such as board or city council members or the university president, so that they know who deserves "special treatment." While this request may be well intentioned, fulfilling it can detract from high-quality customer service. If the library staff treats every patron as if he or she is a member of the city council or the university president, everyone will receive "special service."

The old adage says, "What goes around comes around." A 1995 column in *The Christian Science Monitor* describes a young school library user in the Seattle area and the relationship that he built with his school librarian, who wrote the article. The boy is described to be like any other student. However, that student was Bill Gates, current president of Microsoft Corporation.[3] Today, Gates is one of the nation's leading philanthropic contributors to library programs. Perhaps his positive experiences as a child had some influence over his philanthropic decisions as an adult.

Of course, not every patron who has a positive experience at your library will someday be in a position to contribute millions of dollars. But you never know, do you?

Just remember that your patrons already contribute to the support of your library and its services—as taxpayers they fund your public library, as students their tuition helps fund your academic library. They deserve high-quality service and their experiences with your service will influence their decisions about future funding.

# CAN A LIBRARY BE LIKE A BOOKSTORE?

In a recent article in the *Boston Globe*, Patricia Lambert, director of the Dedham (Mass.) Public Library, said, "We need to be like Barnes & Noble. That's really whom we should be looking at as a concept."[4]

Lambert is right on! As a library today, who is your major competitor? Maybe the Internet, but as a destination, your biggest competitors chain are the friendly, inviting chain bookstores that have sprung up in great numbers over the last decade. Granted their materials can't be checked out for free, but the coffee cafes and comfortable seating areas makes it easy for customers to spend hours at Barnes & Noble or Borders looking through books and other materials. And at a bookstore, it is often easy to find a copy of the current bestseller on the shelf—rather than having to wait on a list with other library patrons.

But your library isn't a for-profit business. How would you possibly ever be like Barnes & Noble or Borders? Well, just like a bookstore, you have physical space and customer policies. You can create an inviting physical environment and develop customer-friendly policies that make your library a place that people want to visit, hang out in, and return to again and again.

## WARM, INVITING PHYSICAL ENVIRONMENT

The physical environment of your library will support or detract from your communications efforts. A clean, well-cared-for library looks valued; chances are that your patrons will treat it with care. A messy environment with unemptied trash cans and worktables littered with books appears unvalued, and will cause patrons to treat the furniture and the rest of the physical environment without much care. If books fall on the floor, why pick them up? The place is already a mess.

A warm, inviting library also has places for people to gather—both in small and large groups. And places for people to go off by themselves and read or think quietly. You may immediately think that you can't afford to do this type of renovation, but often it just requires thinking about rearranging your current furniture or perhaps creating some small sitting areas with furniture from a second-hand store or donated by your Friends of the Library. (One note: check out any donations first and be sure that they will fit in your library and are in good enough shape to sustain patron use.)

Even more important to the atmosphere in any library is the signage. Restrictive signage with lots of negatives—don'ts and nos—will provoke an immediate negative reaction from library users. In an effort to protect their materials and physical environment, libraries have a tendency to use such signage.

It is important to have clear, effective signage that helps patrons use the library. Shelf signs and directional signage are critical for the independent library user. When developing wording for any sign, however, think carefully about the message. Even if what you are trying to communicate is restrictive, you can put it in a positive light. Rather than posting signs that say "No food or drink," post signs that says "Food and drink may be enjoyed in the student lounge." Or in your special collection room, signs that read "Pencils only" are much more positive than "No pens." In both examples, the messages are exactly the same, yet the positive statements evoke more positive reactions.

Lambert says that one of her first decisions at the Dedham Public Library was to take down the sign that said, "No food or drink." She goes on to say, "You can eat and drink in Barnes & Noble. You should be able to do that at the library."[5] Now you may not want to allow food and drink in all areas of your library, but are there spaces where it would be okay? And considering the fact that everyone today carries around a bottle of water, is it realistic to restrict it at the library? Twenty-years ago, when I first started working in libraries, a good friend of mine didn't like to visit me there because of what she called the "pop detectors." Her experience was that every time she went to visit a library, she got in trouble for having a soda with her. Subsequently she was never much of a library user. However, today as a mother with two small children, she is a frequent visitor to the library; she credits the more lenient policies as making it a much more pleasant and inviting experience for both her and the children.

Watch out for sign pollution. Sometimes in an effort to be helpful and provide lots of information, libraries put up so many signs that patrons are confused. Keep the quantity of signs to a minimum and keep the message simple. Stick with signs that provide direction and use other communications tools, such as brochures and newsletters, to communicate policy and share program and service information.

## IMAGE

The bottom line is that public relations is about image! It is about the image that your library projects and, therefore, it is about the image projected by you and by every member of your library's staff. This can be a touchy area to discuss because it is related to people's individual style and behavior. But when your staff carefully consider their personal image and its impact on their job success and the success of the library, they will probably admit that changes—small or large—will help them progress toward their personal goals and help the library progress toward its public relations goals.

## A PROFESSION WITH AN IMAGE PROBLEM?

Is librarianship a profession with an image problem? If you read the professional journals and follow the Internet listservs and newsgroups, you would certainly think so. Librarians are constantly talking about the profession's image problem and what the media and advertisers do to perpetuate it. But, let's be frank! Do lawyers have an image problem? Do doctors? Have you heard more insulting jokes in the past year about lawyers or about librarians?

In many ways, librarians and libraries have an image advantage. While comic strips and television shows may sometimes perpetuate the image of the old-lady librarian with a bun and half-glasses and a QUIET sign on the front of her desk, ask anyone you meet on the street how they feel about libraries. Most likely people will tell you a warm, fuzzy story from their childhood or confess to you some deep, dark secret about an overdue book. In general, our society places a positive value on libraries and books, and librarians are in a position to capitalize on that part of our culture. So, don't spend your time behind the desk, complaining about the image of librarians, and, in the end, perpetuating it—get out on the other side, meet and greet the public, and capitalize on the cultural value that our society places on libraries.

## DRESS FOR SUCCESS

Dressing for success is important in this society—ask any lawyer preparing a client for court. In *The Pursuit of Wow!* Tom Peters recommends that readers develop their own style and "show care and show confidence."[6] Be sure that the clothes you wear match the task you are completing. A power suit is as inappropriate for moving the library collection as shorts are for a library board meeting. Think carefully about the image your clothes project based on the situation. And, when in doubt, dress up! People will know that you think what you are doing is important—important enough to take time and care with your appearance.

This advice may sound trivial, but people will perceive your library in a much more positive light if they see staff who care about their appearance. Patrons will believe that they are in an important place—because the people who work there think it is important.

# DEVELOP YOUR COMMUNICATIONS SKILLS

Developing your personal communications skills and helping other library staff to develop their skills will contribute to the success of your public relations efforts. Effective communication is a growing edge for many people and lots of resources are available for improving those skills. Toastmasters and the Dale Carnegie course are just two options that may be available in your local area. In addition, there may be trainers in your community who can provide ongoing staff development training for your library in the areas of image and communicating effectively.

As you and your library staff become more effective communicators, you will find that the job of telling your library's story is a more enjoyable one. Participating in radio and television interviews will be fun and a challenge, instead of a cause of knocking knees and sweaty palms. Even dealing with patrons (particularly the difficult ones) across a public service desk will become an easier task. Improving the communications skills of library staff will ultimately improve customer service.

# SCAN YOUR SURROUNDINGS

After you have developed your public relations/communications goal, take a walk through your library. Look at the furniture, the paint, the signage, the demeanor of the library staff. Think about all of these environmental influences in terms of the impact that they can have, and consider whether they support or detract from your communications goal. Then, set about changing those that detract from your efforts—and enhancing those that support your efforts. When community members, students, or patrons who have learned about your library decide to visit, they will encounter an environment and staff that support the message you have communicated.

# CONCLUSION

Libraries and the environments that house them have changed a great deal—for the better—since the 1990s. Gone are the staid, lofty looking buildings with high service desks and aisle after aisle of stacks. Some of this change has been the result of fewer reference volumes and more computer terminals. But it is also the result of a change in perception on the behalf of both the library community and the public about the type of space a library needs to have and its role in the community.

In spring 2004, *New York Times* architectural critic Herbert Muschamp reviewed the new Seattle Public Library. The headline: "The Library that Puts on Fishnets and Hits the Disco." His description of the building: "Seattle gets a rock-candy masterpiece, wrapped in glittering crystal and folded like origami."[7] That's definitely not your grandfather's library, is it?

# NOTES

1. "Internet Use in Public Libraries," American Library Association, 2002. *www.ala.org*
2. Tibbett L. Speer, "Libraries from A to Z," *American Demographics* (September 1995): 48.
3. Blanche Caffiere, "Hints of Future Heights in Extraordinary Little Boy," *Christian Science Monitor* (July 20, 1995): 17.
4. Maria Cramer, "In Changing Times, Libraries Test New Survival Strategies," *Boston Globe*, March 11, 2004.
5. Ibid.
6. Tom Peters, *The Pursuit of WOW! Every Person's Guide to Topsy-Turvy Times* (New York: Random House, 1994), 42.
7. Herbert Muschamp, "The Library that Puts on Fishnets and Hits the Disco," *New York Times* (May 16, 2004) Section 2, 1.

# 15 PROMOTING YOUR LIBRARY THROUGH PROGRAMS, SPECIAL EVENTS, AND EXHIBITS

While you may view presenting programs and hosting special events as contributions to fulfilling the library's overall mission, you should also view such activities as great public relations opportunities. You can use these activities to tell your library's story, to attract new audiences to your library, to make new connections in the community, and to have a lot of fun!

Programs and special events tell your library's story—both directly and indirectly. Sometimes the program or special event will blatantly communicate the message; at other times it will communicate it subliminally. For example, if your library's message is to encourage use of its local history collection, a series of adult programs on topics related to the resources in the collection directly communicates your public relations message. On the other hand, if you want to communicate that your library is a community center, you might encourage a variety of community groups to sponsor programs in your meeting room. While the topics of these programs may or may not be related to materials in your library's collection, such programming quietly communicates your "library as community center" message.

One advantage of carefully planned programs and special events is that they bring people into your library. For example, a series of evening workshops appealing to parents of preschoolers, with an accompanying storytime, is an effective strategy for helping parents develop the "library habit" and will, ultimately, increase your library's circulation and gate count. Or, if you want parents to see the resources and excitement of your school library media center, hosting a special evening reception during National Library Week that showcases student work may be one strategy for communicating your message.

In addition to reaching out to the audience targeted for the event, public relations activities promoting your library's programs and special events also have the possibility of reaching a broader audience. Senior citizen likely don't have any children attending the neighborhood elementary school, but when they see an article in the newspaper promoting your school library's National

Library Week events, they are assured that their tax dollars are being spent in a positive way. Members of the city council might not be targeted for your teen summer reading program, but when they see the flyers publicizing it, they are pleased that the city library is offering positive activities for teenagers during the summer.

# WHAT ARE PROGRAMS?

Library programs disseminate information to participants. They are public relations tools, but they are also part of any library's services to the community. Therefore, it is important that library programming not be planned in isolation by the individual or team responsible for public relations. Library staff in service areas should be involved in the program planning process. In fact, they may bring program ideas to the public relations team and ask for help in developing and promoting them. For example, the business reference librarian at your library may want to do a series of programs on the services and resources that your library can provide to small businesses. She might be willing to design the content for the programs, but be stuck when it comes to targeting audiences or developing promotional materials. This is an excellent opportunity for staff collaboration.

As the public relations manager, you might know that one of your librarians has a deep personal interest in the history of the region. You can approach him and, with a bit of encouragement, help him develop a public program that showcases your library's local history materials and reaches out to community members who are interested in learning more about your city's roots.

## TYPES OF PROGRAMS

The types of programs that libraries can present go far beyond the traditional story hours and book discussion groups. Libraries host informational presentations on a myriad of topics, sponsor film festivals and special showings of movies, provide free concert opportunities—the possibilities are endless. Computer and Internet training programs seem to be on the calendar of every public library today. These workshops provide customers with important free training and also ensure that they are able to use the library's online resources.

Library programs can be geared for a wide variety of audiences, too—children, young adults, parents, senior citizens, small busi-

---

**Sources for Great Library Programming Ideas**

---

Benton, Gail and Trisha Waichulaitis. *Low-Cost, High Interest Programming: Seasonal Events for Preschoolers.* New York: Neal-Schuman, 2004.

Honnold, RoseMary. *101+ Teen Programs that Work.* New York: Neal-Schuman, 2003.

Honnold, RoseMary. *More Teen Programs that Work.* New York: Neal-Schuman, 2005.

Honnold, RoseMary and Saralyn A. Mesaros. *Serving Seniors: A How-To-Do-It Manual for Librarians.* New York: Neal-Schuman, 2004.

Lear, Brett W. *Adult Programs in the Library.* Chicago: ALA Editions, 2002.

Reid, Rob. *Cool Story Programs for the School-Age Crowd.* Chicago: ALA Editions, 2004.

Wilson, Patricia Potter and Leslie Roger. *Center Stage: Library Programs that Inspire Middle School Patrons.* Littleton: Libraries Unlimited, 2002.

---

ness owners, corporate executives, homemakers, college students. Again, the possibilities are endless. The sidebar above includes titles of some of the newest and best titles available to help you develop great programming ideas for library users of all ages.

When planning successful library programs, the key is to think creatively and try not to duplicate the effort of other community organizations. For example, if your library would like to offer a program on how to build bluebird houses and attract bluebirds, do some research to find out if anyone else in the community offers a similar program. You may discover that the Audubon Society has offered that program twice in the past; planning and hosting your own program on that topic would duplicate its efforts. You may also discover that the Audubon Society is looking for a location for this year's program and you might offer them your library's meeting room for their presentation. In addition, if you offer to help promote the program and develop a booklist of ornithology-related topics, the society might be willing to list your library as a cosponsor for the program. This turns out to be a positive solution for everyone—you don't spend time developing a program that already exists and the Audubon Society gets a free location and increased promotion for a program they were considering doing anyway. Best of all, you get yet another chance to promote your library's services and resources.

At other times, you may discover, for example, that a program is already being sponsored by another organization and that they already have a location. This is your opportunity to offer to develop a resource list for distribution at the program. Such a list promotes your library and highlights its resources on the program topic. Maybe your high school's history department is sponsoring a major history fair and essay competition. You can contact the chair of the history department and offer to do a list of books and online resources that support the topics for the history fair and maybe offer extended library hours during the two weeks that the students are writing their essays. Again, you aren't duplicating their efforts—you are demonstrating how the library supports them.

## PROGRAM DEVELOPMENT AND PLANNING

To communicate effectively for your library, programs must be carefully planned and effectively promoted. It is futile to plan an informative adult or children's program if you don't put equal effort into recruiting an audience for it. On the other hand, you don't want to promote a program until you are sure that you can give participants what your promotional materials promise. Time is precious and when you ask people to attend a program, you are asking them to give up some of their time. If participants don't feel the program they attended was worth their time, you may create a negative public perception of your library; the next time you try to host a similar program, they may dismiss it without even considering the topic or presenters. In addition, if community volunteers develop a wonderful program but no one shows up because you failed to promote the program, you have damaged their perception of your library also. You must commit time and energy to both content planning and promotion for a program. If you cannot make this commitment, you should consider using a different communications tool.

On the other hand, just like any aspect of public relations/communications, program planning and promotion is not an exact science. You can plan the best program in the world, and promote it in a targeted and informative way, but if, for example, there is a blizzard on the night of the program, the success of the program in terms of attendance is really out of your control. There are things that you can do, however, when planning your program to help ensure your success.

---

**FIGURE 15.1 Program/Special Event Development Form**

Program/special event name:

Program/special event content or activity:

Public relations goal or objective related to this program/special event:

Need: Why should we plan this program/special event?

Audience: Who are we targeting with this program/special event? What age range?

Format: What format should the program/special event take? Should it be held in the morning, afternoon, or evening? Should it be lecture-only or interactive? Will there be a movie or other performance?

Resources: What resources are required to present this program/special event? Does the presenter or performer require a fee? Approximately how much staff time will be consumed by planning, promoting, and hosting the program/special event? Will we need to rent any equipment? Will we need to rent a space to hold the program/special event in?

---

Before you decide to do a program, make sure it has a specific purpose and relationship to your public relations goal. Programming for the sake of programming (or a special event planned with no clear goal) has the potential to send you on a damaging detour on the road to your public relations goal.

Need, audience, format, and necessary resources are the first things that you should think about when planning any library program. Each time you consider holding a program you should complete a program development form similar to the example in Figure 15.1.

After completing the form, think carefully about the program you are considering. Will you get enough bang for your buck? Is the potential audience large enough to justify the staff time and other resources that the program will need? Does the program help you achieve your public relations goal? This is basically a judgment call. If you or your programming planning committee answers "yes" to these questions, then planning must begin in earnest.

Plenty of lead time for planning and promotion is a key to the success of your program. At least three months is usually best. Sometimes, however, you may get an opportunity to present a program that is too good to ignore even though you won't have sufficient planning time. Maybe a best-selling author is visiting your town and is willing to make a presentation, or a popular jazz group wants to donate a performance. You may decide the opportunity is worth working overtime to pull off the program. In general, however, you will want to work with 12 weeks of lead time.

Planning a program requires certain basic steps. If you follow these steps with sufficient lead time, you have a good chance of success. A basic program/special event planning checklist, based on 12 weeks of lead time, appears in Figure 15.2.

## PROGRAM EVALUATION

Evaluation of your programs will provide you with an important tool for future program planning. Using a simple evaluation form, you can learn what participants thought about your program and what other types of programs they would like your library to offer. Keeping your evaluation form short and easy to complete will increase the number of participants who fill it out. Think carefully about what you want to learn, and then design your evaluation form to get that information. See Figure 15.3 for a sample program evaluation form.

If you ask your participants to take the time to complete this evaluation, take their input seriously. Compiling the results and relying on them to plan your library's future programming is important to your success. Your result will be library programs that have developed from community interest and need. Through continual evaluation you will learn what you are doing right and what you need to improve in future programs.

Plus, you may want to use some of the positive comments to promote future events. Allow attendees to complete the evaluation anonymously, but also ask them if they give you permission to use their comments.

---

**FIGURE 15.2 Program/Special Event Planning Checklist**

**12 weeks before program/special event**
Complete Program/Special Event Development Form.
Determine date, time, and location for program/special event. Check that there aren't any
    competing activities planned for the same date.
Secure any necessary funding for the program/special event.
Develop promotional plan for program/special event.

**8 weeks before program/special event**
Confirm in writing presenters and other involved participants.
Decide if the program/special event has any direct links to materials in your library's col-
    lection and whether you will prepare a booklist or display for the function.
Develop evaluation form.

**1 week before program/special event**
Contact presenter to confirm audiovisual and other needs.
Make name badges for presenters and other special guests.

**3 hours before program/special event**
Check space to be sure that audiovisual equipment is set up and working, and that room
is set up correctly.

**1 hour before program/special event**
Be available to greet presenters and participants.

**Day after the program/special event**
Write thank-you notes to everyone who helped make the program/special event possible.
Compile results of evaluation and analyze the implications for the future.

---

**FIGURE 15.3 Program Evaluation Form**

Please circle the number that most closely describes your evaluation of this program.

This program was informative.

| Very | | Moderately | | Not at all |
|---|---|---|---|---|
| 5 | 4 | 3 | 2 | 1 |

This program was entertaining.

| Very | | Moderately | | Not at all |
|---|---|---|---|---|
| 5 | 4 | 3 | 2 | 1 |

**Figure 15.3** *continued*

I would recommend this program to my friends.

| Very | | Moderately | | Not at all |
|---|---|---|---|---|
| 5 | 4 | 3 | 2 | 1 |

The location for this program was convenient.

| Very | | Moderately | | Not at all |
|---|---|---|---|---|
| 5 | 4 | 3 | 2 | 1 |

The time for this program was convenient.

| Very | | Moderately | | Not at all |
|---|---|---|---|---|
| 5 | 4 | 3 | 2 | 1 |

Overall, I rate the program as

| Excellent | | Average | | Poor |
|---|---|---|---|---|
| 5 | 4 | 3 | 2 | 1 |

Other programs that I would like to attend (please list):

_____

_____

_____

Other comments:

_____

_____

_____

Please add my name and address to your mailing list for future programs:

Name _____

Address _____

City, State, Zip Code _____

_____

You have permission to use my comments in Anytown Public Library promotional materials.

Signature _____ Date_____

Thank you for attending Anytown Public Library's program!

# WHAT ARE SPECIAL EVENTS?

Special events may or may not be an opportunity to share information with participants. They may or may not raise funds for your library. All special events, however, are "special"—they are unique or different activities from what your library offers on a regular basis. A special event occurs once and has a particular purpose. Examples of special events include groundbreaking or ribbon-cutting ceremonies for a new library building, a reception or banquet, or a special fund-raising event, such as a theater benefit or a fun run.

If planned carefully and used sparingly, special events can put the community spotlight on your library and can reward library users, attract new users, and, in some cases, raise funds for your library. However, if the event is a disappointment for attendees, or if it seems as if your library is hosting a special event every week, the impact of this communications tool will be diminished. You rarely have a second chance with a special event.

Before you begin to plan a special event, ask yourself if it is truly worthy of your time and energy and the focus of the community. Think about how long it has been since your library sponsored a similar event. What was the community reaction? What should you do differently this time? For example, cutting the ribbon on your new library building definitely merits a celebration, media coverage, and lots of hoopla. In contrast, the addition of 250 new titles to your video collection might be celebrated in a different, more low-key manner, such as a newsletter article or a special in-house display. Don't "cry wolf" with your special events. When your library says it has something to celebrate or focus on, make sure it is worthy. Planning special events takes lots of time and hard work, too; be sure that the purpose of the event merits the effort.

## SPECIAL EVENT DEVELOPMENT AND PLANNING

The same steps to plan a program for your library should be used to plan a special event. The key is to give yourself plenty of lead time and to be sure that there is a relationship between your event and your public relations/communications goal.

No detail is too small to write down and assign someone to be responsible for. Careful attention to detail will help make your event special. It will be obvious to participants that nothing was overlooked and that this event is very important to your library and your community.

## SPECIAL EVENT SPONSORSHIPS

Special events offer local businesses and corporations the opportunity for relationship building through sponsorships. By providing support for your event, either in terms of fiscal or human resources, a business or corporation can, by association, cash in on your library's goodwill and good reputation—and you get to put on your event. If you work with a sponsor, you can develop a mutually beneficial relationship.

Once you have decided that you want to have a special event, you may want to approach a local business or corporation for sponsorship. Think carefully about who might be most interested in your event. For example, the local electric power utility might have expressed a strong interest in children and education and you are planning a huge end-of-summer reading rally. Sounds like a perfect match! Develop the plan for your event, put a price tag on it, and make an appointment to see the appropriate person at the company. Better yet, do you know someone who has a connection with the company? Is one of your board members on the company's board? Explore all of these connections before going blithely off to pitch your event.

Also, think carefully about whether the company that you are approaching can actually afford your event. Design your proposal in such a way to indicate that you are offering the opportunity for sole sponsorship, but that, if necessary, you will work with multiple sponsors. Develop and pitch a realistic budget. Above all, don't undersell the value of being associated with your library and your event. Some events-marketing consultants recommend putting a price tag on being associated with your library's name. Your level of involvement with corporate sponsors and the actual promotional market may not be big enough or sophisticated enough to merit this type of sponsorship fee, however. A proposal outline for a special event sponsorship appears in Figure 15.4.

Make sure that the recognition that you provide sponsors is commensurate with their contribution. If a sponsor gives you $500, for example, to fund an event that costs $5,000, putting its name on a billboard is probably excessive. In addition, if you begin offering a lot of corporate-sponsored events, you may want to develop a plan of levels of sponsorship. Such a plan ensures equity in your recognition program. Sponsorship levels are usually based on dollar amounts. A simple example appears in Figure 15.5.

**FIGURE 15.4 Special Event Sponsorship Proposal Outline**

**Name of special event:**

**Purpose:**

**Date, time, location:**

**Description of event:** Include names of participants, types of activities that will be included, etc. For example, if you are planning a fun run, discuss who your target audience will be. If you are planning an open house, describe the activities that will be happening in the library during the open house, who the celebrity guests might be, and who will be providing the entertainment.

**Promotional plan for event:** Develop your promotional plan before approaching the sponsor. This plan will help the sponsor see the opportunities for recognition of sponsorship.

**Sponsor recognition opportunities:** Detail the times and places where the sponsor will be recognized. Examples include listing the sponsor's name on all special event promotional materials and/or introducing the sponsor's representatives during the event. Be very specific about the types of recognition you are prepared to provide.

**Budget:** Include the total budget for the event—not just the amount that you are asking the sponsor to fund. Include the time and materials that your library is providing for the event as "in-kind." This itemization shows the sponsor that the event is important enough for the library to dedicate resources to it.

## SPECIAL EVENT EVALUATION

While it is important to evaluate your library's special events, the activities involved may not be conducive to the completion of a formal evaluation form. It is hard to ask participants at an open house or a fun run to fill out a form. In fact, it may detract from the festive atmosphere and your completion rate may suffer. The easiest way to evaluate a special event may be to set some goals and then evaluate the success of the event in relationship to these goals.

---

**FIGURE 15.5 Sample Sponsorship Recognition Program**

## MIDDLEFIELD PUBLIC LIBRARY
## SPONSORSHIP RECOGNITION PROGRAM

**Platinum Sponsor ($10,000–$25,000)**
- Name on plaque in Main Library lobby
- Special sticker for corporate officers' library cards recognizing their support of the library
- Name of corporation included on all program or event promotional materials and on library Web site
- Announcement of sponsorship at program or event
- Listed as Platinum Sponsor once per year in monthly newsletter

**Gold Sponsor ($5,000–$9,999)**
- Special sticker for corporate officers' library cards recognizing their support of the library
- Name of corporation included on all program or event promotional materials and on library Web site
- Announcement of sponsorship at program or event
- Listed as Gold Sponsor once per year in monthly newsletter

**Silver Sponsor ($2,000–$4,999)**
- Name of corporation included on all program or event promotional materials and on library Web site
- Announcement of sponsorship at program or event
- Listed as Silver Sponsor once per year in monthly newsletter

**Bronze Sponsor ($500–$1,999)**
- Announcement of sponsorship at program or event
- Listed as Bronze Sponsor once per year in monthly newsletter

**Sponsor ($100–$499)**
- Listed as Sponsor once per year in monthly newsletter

---

For example, if your school library is having an open house, you could set the following goals:

- To have a minimum of 125 parents attend the event.
- To have the community newspaper and at least one television station cover the event.

Then you can measure your success against these goals. Asking attendees to sign a guest book is a nice way to measure your attendance, and you can monitor media coverage of the event. In addition, you may want to add some qualitative information to your evaluation of the event. When you meet to discuss what worked about your event and what didn't, ask school faculty members and students to share their impressions of the event. This information will help you evaluate the success of your event and thus will help you with future planning.

## DON'T FORGET YOUR FRIENDS

While your Friends organization may plan and host its own programs and special events, members may also be interested in helping out with the library's programs and special events. Such involvement gives them the opportunity to promote membership in their organization and it is a chance for them to contribute their time.

Friends members can serve as hosts at a library program, handing out programs and welcoming attendees. They can serve punch at a reception honoring the new school librarian or they can serve as aids during an Internet training workshop, circulating to help attendees during the workshop. As you plan your programming, be sure to check in with the Friends and find out if they are interested in participating.

# PROMOTING PROGRAMS AND SPECIAL EVENTS

You promote programs and special events to get people to act. You want them to participate in your program or to attend your special event. In most cases, you aren't simply trying to create a positive perception of your program or event. Therefore, you will want to develop a promotional plan that will encourage people to take some type of action.

## CHOOSING YOUR PROGRAM/SPECIAL EVENT PROMOTIONAL TOOL

All of the communications tools described in this book are possibilities for promoting your library's program or event. You will have to decide which ones to use based on the audience you want to reach, the lead time you have before the program or event, and the budget that is available to you.

The key to encouraging people to attend your program or spe-

---

**FIGURE 15.6 Program/Special Event Promotional Materials Information Checklist**

- Clear description of the program or event
- Date and time
- Location
- Cost (if any)
- How to register (if required)
- Age that the program or event is geared to (especially important for children's programs)
- Where to call/e-mail for more information; Web site for event
- Event sponsors

---

cial event is to be sure that whatever communications tool you select includes all of the information that a person needs in order to attend your program or event. Use the checklist in Figure 15.6 to review your promotional materials.

Each time you design a flyer or brochure for a program or event, review it against this information checklist or an expanded one that you may develop. It may seem obvious that you would include all of this information, but even the most experienced event planner or public relations person can tell you about a time when critical information was omitted from promotional material—and the unfortunate result.

Another important factor in promoting your library's program or special event will be to think carefully about where the promotional materials should be distributed. Flyers promoting summer reading are a natural for distribution through the public schools. If your university library is hosting an open house, flyers should be stuffed in student mailboxes or a broadcast message sent to their e-mail accounts. You probably won't reach the audience you want if you just make the promotional materials available in your library—particularly if one of your goals to encourage library use by nonusers.

## EXHIBITS AND DISPLAYS

Like programs and special events, library exhibits and displays are both an information service and a public relations activity. They can help increase your library's visibility and promote its services and collections. In addition, by allowing schools and other community groups to exhibit in your library, you can increase library use and bring in new audiences. Most parents will want to visit the library to see their child's artwork displayed there, even if they don't normally use the library. While they are there, they may see the available resources and services and change their perception of your library. In some cases, they may even become library users.

Before you begin to plan an exhibits program for your library, decide whether you have the space available. You need room for both the exhibit and for participants to view it. The exhibits that you book for your library may come with display boards or you may have to look into building or purchasing some for your own use.

You must decide the goal of your exhibits program. Where does it fit in terms of your overall public relations/communications plan? What goals and objectives does it help you fulfill? Again, like all other communications tools, an exhibits program needs to have a purpose and a plan.

If you decide that an exhibits program will help you achieve your public relations/communications goals, the next step is to develop an exhibits policy. The principles in the American Library Association's "Exhibit Spaces and Bulletin Boards: An Interpretation of the Library Bill of Rights" will help you develop this policy. The policy should include your procedure and criteria for accepting exhibits, the length of time that exhibits will be on display, and the security and insurance that your library will or will not provide for exhibits.

Finally, you need to develop an application for exhibit space. The application will help you select exhibits for display and can also be used when you are promoting the fact that your library has exhibit space available. A sample application for exhibit space appears in Figure 15.7.

## EVALUATING YOUR EXHIBITS PROGRAM

You will want to evaluate the success of your exhibits program on an annual basis. One way to get continual qualitative feedback on your exhibits is to provide a guest book for visitors to sign and write comments in. This information will help you plan future exhibits and decide which exhibits were particularly successful and should be booked again. In addition, you may wish to send your exhibitors an evaluation form after hosting their exhibit. Their feedback may also help you with future planning.

Another way to evaluate the success of an exhibit is to com-

---

**Figure 15.7 Application for Exhibit Space**

Name _____

Organization (if any) _____

Address _____

Phone _____ Fax _____ E-mail _____

Preferred dates for exhibit _____

Title of exhibit _____

Number of pieces in exhibit _____

Average size of pieces_____

Have you exhibited at Middlefield Public Library in the past?_____

If yes, what dates?_____

I have read and will abide by Middlefield Public Library's exhibits policy. I understand that Middlefield Public Library does not provide any insurance or security for its exhibits. My artwork will be displayed at my own risk.

Signature_____ Date_____

Return to:  Middlefield Public Library Exhibits
123 Main Street
Middlefield, Ohio 44444

### DO NOT WRITE BELOW THIS LINE

Application status:

_____ Accepted             _____ Denied

Date booked _____

Date letter mailed to applicant_____

---

pare your library's gate count during the exhibit to the gate count for the same dates in the previous year. If there is a significant increase, this increase might be linked to the popularity of your exhibit.

## CONCLUSION

Well-planned and well-executed programs, special events, and exhibits, such as the ones included as examples in this chapter, are great opportunities to tell your library's story. They provide an important information resource for your community while furthering your public relations goals. They bring people into your library who might not normally visit, giving them a chance to see the services and materials that your library provides. Best of all, programs, special events, and exhibits have the potential to enhance the public's perception of your library and to create new library users.

## PROGRAMMING EXAMPLES

### PROGRAMMING EXAMPLE 1: MILL VALLEY PUBLIC LIBRARY, MANN COUNTY, CALIF.

The Mill Valley Public Library doesn't have branch libraries so communicating to the public about where and when an event takes place is less of a challenge than for the library's neighbors across the Golden Gate Bridge—San Francisco Public Library. However, as a small library serving a small community—about 13,500 residents—the library offers an abundance of fine programs. To promote those programs, Mill Valley Public Library developed a printed calendar with all of the important details; staff members give a copy of the calendar to patrons when they apply for or renew a library card. The calendar is also made available around the library, on the library Web site, and at city hall and the community center. One year, in celebration of National Library Week, the library mailed a copy of the calendar, along with a library card application, to every home and business in Mill Valley.

## SAMPLE 15.1

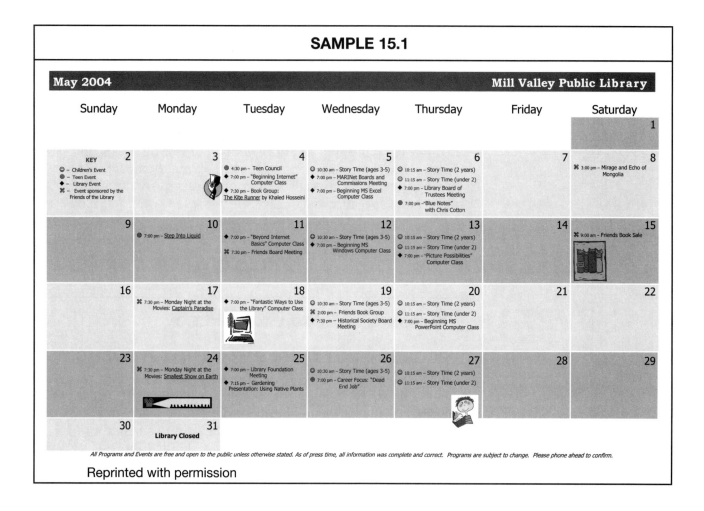

**May 2004**                                          **Mill Valley Public Library**

| Sunday | Monday | Tuesday | Wednesday | Thursday | Friday | Saturday |
|---|---|---|---|---|---|---|
| | | | | | | **1** |
| **2** KEY<br>☺ – Children's Event<br>◉ – Teen Event<br>◆ – Library Event<br>⌘ – Event sponsored by the Friends of the Library | **3** | **4** ◉ 4:30 pm – Teen Council<br>◆ 7:00 pm – "Beginning Internet" Computer Class<br>◆ 7:30 pm – Book Group: The Kite Runner by Khaled Hosseini | **5** ☺ 10:30 am – Story Time (ages 3-5)<br>◆ 7:00 pm – MARINet Boards and Commissions Meeting<br>◆ 7:00 pm – Beginning MS Excel Computer Class | **6** ☺ 10:15 am – Story Time (2 years)<br>☺ 11:15 am – Story Time (under 2)<br>◆ 7:00 pm – Library Board of Trustees Meeting<br>◉ 7:00 pm – "Blue Notes" with Chris Cotton | **7** | **8** ⌘ 3:00 pm – Mirage and Echo of Mongolia |
| **9** | **10** ◉ 7:00 pm – Step Into Liquid | **11** ◆ 7:00 pm – "Beyond Internet Basics" Computer Class<br>⌘ 7:30 pm – Friends Board Meeting | **12** ☺ 10:30 am – Story Time (ages 3-5)<br>◆ 7:00 pm – Beginning MS Windows Computer Class | **13** ☺ 10:15 am – Story Time (2 years)<br>☺ 11:15 am – Story Time (under 2)<br>◆ 7:00 pm – "Picture Possibilities" Computer Class | **14** | **15** ⌘ 9:00 am – Friends Book Sale |
| **16** | **17** ⌘ 7:30 pm – Monday Night at the Movies: Captain's Paradise | **18** ◆ 7:00 pm – "Fantastic Ways to Use the Library" Computer Class | **19** ☺ 10:30 am – Story Time (ages 3-5)<br>⌘ 2:00 pm – Friends Book Group<br>◆ 7:30 pm – Historical Society Board Meeting | **20** ☺ 10:15 am – Story Time (2 years)<br>☺ 11:15 am – Story Time (under 2)<br>◆ 7:00 pm – Beginning MS PowerPoint Computer Class | **21** | **22** |
| **23** | **24** ⌘ 7:30 pm – Monday Night at the Movies: Smallest Show on Earth | **25** ◆ 7:00 pm – Library Foundation Meeting<br>◆ 7:15 pm – Gardening Presentation: Using Native Plants | **26** ☺ 10:30 am – Story Time (ages 3-5)<br>◉ 7:00 pm – Career Focus: "Dead End Job" | **27** ☺ 10:15 am – Story Time (2 years)<br>☺ 11:15 am – Story Time (under 2) | **28** | **29** |
| **30** | **31** Library Closed | | | | | |

*All Programs and Events are free and open to the public unless otherwise stated. As of press time, all information was complete and correct. Programs are subject to change. Please phone ahead to confirm.*

Reprinted with permission

## PROGRAMMING EXAMPLE 2: PLYMOUTH PUBLIC LIBRARY, PLYMOUTH, MASS.

The Plymouth Public Library offers its adult patrons a wide variety of programming from jazz and classical music concerts to presentations on dressmaking and flower arranging. All of the programs are promoted using simple one-page 8-1/2-by-11-inch flyers. The flyers are printed in one color of ink on colored paper. This format keeps costs down, while the result is eye-catching promotional materials.

**SAMPLE 15.2**

Courtesy of the Plymouth Public Library, Plymouth, MA.

**SAMPLE 15.3**

*Posies and Portraits*
*Celebrating*
*Mother's Day*
*in Flowers and Art*

*Presented by:*
*Carol Barnes, floral designer for "Thyme & Time Again"*
*and Mary Waring Barnes award winning artist*

*The presentation will include a discussion on*
*Mother & Daughter portraits with a demonstration*
*on how to design a rose topiary, other fresh topiaries,*
*a living wreath and various spring flowers.*

*Monday*
*May 3, 2004*
*7:00pm – 8:30pm*

*Plymouth Public Library*
*Otto Fehlow Meeting Room*
*132 South St., Plymouth, MA*

This program is free and no registration is required. It is sponsored by the Plymouth Public Library Corporation.
The library is fully accessible; please let us know if you need special accommodations to attend.

*If you have any questions, contact Jennifer Harris at Plymouth Public Library by calling 1-508-830-4250,*
*TTY 1-508-747-5882, or visit our homepage at www.plymouthpubliclibrary.org*

Courtesy of the Plymouth Public Library, Plymouth, MA.

**SAMPLE 15.4**

Courtesy of the Plymouth Public Library, Plymouth, MA.

**SAMPLE 15.5**

Reprinted with permission

## PROGRAMMING EXAMPLE 3: JULIA ROGERS LIBRARY, GOUCHER COLLEGE, BALTIMORE, MD.

The Julia Rogers Library at Goucher College won a 2003 John Cotton Dana award for its public relations program "25 Years of Jane Austen," designed to bring attention to the library's unique collection of books related to Jane Austen and her times. Special programming for the celebration was promoted through these one-color direct-mail pieces that also worked as flyers. Note that some of the events were cosponsored by the Friends of the Goucher College Library.

---

### SAMPLE 15.6

"Jane Austen's Body"
A lecture by Claudia Johnson
Burke Scholar in Residence, Fall 2003.

Tuesday, November 4, 2003
7:00 p.m.
Kelley Lecture Hall
Goucher College
1021 Dulaney Valley Road
Baltimore, MD 21204

Light refreshments will follow the program.
Books will be available for sale and signing.

at Julia Rogers Library, Goucher College

Claudia Johnson is the Murray Professor of English Literature at Princeton University, where she has taught since 1994. In addition to editing several editions of Jane Austen's novels, Johnson has authored a number of scholarly texts, including *Jane Austen: Women, Politics, and The Novel*, *The Cambridge Companion to Mary Wollstonecraft*, and *Equivocal Beings: Politics, Gender, and Sentimentality in the 1790s*, which was a James Russell Lowell finalist for outstanding book published during 1995.

The Burke Scholar in Residence program was established by Goucher College to honor Alberta and Henry Burke, who bequeathed their extensive Austen collection to the Julia Rogers Library in 1975. Mr. Burke was a co-founder of the Jane Austen Society of North America. Johnson's visit is further supported by the Stella Platnick Yousem '54 Jane Austen Special Collection Fund.

Johnson is one of two Burke Scholars in Residence selected to present public lectures this year. The Spring 2004 scholar, Peter W. Graham, will appear in March. This biennial residency will next be offered in 2005–06.

Reprinted with permission.

**SAMPLE 15.7**

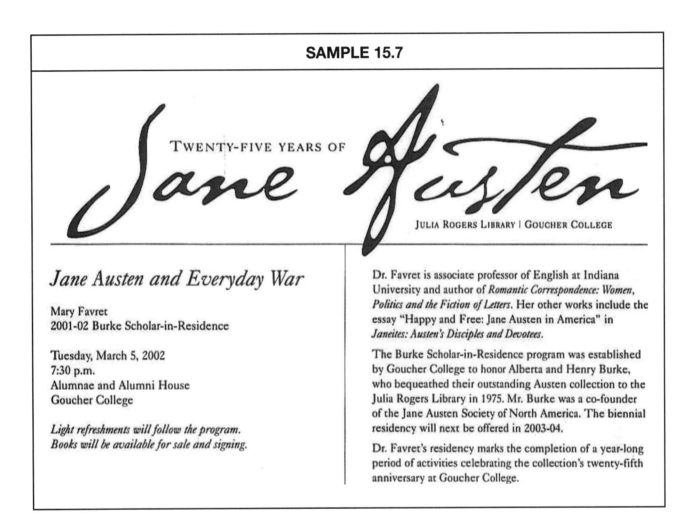

TWENTY-FIVE YEARS OF *Jane Austen*

JULIA ROGERS LIBRARY | GOUCHER COLLEGE

*Jane Austen and Everyday War*

Mary Favret
2001-02 Burke Scholar-in-Residence

Tuesday, March 5, 2002
7:30 p.m.
Alumnae and Alumni House
Goucher College

*Light refreshments will follow the program.*
*Books will be available for sale and signing.*

Dr. Favret is associate professor of English at Indiana University and author of *Romantic Correspondence: Women, Politics and the Fiction of Letters*. Her other works include the essay "Happy and Free: Jane Austen in America" in *Janeites: Austen's Disciples and Devotees*.

The Burke Scholar-in-Residence program was established by Goucher College to honor Alberta and Henry Burke, who bequeathed their outstanding Austen collection to the Julia Rogers Library in 1975. Mr. Burke was a co-founder of the Jane Austen Society of North America. The biennial residency will next be offered in 2003-04.

Dr. Favret's residency marks the completion of a year-long period of activities celebrating the collection's twenty-fifth anniversary at Goucher College.

**SAMPLE 15.8**

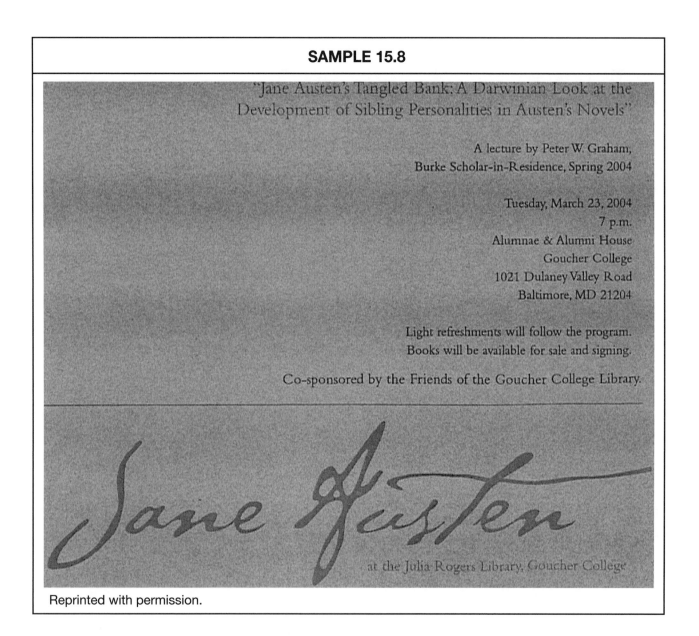

"Jane Austen's Tangled Bank: A Darwinian Look at the Development of Sibling Personalities in Austen's Novels"

A lecture by Peter W. Graham,
Burke Scholar-in-Residence, Spring 2004

Tuesday, March 23, 2004
7 p.m.
Alumnae & Alumni House
Goucher College
1021 Dulaney Valley Road
Baltimore, MD 21204

Light refreshments will follow the program.
Books will be available for sale and signing.

Co-sponsored by the Friends of the Goucher College Library.

at the Julia Rogers Library, Goucher College

Reprinted with permission.

### PROGRAMMING EXAMPLE 4: DULUTH PUBLIC LIBRARY, DULUTH, MINN.

The Duluth Public Library published this great booklet to promote its 2004 "Reading: Bridges to a Wider World" project. In its third year, the project focused on "The Adventures of Huckleberry Finn," and was sponsored by the Duluth Library Foundation. In addition to a list of events, the guide included a short biography of Mark Twain, a list of his work, a discussion guide, a list of Web resources and, of course, an evaluation form.

**SAMPLE 15.9**

# The Adventures of Huckleberry Finn

## Resource Guide and Schedule of Events

2004

*Reading.*

Bridge to a Wider World

Sponsored by the Duluth Library Foundation

Reprinted with permission

## PROGRAMMING EXAMPLE 5: BLOOMINGTON PUBLIC LIBRARY, BLOOMINGTON, ILL.

Bloomington Public Library promotes its ongoing "Itty Bitty Lapsit" storytimes with this eye-catching little brochure shaped like a baby block.

**SAMPLE 15.10**

Reprinted with permission of Bloomington Public Library, Bloomington, IL.

## PROGRAMMING EXAMPLE 6: PIONEER LIBRARY SYSTEM, NORMAN, OKLA.

The Pioneer Library system won a 2004 John Cotton Dana award for the "Red Dirt Book Festival," celebrating the Oklahoma literary experience. The beautiful four-color materials to promote the festival included a large poster, an 8-1/2-by-11-inch poster and a booklet of programs and events.

**SAMPLE 15.10  Pioneer Library System Red Dirt Festival Promotion**

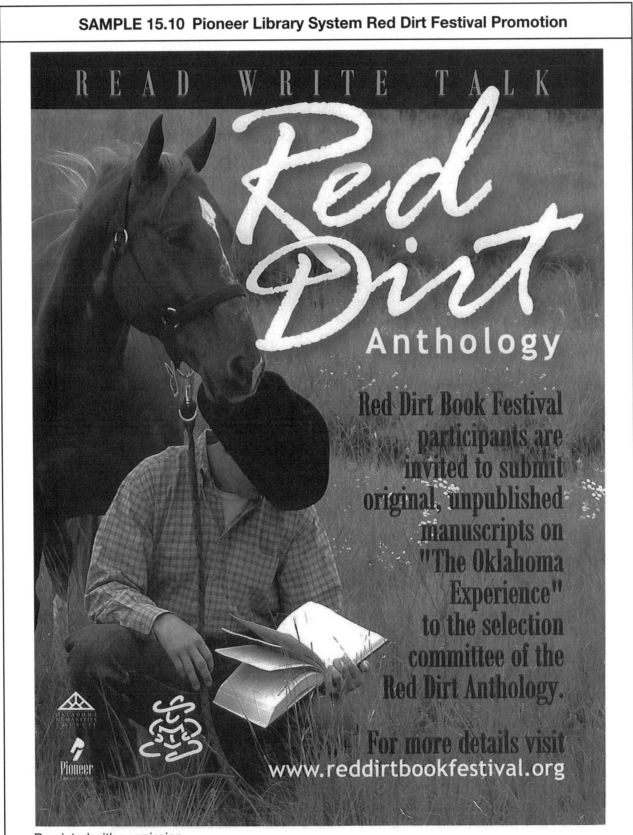

# SPECIAL EVENT EXAMPLES

### SPECIAL EVENT EXAMPLE 1: BLOOMINGTON PUBLIC LIBRARY, NORMAL PUBLIC LIBRARY, AND PONTIAC PUBLIC LIBRARY, ILL.

These three rural Illinois libraries came together with the local radio station, Star 107.7, to collect hats, mittens, and scarves for area shelters, schools, and day-care centers. They promoted the campaign, dubbed "The Mitten Tree," with this clever and attractive bookmark. What a great way to promote library services and give back to the community at the same time!

**SAMPLE 15.12**

# The Mitten Tree

Nov. 24, 2003 - Jan. 5, 2004

*The library has oh so many books piled high*

*It is fun to read, read, read them oh my!*

*But that's not all a library can do It can also help people with a little help from you*

*They put up a tree Oh what a sight As they lit it up with tinsels and light I will not let you shiver I will not let you be cold As I ask people To bring mittens for the little tree to hold*

*The winter is cold, as cold as could be As we dance merrily about the library Tree It's colors are bright and as happy as we For it's branches held mittens as high as we could see*
*by Patti Donsbach*

Star 107.7 FM has joined forces with Bloomington Public Library, Normal Public Library, and Pontiac Public Library to help collect scarfs, hats, and mittens to help keep little fingers warm and cozy.

Join us in collecting for area shelters, schools, and day care centers. The hats, mittens, and scarfs will be passed out to kids who don't have any of their own. Together, we can bring enough warmth to Central Illinois to last the whole winter long.

Mitten Tree locations:

Bloomington
Public Library
205 E. Olive St.

Normal
Public Library
206 W. College Av.

Pontiac
Public Library
211 E. Madison

Reprinted with permission of Bloomington Public LIbrary, Bloomington, IL.

## SPECIAL EVENT EXAMPLE 2: ST. PAUL PUBLIC LIBRARY, ST. PAUL, MINN.

The St. Paul Public Library celebrated the opening of its newly renovated central library with many impressive promotional materials. Items included a beautiful glossy booklet (sponsored by the Friends of St Paul Public Library) on the history of the library and a "Shout it Out! Central Library Is Open!" button.

**SAMPLE 15.13**

Courtesy of Saint Paul Public Library and the Friends of St. Paul Public Library.

---

**SAMPLE 15.14**

Courtesy of Saint Paul Public Library and the Friends of St. Paul Public Library.

---

# EXHIBIT EXAMPLE

## EXHIBIT EXAMPLE: HIGHLAND PARK PUBLIC LIBRARY, HIGHLAND PARK, ILL.

The Highland Park Public Library was one of 40 libraries nationwide to host "Forever Free: Abraham Lincoln's Journey to Emancipation," a traveling exhibition. To promote the exhibit, the library developed this attractive two-color brochure, which listed all of the associated special events and programs and also thanked the exhibit's financial sponsors.

**SAMPLE 15.15**

Courtesy of Highland Park Public Library, Highland Park, IL.

# 16 COPING WITH COMMUNICATIONS DURING A CRISIS

This may be one of the shortest chapters in this book, but that doesn't mean it is the least important. If you have followed all of the developmental steps to plan and implement a public relations communications program for your library, then you already have a firm foundation for crisis communications. However, the reality of running any kind of an organization is that emergencies and crises arise, and when they do you will benefit from having thought through the possibilities and the communications strategies for dealing with them.

## A CRISIS? IN A LIBRARY?

Crisis communications. Why would a library ever need crisis communications? Libraries are warm, friendly places where only good things happen, right? Anyone who has worked in libraries for any amount of time knows that the answer to that question is a resounding, "NO!"

Libraries face crises and challenges every day. There are intellectual freedom challenges, the USA Patriot Act, the Children's Internet Protection Act—the list is endless. Then there are times when things happen at the library that can happen in any public building—fire, flood, assault—again another long list of possibilities. Part of an effective public relations program is having a strategy for dealing with those situations, if and when they arise.

### HOW TO PLAN FOR THE UNEXPECTED

In the midst of the crisis is not the time to develop your crisis communications plan. Every organization should outline a plan for how to deal with communications during a crisis. Develop this plan, have the appropriate people become familiar with it, and then hope you never have to use it.

## ELEMENTS OF A CRISIS COMMUNICATIONS PLAN

First, determine "who" will be the point person for communications during a crisis. The fire may occur at night when the library director or PR person is not available, so what is the chain of command when it comes to talking to the media? Is it the most senior person available? Or do you wait until a key library spokesperson is available? Your library system, school district, college, or university likely has a crisis management team so perhaps the point people should be the members of that team.

Have a designated "crisis communications headquarters." Obviously, if the location is compromised by the incident, you will need to change locations, but having a place where the media can go is critical to ensuring that the information that needs to get out does.

Then have a list of facts that need to be gathered about the crisis:

- What happened?
- Who did it happen to?
- Where did it happen?
- When did it happen?
- How did it happen?
- Is the crisis over, or when will it be over?

These facts will help you quickly develop your message and communicate it to the media. Just having a simple plan like this will help you to jump into action.

Your PR committee or executive committee may also want to brainstorm the types of crises that could arise in your library and then talk through strategies for dealing with them. Possibilities include:

- fire
- flood
- union strike
- bomb threat
- death of a top employee
- robbery
- major intellectual freedom challenge
- assault in a library building
- earthquake
- law suit
- closing libraries

This is a daunting list, and it could be even longer. In today's world, we even need to think about the possibilities of terrorist attacks in our public buildings. That is why it is so critical that you and your library's crisis management team think through and talks about the possibilities. You do not want to be caught off guard when the unexpected happens.

# ONCE THE CRISIS HAPPENS

Depending on the type of crisis, there may be issues of safety and security. Always, always put safety above media relations or communications. Keep the press out of unsafe areas and don't serve as the spokesperson in circumstances that aren't safe.

Then prepare yourself to communicate with the media. Develop your messages based on what happened and what is being done to resolve the situation. Work with colleagues to brainstorm a quick list of "Rude Questions and Answers" so that you are not caught off guard in a press conference or interview. And be prepared to tell the truth—no matter what.

One of the most lauded instances of crisis communications was the Tylenol poisoning scandal of more than a decade ago. Many PR pros in Chicago claim to have worked on that communications program because it was so effective. It was successful because Tylenol told the truth about what had happened, both through media relations and advertising, and then took steps to ensure that the situation would not happen again and communicated that action. The result was that the product came through the incident relatively unscathed in the marketplace.

The lesson to be learned here is that in any crisis, it is important to communicate quickly, honestly, and accurately. Tell the media what happened, how it happened, who it happened to, and what steps your library is going to take to ensure that it doesn't happen again.

## DELIVERING THE BAD NEWS: A FABLE

The following story describes the dilemma faced by anyone who has to deliver bad news:

> Allan went away for six months and left his cat with his younger brother Sam. After about a week, Allan called Sam and asked about the cat. Sam said, "Sorry, Allan, the cat fell of the roof and died." Allan was devastated, but after he composed himself, he told his brother, "Sam,

that was a terrible way to tell me that. You should have told me in stages. One time, when I called you could have said the cat is up on the roof and he won't come down. And the next time, you could have told me he fell and was seriously injured. And then the next time, it would have been okay to tell me he was dead." Sam thoughtfully said okay and they continued to chat for a while. Finally, Allan asked, "How's Mom?" Sam responded, "Mom's up on the roof and she won't come down."

The moral is: There is no good way to tell bad news!

Be forthright. Tell the whole story or as much as you can share. If there has been a bomb threat and that is why your building has been evacuated, tell the reporter just that. If a book is being challenged by the parent of a student in your school and a reporter has been contacted, share the reviews you used in selecting the book with the reporter. Remember that it is always better that they come to *you* for information pertaining to your library. Be honest and frank, and you will ensure that they will return in the future.

In crisis situations, you may want to prepare a written statement for release to the press. You can have it reviewed by the library director, legal counsel, and even the police, depending on the situation. By preparing a written statement, you ensure that the same information is released to all media. You may still want to answer specific questions, but when things are hectic because of the nature of a situation, a written statement helps you communicate your message.

You must also be careful not to share information that is legally protected. For example, in most states you wouldn't allow anyone to have access to your patron database without a court order. Other areas to be careful about are those having to do with negotiations and personnel. If a personnel matter is of interest to the press, consult legal counsel before releasing any information. Find out exactly what you can and can't share, and what you should and shouldn't say. In matters of confidentiality, it is important to be careful about the information that you release.

Finally, be sure to let the press know when will be available to update them on the situation. Then show up for those press briefings, even if you don't have anything new to say.

# DON'T MAKE IT NEWS IF IT ISN'T

If a patron is assaulted at your main library, that is a crisis. However, if the media doesn't hear about it and you believe it was an isolated incident, you may not want to talk about it. Gather the details and develop your messages (including what the library has done to ensure that it won't happen again), so that you are ready if someone calls—but you may not want to communicate about this incident proactively.

If you think that something similar might happen again, then consider carefully how you want to manage the communications regarding the incident. You should explain what happened, state when and where it happened, and then describe the steps that your library took to deal with the situation. For example, maybe you hired extra security guards or put in new surveillance cameras. Or perhaps the police have offered to post an officer in your library building. Managing communications in such a crisis is a delicate balance. You should warn your customers and staff that they should take the same safety precautions in the library that they would in any public building; but you also want to reassure them that the library is doing everything in its power to offer a safe environment.

The same thing goes for an intellectual freedom challenge. If a parent doesn't like the fact that your school library has *Heather Has Two Mommies* in its collection and has asked you to reconsider it, it isn't necessarily news. Obviously if the issue reaches the level of the school board, it will become news—but when a title is under reconsideration by a building-level committee, it is an internal issue. Unless, of course, the parent calls the press. But that's why you should develop your message as soon as the parent raises the issue—just in case it ceases to be an internal issue. At the same time, you may want to consider launching a public education campaign for your school's parents about how materials are selected for your library and about overall issues of intellectual freedom.

# CONCLUSION

With careful planning and message development, you can establish a crisis communications plan for your library that will help you turn a distressing situation into a positive opportunity to communicate with your audiences. For example, if you have a fire at one of your branch libraries, the press might be interested in doing a follow-up story on the neighborhood volunteers who helped you with cleanup. A television station might want to feature the heroic efforts of a library staff person who performed CPR on the man who had a heart attack in the stacks. After a story on the series of purse-snatchings at your library, you might be able to convince a reporter to do a follow-up story on the new security measures, urging patrons not to leave their belongings unattended.

The key is to plan ahead, know your messages, and communicate clearly, honestly, and consistently. With those important steps, every crisis, every challenge can be a positive opportunity for your library when it comes to telling your story.

# 17 BUILDING YOUR NETWORK OF PR PROS

When you first begin your library public relations program, books such as this one, as well as workshops and seminars, will help you develop your plan, strategies, and materials. But you will get your ongoing inspiration, support, and new ideas from the relationships you create within a network of peers who are doing communications work both in libraries and other organizations. Making connections with other individuals will give the chance to share experiences, discuss challenges, and develop creative new approaches to promoting your library and its programs, services, and resources. The opportunity for creating that network can be found in state library associations, through the American Library Association, in public relations and communications professional associations, and on the Web.

By becoming involved in these groups, you will have the opportunity to connect with other library staff who do PR. You can also take advantage of the many training workshops and printed and online resources that these groups offer. Best of all, you will have colleagues all around the country to call on when you need help dealing with a communications crisis or want to share the success of a new program.

## @ YOUR LIBRARY AND THE AMERICAN LIBRARY ASSOCIATION

In addition to managing its own library PR efforts, the American Library Association (ALA) has always demonstrated a strong commitment to helping its members promote their libraries and services. However, over the past several years those efforts and the resources that ALA offers libraries have increased ten-fold. Through its "@ your library" advocacy campaign, ALA now offers suggested PR activities, downloadable artwork, sample press materials, and other tools for implementing the library advocacy campaign in your local community. And, best of all, the materials are designed to work for all different types of libraries. Individual ALA divisions, such as the American Association of School Librarians and the Association of College and Research Libraries, have also developed "type of library" advocacy campaigns

---

**FIGURE 17.1  @ Your Library Logo**

# @ your library®

---

that dovetail nicely with the overall ALA campaign. Starting in 2005 ALA is planning a series of Advocacy Institutes at its Midwinter Meeting and Annual Conference—with the hope that these institutes become annual events. ALA hosts several online listservs where members discuss issues of library PR and advocacy. These lists are treasure troves of information and allow you to connect instantly with colleagues around the country and the world.

ALA Graphics offers lots of materials, such as bookmarks and posters, that you can buy at a quantity discount. If you don't have the resources to develop local materials, these ready-made PR materials are a great alternative.

ALA also sponsors national events to celebrate libraries and offers tools to implement them locally. Library Card Sign-Up Month, Banned Books Week, and, of course, National Library Week all offer a national platform for promoting your local library.

In addition to information and resources, ALA offers opportunities to get involved with PR-related committees. Two are the Public Relations Section of the Library Administration and Management Association and the Marketing Section of the Public Library Association. Most of ALA's other divisions also have that focus on public relations committees and task forces. Involvement in these groups will provide you with another level of networking beyond your state organization and with the opportunity to learn about what is happening in library public relations throughout the nation.

The public relations–focused programming offered at ALA's Annual Conference will offer you learning opportunities. You will see exemplary programs, learn about ALA's support for your local public relations efforts, and have a chance to judge your efforts against those in other libraries. In some instances you will glean terrific new ideas, and in other cases you will learn that what you are doing is exceptional compared to what others are doing. Both are valuable reasons for being involved in ALA.

Visit the ALA Web site at *www.ala.org* or contact the association at 800-545-2433 for more information about this wealth of PR training opportunities and resources.

## STATE LIBRARY ASSOCIATIONS

Most state library associations have committees or sections that focus on public relations. The individuals involved in these groups include both librarians who do public relations work as an additional duty and full-time library public relations people. The activities of these groups range from planning conference programs and workshops to producing newsletters and tip sheets. In addition, many of these groups function as a support group for people who do the same work in different libraries. This support group provides you with an opportunity to discuss—with individuals other than those you deal with on a day-to-day basis—the challenges that you face in your library and community. Plus, it provides you with a chance to share your creative solutions to challenges that you have faced.

Contact the library association in your state for information about the type of public relations networking opportunities available. If there aren't any, you might wish to form a section or interest group with some of your colleagues who are doing similar work. Be proactive!

## PUBLIC RELATIONS AND COMMUNICATIONS PROFESSIONAL ASSOCIATIONS

There are many associations, on both a local and national level, for public relations and communications professionals. Their members, like those of library organizations, include both full-time public relations professionals and individuals who have public relations duties as part of another position. Involvement in these groups will help you see your communications efforts in a different way. You will have the chance to network with people working in public relations and communications, in areas ranging from nonprofits to corporations and government. In addition to learning more about effective ways to communicate your library's message, you may make valuable contacts for your library by being active in one of these groups.

The Public Relations Society of America (PRSA) is the world's largest society for public relations professionals. PRSA has nearly 20,000 members in 116 local chapters. PRSA members work in business and industry, technology, PR agencies, government, associations, hospitals, schools, nonprofits, and, yes, even libraries. The association has 18 practice-specific groups designed to focus on public relations trends. Like most professional associations, PRSA hosts local and national conferences and professional development workshops.

One of the greatest values that you may get from a national PRSA membership, however, is access to its PR and media relations tools and resources. Some are made available to you in print—others through its secure member Web site.

While you need to join the PRSA national to belong to your local chapter, you can likely find a PRSA member in your community to host you at a local chapter event or two so you can try it out and see if it will meet your networking and professional development needs. For more information about PRSA, visit *www.prsa.org* or call 212-460-1400.

The International Association of Business Communicators (IABC) has a broader membership than PRSA. Its 13,000 members are communications professionals from more than 60 countries who work in many different areas of communications—public affairs, government relations, marketing communication, community relations, editing, advertising, and, yes, of course, public relations. In fact, the largest percentages of IABC members work in some type of PR. IABC has about 100 chapters worldwide, so there could be opportunities for you to become involved locally. Again, you might want to visit a local meeting as a guest of a member from your community. For more information about IABC, visit *www.iabc.com* or call 415-544-4700.

# PROFESSIONAL DEVELOPMENT

Taking advantage of high-quality professional development opportunities is important in communications, as in any professional area. It is particularly important constantly to be learning more about communications and public relations because the available technology and communications techniques are changing so rapidly and are becoming increasingly sophisticated. This learning process is a two-way street; you will want to participate in professional development opportunities and provide such opportunities for others.

## PARTICIPATING

Organizations such as the ones described above will provide a wide variety of professional development and training opportunities. Some will be "how-to-do-it" presentations and others will focus on the more theoretical and philosophical aspects of communications. You will want to take advantage of both. Understanding how and why people retain information and react to different communications techniques will be as important to your work as honing your skills for speech writing or developing effective printed promotional publications. Develop a communications professional development plan for yourself that includes a mixture of both the practical and the theoretical. Then use the theory that you learn in the practical application of your work.

Best of all, with today's online technology, groups like PRSA now offer "Webinars"—online workshops and seminars—which you can attend without the expense or time investment of travel.

## PROVIDING

Sharing your library public relations and communications experiences with your colleagues through conference programs and other professional development events will provide you with another learning opportunity. By sharing your "lessons learned," you can help others to develop effective communications programs for their libraries. At the same time, they can provide you with tips for avoiding problems that they have encountered. In addition, presenting at local, state, and national meetings is good public relations for your school, community, or university. Through your presentation, you can demonstrate the exciting things that are happening at your institution and you create a positive public perception of your library and community. Community leaders and people who hold the purse strings will be impressed when they learn that an activity at your library has been selected for presentation at a national, state, or local conference.

# INFORMAL NETWORKING AND SHARING

Some of your most valuable networking opportunities will be informal. You may learn more from the person you meet on the shuttle bus at a conference than you do during a formal presentation. Talk to the people you meet, ask them about their work, listen, learn, and share. Not only will you get valuable information during the encounter, you may also develop a relationship with a peer whom you can later call for assistance or advice. Collect your colleagues' business cards and nurture those relationships. Ask them to send you samples of their materials and send them copies of yours. These relationships will be invaluable, particularly when you face such public relations challenges as censorship attempts or funding decreases. Your colleagues will be able to provide ideas and support, and, when needed, they can be understanding friends.

Keeping your eyes open for great communications techniques—in all aspects of your life—will also provide you with great new ideas. When you walk down the street, look at the billboards you encounter. What interesting techniques do they employ in their communications efforts? What new, compelling approach do television or radio commercials use? Look at the travel brochures that you pick up at a hotel, the direct-mail pieces that you receive, and other people's news releases. You'll see things that don't work and you'll know to avoid them. You'll see things that do work and you may be able to integrate them into your future efforts.

Start a file of samples of printed pieces that you find particularly appealing and a file of those that you think have problems. These will basically become your printed materials "do's" and "don'ts" files. When you are ready to develop a new publication, flipping through these files will help spark ideas and remind you of things to avoid.

Along the same line, when you get a great idea from a television ad or another communications tool, jot a few notes on a piece of paper and stick it in an ideas file or start a computer file folder for those ideas. You may not have an application for the idea the moment you see it, but down the road it may fit the bill for a promotion.

# ENTERING CONTESTS AND WINNING AWARDS

Many public relations and communications awards opportunities are available, and several at the national level are specifically for library public relations. Entering these contests can be a valuable experience. It will help you to see how your work stands up against the work of others nationally, and the application process may help you evaluate your efforts. In addition, when you win an award it emphasizes the quality of your public relations communications efforts to the individuals who are funding it, such as your library board, your principal, or your university administrator. It also demonstrates to your community the quality of the work being done by the library.

## LIBRARY PUBLIC RELATIONS AWARD OPPORTUNITIES

Several important library public relations award opportunities are described below. By applying for them, you will share your library's work with the national network of libraries and will be able to learn more about what other libraries are doing to communicate their message to their communities.

### John Cotton Dana Public Relations Awards

These awards, sponsored by the H. W. Wilson Company and ALA's Library Administration and Management Association, are the most prestigious library public relations awards. All types of libraries are eligible to apply for the award by submitting a scrapbook describing their public relations program. Developing a scrapbook based on the application guidelines is time-consuming, so it is best to begin several months before the early February deadline. Even if you aren't an award winner, compiling a John Cotton Dana Award scrapbook will provide you with a complete record of your public relations program and an opportunity to evaluate your program. An award is given to the best overall public relations program, and citations are given for specific public relations projects.

### Library Public Relations Council Awards

The "L. PeRCy" and "Share the Wealth" awards are sponsored by the Library Public Relations Council (LPRC). The L. PeRCy award recognizes excellence in six categories: newsletter, annual report, service brochure, book/material lists, summer reading program, and logo.

Also sponsored by LPRC, the Share the Wealth award judges "PR Bests," which are assembled and distributed to council members. To enter, submit five copies of any public relations item, such as a bookmark, flyer, annual report, or brochure. If your item is selected for the packet, you will be asked to provide 300 copies of your item.

For more information about LPRC, contact Kay Cassell, Office of Programs and Services, New York Public Library, kcassell@nypl.org.

### ALA Swap and Shop

Share your public relations materials at the annual Swap and Shop, sponsored by the Public Relations Section of the Library Administration and Management Association at ALA's Annual Conference. You must submit 300–500 copies of each item. Visit the event and take home examples of library public relations materials from throughout the country.

Submit your best materials for the Swap and Shop "Best of Show." Certificates are awarded in such categories as bookmarks, annual reports, service brochures, and summer reading materials.

For more information about Swap and Shop and its Best of Show competition, visit the ALA Web site at *www.ala.org* or call 800-545-2433.

## OTHER AWARDS

Communications professional organizations, such as PRSA and IABC, also have local and national award opportunities for public relations and communications efforts. You can learn more about them by contacting the associations or accessing their home pages on the Web. In addition, you may want to explore other local public relations awards offered by your community's advertising council or other groups. By applying for these awards, you will have the opportunity to compare your communications efforts to nonlibrary programs; you may learn that what you are doing holds up pretty well even in comparison to well-funded corporate efforts. High-quality, effective communications efforts win awards more often than slick, high-budgeted programs that do not communicate well.

## WINNING AN AWARD AS A PR OPPORTUNITY

When your school, public, or academic library wins any type of award, you are presented with a wonderful public relations opportunity. You can issue a news release, hold an awards ceremony, or publish an article in your newsletter. You will want to strategize carefully how promoting your award-winning status fits into your overall communications plan. However you proceed, this type of recognition builds community pride and is a terrific "pat on the back" for staff who have dedicated a great deal of time and energy to your communications efforts.

## THE AWARDS TRAP

While there are many beneficial reasons for submitting materials and winning public relations awards, be careful of falling into the awards trap—developing materials with a specific award in mind. Remember that the compelling factors in the development of your public relations/communications efforts must be your goals and the message that you want to communicate, not the criteria for a particular award. Make "We don't do public relations to win awards, we do public relations that wins awards!" your motto. Then when you do something that is really effective and that you are really proud of, submit it and win an award!

## CONCLUSION

When you become involved in professional associations that offer you the opportunity to build your PR and communications skills, you will quickly find not only that you are learning a lot, but that you have a lot to share with your colleagues as well. However, this involvement takes time and energy to maintain. Attending meetings, following up with colleagues, and keeping abreast of the organization's programs and activities are time-consuming. Weigh the time you invest against the benefits you get in terms of gathering new ideas, avoiding pitfalls, and gaining personal and professional support. Chances are you will find that the returns are worth many times your investment. And there is an even greater chance that you will develop professional relationships and friendships that will support you for the rest of your career and life.

# APPENDIX: PUBLIC RELATIONS/ COMMUNICATIONS PLAN

---

## PLAN OUTLINE

**Goal:** What is the purpose of this plan? What do you want to achieve?

**Time Frame:** What is the implementation period for this plan? It might be six months or two years, depending on what you want to achieve. The broader your goal, the more time and energy will be required to achieve it.

**Major Target Audience:** Who do you primarily want to communicate with and promote your services to?

**Minor Target Audiences:** Who are the secondary audiences for this plan? Do you want your library colleagues in other communities to know what you are doing?

**Objectives and Activities:**

### A. OBJECTIVE:

You can have as many objectives as you want. The number depends on how broad your goal is and what it will take to achieve it. Promoting use of the video collection to children may take only 3 simple objectives with a few supporting activities. Communicating the services and programs of your entire system to the community might involve 20 objectives with 10 activities each. The key is to keep the plan manageable. Don't set yourself up not to complete it. Examine each objective and its supporting activities and think carefully about the human and fiscal resources needed to complete each one.

**Time Frame:** It is important to describe the time frame for the completion of each objective. Some objectives might continue for the full time frame of your public relations/communications plan. Others will be completed at various times during the implementation of the plan.

**Person Responsible:** For each objective in your plan specify who has overall responsibility for seeing that this objective is achieved. The person responsible may not accomplish the objective alone, but he or she is the accountable individual. This is particularly important if you are in a library without a designated public relations or communications staff person.

1.  **Activity:** Activities are what you will do to achieve the objective. Think carefully about what communications tools or strategies might best help you achieve the objective. Such activities as newsletters, flyers, and news releases support communications objectives, and so do displays and public-speaking engagements. Now is a good time, as you are developing your activities, to review carefully the results of your research. What did people say about the things you are already doing? Did the majority of the people that you interviewed say that your newsletter was too cute and didn't include enough information about services? If so, your activity might be to change the focus of your newsletter, rather than to create a whole new newsletter.

**Time Frame:** Each activity should be assigned a time frame within the time period designated for completion of the objective.

**Person Responsible:** You may wish to designate the person responsible for each activity—unless it is the person responsible for the overall objective.

**Evaluation:** Describe how you will evaluate your plan's success. For example, rather than simply reviewing the plan to make sure you completed each activity, it might be more effective to conduct another survey or hold another round of focus groups to see if you really succeeded in changing perceptions.

# SAMPLE PLAN: SCHOOL LIBRARY

**Goal:** Communicate to parents and school board members the role that the Internet can play in education for children. Demonstrate the Internet's valuable educational resources in order to secure funding for more online resources for services in the school library media center by June 2006.

**Time Frame:** September 2005–June 2006

**Major Target Audiences:** Parents of students enrolled in our school
Teachers
School board members

**Minor Target Audiences:** Other community members

**Objectives and Activities:**

**A. Objective:** Plan, promote, and host two brown-bag teacher lunches per month in the school library media center. Use the time to demonstrate Internet resources in particular curriculum areas. Cover a different subject (such as space, rain forests, music, or art) each time.

**Time Frame:** September–December 2005

**Person Responsible:** School library media specialist

1. **Activity:** Publish item announcing lunches in bimonthly faculty newsletter.
   **Time Frame:** September and November 2005
   **Person Responsible:** School library media specialist
2. **Activity:** Produce and distribute to all faculty members a flyer announcing each lunch and the topic that will be the focus of the Internet demonstration.
   **Time Frame:** September and November 2005
   **Person Responsible:** School library media specialist
3. **Activity:** Develop and distribute a questionnaire evaluating the luncheon series and use the responses to develop a spring series.
   **Time Frame:** December 2005
   **Person Responsible:** School library media specialist

**B. Objective:** Work with students to develop and present a demonstration of online resources at Parents' Night in January.

**Time Frame:** September 2005–January 2006

**Person Responsible:** School library media specialist

1.  **Activity:** Identify teachers willing to have their students work on a research project using Internet resources. Work with them to plan and implement the project.
    **Time Frame:** September 2005–January 2006
    **Person Responsible:** School library media specialist and identified teachers
2.  **Activity:** Promote the demonstration in the library media center as a special feature of Parents' Night by publishing an article in the school newsletter. Include information on the Parents' Night flyer that is sent home with all students.
    **Time Frame:** January 2006
    **Person Responsible:** School library media specialist
3.  **Activity:** Encourage press coverage of the demonstration by sending a news release announcement to the local newspaper and to the television and radio stations. Identify specific students for interviews with reporters.
    **Time Frame:** January 2006
    **Person Responsible:** School library media specialist and identified teachers

**C. Objective:** Work with teachers and principal to prepare and make a presentation to the school board demonstrating the cost-effectiveness of purchasing online rather than printed reference materials. Use examples of student work and a live demonstration in the presentation.

**Time Frame:** September 2005–February 2006 (preparation), March–June 2006 (presentation March–June 2006 at school board meeting)

**Person Responsible:** School library media specialist and identified teachers and students

1.  **Activity:** Prepare a press kit that includes examples of student research using Internet resources and the cost comparison. Distribute to local media, announcing the presentation at the school board meeting.
    **Time Frame:** February 2006

       **Person Responsible:** School library media specialist working with district communications director

2.  **Activity:** Provide a copy of the press kit to each school board member and all PTA board members.
     **Time Frame:** February 2006
     **Person Responsible:** School library media specialist

3.  **Activity:** Schedule a minimum of five other times to repeat this presentation, including to a PTA meeting and meetings of such community groups as Rotary or Kiwanis.
     **Time Frame:** March–June 2006
     **Person Responsible:** School library media specialist and identified teachers and students

**Evaluation:** Prior to implementing this plan, we will survey the teachers, parents, and school board members about their perceptions of the value of Internet resources in the curriculum. Following the completion of the plan, we will repeat the survey and compare results. In addition, the true measurement of the plan's success will be if, at the June 2006 budget meeting, the school board approves our request for funds to purchase additional computers, install more phone lines, and increase Internet access.

# SAMPLE PLAN: ACADEMIC LIBRARY

**Goal:** Create faculty and student awareness of the university library's expanded hours by launching a multidimensional public relations campaign. Achieve a 15 percent increase in the library's overall gate count.

**Time Frame:** September–December 2005

**Major Target Audiences:** Faculty members and students

**Minor Target Audiences:** University staff

**Objectives and Activities:**

**A. Objective:** Inform all students and faculty of the new library night hours by developing and implementing a "Night Owl" study-hour campaign.

**Time Frame:** August–December 2005

**Person Responsible:** Manager of reference services

1. **Activity:** Develop a logo and slogan for the "Night Owl" campaign.
   **Time Frame:** August 2005
   **Person Responsible:** Manager of reference services working with university graphic designer

2. **Activity:** Design and print a magnet—use the campaign logo and list the library's new hours and phone numbers. Distribute to all students and faculty via the campus mail.
   **Time Frame:** August 2005
   **Person Responsible:** Manager of reference services

3. **Activity:** Develop posters that use the "Night Owl" logo and list library hours. Post in all dorms and university buildings.
   **Time Frame:** August–September 2005
   **Person Responsible:** Manager of reference services

4. **Activity:** Write and send a press release to the campus paper and television and radio stations announcing the new library hours.
   **Time Frame:** August 2005
   **Person Responsible:** Manager of reference services

5. **Activity:** Plan, promote, and host a midnight open house at the library during midterm exams. Promote via flyers in all student and faculty mailboxes, on campus bulletin boards, and as an insert in the campus newspaper. Provide students with refreshments and additional magnets listing the library's hours and phone numbers.
   **Time Frame:** October 2005
   **Person Responsible:** Manager of reference services

**B. Objective:** Work with the campus newspaper to develop a regular weekly feature on "Night Owls at the Library," focusing on the unique adventures of students who take advantage of our night hours. Highlight the advantages of studying at night.

**Time Frame:** September–December 2005

**Person Responsible:** Manager of reference services

1. **Activity:** Identify a student reporter interested in the library and its services. Provide the reporter with a special tour and orientation.
   **Time Frame:** September 2005

**Person Responsible:** Manager of reference services

2. **Activity:** Work with the reporter to identify students to be featured in the "Night Owls" column.
**Time Frame:** September–December 2005
**Person Responsible:** Manager of reference services

**C. Objective:** Promote the library, its new hours, and its resources to university faculty.

**Time Frame:** August–September 2005

**Person Responsible:** Manager of reference services

1. **Activity:** Develop a packet of information about the library and its services and resources for all university faculty members. Include a suggestion slip and a request form to add materials to the collection.
**Time Frame:** August 2005
**Person Responsible:** Manager of reference services

2. **Activity:** Have the packet for each faculty member hand-delivered by the librarian responsible for library service in that faculty member's subject area.
**Time Frame:** August–September 2005
**Person Responsible:** Manager of reference services working with librarians

**Evaluation:** Prior to the implementation of this plan, a brief survey of 100 students and 50 faculty, assessing their perceptions of library services and resources, was conducted. Following the fall semester, this survey will be repeated. In addition, gate counts for the previous fall semester will be compared to those for this fall to determine if the promotion resulted in increased use. The targeted increase is 15 percent.

# INDEX

# ABOUT THE AUTHOR

LISA A. WOLFE is a public relations professional with more than 20 years of award-winning communications, journalism, and public relations experience, with particular expertise in libraries and education. She is currently the president and principal of L. Wolfe Communications, a Chicago-based public relations agency focused on serving the education and library markets.

Before founding L. Wolfe Communications in 2000, Wolfe was Senior Vice President at Grant/Jacoby, Inc., heading the agency's Microsoft team, which was responsible for Microsoft's education public relations worldwide. As Microsoft's "agency of record" for education public relations, Wolfe and her team developed Microsoft's position for the role of technology in K–12 and higher education, managed all education-technology analyst and media relations, launched products in the education market, and planned and implemented speeches and special events involving Microsoft's company executives, such as Bill Gates and Steve Ballmer.

Wolfe's public relations career has its foundation in school and public libraries. After working briefly as a newspaper reporter in northern Idaho, she began her career in libraries in 1985 as the Public Information Officer for Spokane Public Library, Spokane, Washington. She developed the position into the senior-level administrative post of Manager of Community Relations. Highlights of her accomplishments during her eight-year tenure were developing and implementing a major capital campaign and earning numerous awards for public relations, promotions, and communications, including two of the American Library Association's prestigious John Cotton Dana Awards for Outstanding Library Public Relations.

Wolfe also created the position of Coordinator of Communications for the American Association of School Librarians (AASL), a division of the American Library Association (ALA). In addition to managing the communications efforts of this division, she developed and implemented communications strategies for the National Library Power Program, a $45 million school library improvement initiative, funded by the DeWitt Wallace-Reader's Digest Fund and managed by AASL.

After leaving ALA, Wolfe was manager of the Chicago Public Schools Department of Libraries and Information Services, where she coordinated the setup and opening of the school system's new professional library and assisted in the development of the department. She has been active in ALA and served as the editor of *ALKI: The Journal of the Washington Library Association* for three years.

L. Wolfe Communications' current clients include the American Library Association, Inspiration Software, MetaMetrics/Lexile Framework for Reading, Pearson Educational Measurement, and Keystone National High School.